For
Mitchell Sa[illegible] 75

G. B[illegible] Aug. 31

little
wood

recommend, for a glance,
pages 36, 39, 40, 43
147, 172, 193,
300, 317, 320, 322,
344, 349, 353, 400 to the end

THIRD PRINTING

PRINTED IN THE U. S. A. BY J. J. LITTLE & IVES CO., N. Y.

CONTENTS

ILLUSTRATIONS

CHAPTER ONE

THE CRADLE OF STALIN

I

THE Land of Courage . . . The Land of Fear . . . The Caucasus.

A gigantic mountain knot, where Europe and Asia are inextricable; the milling crossroads of the world, where East meets West, where South meets North, where all boundaries merge, all ages converge—

This is the cradle of Stalin.

Here the spawn of a hundred races has been dashed and spattered against the rocky ranges by all the tidal migrations of history. Here civilization and savagery, imperialism and tribalism, pristine beauty and degeneracy, swashbuckling and obsequiousness, gallantry and cowardice, live side by side. Here the aquiline fastnesses harbor, within a radius of a score of miles, a score of different clans, speaking their aboriginal dialects, waging their ancient feuds. Here chivalry braves danger with a scimitar in hand. . . .

Fear is written across the valleys and slopes of this land. Fear is preserved in the ruins of prehistoric fortresses, carved in the ageless faces of the market crowds. Five thousand years of fear, of incessant invasions, of short-lived spells of peace, and of undying conflicts of arms. Here the farmer does not venture into town without a dagger on his hip.

Here the national costume displays pockets with compartments for bullets. Here the wine is cool, the temper hot, and treachery is cut into the soil by a hundred generations of vanquishers and vanquished.

There is no land like it on the face of the earth. The Vikings reached it from the north, the Semites from the desert, the Mongols from the Orient, the Homeric adventurers from Troy. This is the home of the oldest white race of the world, the Iberia of ancient Greece. The legendary Prometheus was bound to its cliffs. Jason went here in search of the golden fleece. Alexander the Great conquered it. General Pompey captured it for Rome. Byzantium sent a viceroy to rule it. The Persians and the Armenians established dynasties here. The Huns, the Arabs, and the Turks inundated it. Here Zoroastrianism, Mohammedanism, and Christianity fought their futile battles for supremacy. Genghiz Khan and Tamerlane swept over the country with fire and sword. The crusaders penetrated it from the south, and their Gallic survivors still cling to its glens. Peter the Great took possession of it and Catherine the Great betrayed it. Here the last Holy War in history was waged less than a century ago with spectacular perfidy and valor.

This is the cradle of Stalin, a caldron of seething hatreds. During the nineteenth century, the tsars of Russia carried on here a relentless campaign of subjugation and Russification. The Armenians, the Tatars, and the Georgians were incited to mutual extermination in a methodical fashion. Predatory warfare and predatory politics followed in the wake of the Muscovite invaders. Occasionally there would be a wholesale exodus of mountaineers to Turkey. Under the crushing and arbitrary weight of the Russian military steam-roller Caucasia was filled with fear as never before and the children drank the sweet milk of sworn vengeance from their mothers' breasts.

II

Stalin was born on the frontier of two eras. The feudal order was still entrenched in his homeland, Georgia. The age-old castes were still in power. But the industrial revolution was dawning already. There was oil in Baku, on the Caspian Sea. There was manganese near Batum, on the Black Sea. There was a frenzied quest for mineral wealth in the interior of the mountains. The Nobels and the Rothschilds, the British, the Belgians, and the Dutch were already on the march to that distant country. They would dig the fabulous treasures out of its petrified bowels. They would span the mountain passes with railroads at a time when great areas of European Russia were still closed to the rest of the world. They would lay a pipe-line overland from the Caspian to the Black Sea, to carry the precious black fluid to remote harbors.

Capitalism was striding across primitive, agricultural Caucasia. Shepherds would learn to drill wells. Horsemen would become miners. Care-free warriors would be chained to the lathe. Peasants would become machine fodder. Barter would give way to modern commercialism. Nobility would yield to money. A new class would arise, a caste not by birth but by acquisition, a capitalist class whose racial origin would be secondary to the size of its fortunes. The tsar's generals and functionaries would learn to respect industrial and commercial princes.

Into the life of the Caucasian peoples, the internationalism of capital brought a new, an almost mystical element. In its train, as usual, came the inevitable twins of modern imperialism—nationalism and socialism. In the atmosphere of cultivated rancor, of bitter oppression prevailing under the Romanov rule, the seeds of western thought were to flourish rapidly and violently.

III

In the mountain hamlet of Didi-Lilo, a peasant cobbler by the name of Djugashvili was pursuing his trade. His parents and grandparents had been cobblers, even as his sons and grandsons would be. But the days of peasant cobblers were drawing to an end. One of the Djugashvilis, Vissarion, left his native village and moved to the neighboring town Gori, to become a shoemaker there. In time he would be forced to go to Tiflis, be hired as a hand in a shoe factory, and turn proletarian.

Vissarion took himself a bride, Ekaterina, a typical Georgian bride. To this day, girls are given away in marriage there at the age of thirteen or fourteen. The Georgian women, like those of Sicily, blossom early. At thirty-five they are old and worn out. Ekaterina Djugashvili became a mother when most western girls are still in elementary school. She had three children in succession. They all died in infancy. The fourth child was expected around Christmas. Ekaterina was a devout woman. If God granted her a son who would live, she would name him Joseph and dedicate him to the church.

Ekaterina was twenty when Joseph was born, on December 21, 1879. One can surmise with what love and care the young mother reared her only child. Joseph was nicknamed Soso, a Georgian pet name. Ekaterina had great plans for her son. The tradition of education is deeply ingrained among the Georgians. To the poorest among them it signifies the only possible escape from privation, the only medium for acquiring position and power in the world. Ekaterina wanted her son to become a great man. She would bring Soso up to be a priest!

Stalin was more his mother's child than his father's. It is to her that he owes the ambition, the repressions, and the inhibitions, characterizing his career. Vissarion was just a mere shoemaker. Not so Ekaterina, his wife. A woman of strong character and unusual vitality, she was determined to make a churchman of her son.

And Stalin lived up to his mother's dream. He grew up to be a priest indeed, the high priest of a hierarchy he helped to shape and perfect. If it was Lenin who conceived the Communist Party as a military order, even as Loyola had declared the church to be in a permanent state of war, it is to Stalin that is due the lion's share of the credit or onus of forging this order into an army of steel. Ekaterina Djugashvili was wrong in one respect; she did not know that the sixteenth century had passed. And she certainly did not suspect, even as the greatest seers of the age did not suspect it, that the twentieth century would produce a modern breed of Torquemadas, Loyolas, and Machiavellis.

IV

Stalin's childhood was spent in Gori, a charming and picturesque town on the railroad to Tiflis, the capital of Georgia. Gori was already a cultured urban center, boasting a high school. It is situated in the midst of a fertile agricultural zone, where the wine is famous and the corn the best in the Caucasus. The town church was built by Capuchin missionaries from Rome. In Gori itself are the remains of a fortress constructed by the Byzantine conquerors. Within five miles is another natural fortress that was cut in the rock by the army of Alexander the Great.

A year before Stalin's birth, the last Russian-Turkish war had come to an end. The tsar had annexed the provinces adjacent to the Tiflis district. Soso was fifteen months old when Alexander II was assassinated in St. Petersburg. He was seven when Lenin's brother was executed for participating in an attempt to assassinate Alexander III. The Caucasus Mountains were still reverberating with the fresh tales of the last rebellion against Russia, when a large force of tribesmen joined hands with the Turks. The exodus of thirty thousand mountaineers to Turkey occurred when Stalin was an infant.

Stalin's mother was proud of him. He excelled in his studies, his deportment was good, and he was his teacher's favorite pupil. Soso was not a strong boy, the family was poor, and food was not always plentiful. At seven he had smallpox. To this day his face shows light pit marks. His mother was bringing him up by virtue of hard work and even harder prayers. He was sent to the local church school when he was nearly eight.

"Soso was always a good boy," his mother declared emphatically, in 1930. "Yes, he was always a good boy. I never had to punish him. He studied hard, was always reading or talking and trying to find out about everything. . . . Soso was my only son. Of course I treasured him. Above everything in the world. . . . His father, Vissarion—well, his father said he would make a good cobbler out of Soso. But his father died when Soso was eleven years old. And then—and then, you see, I didn't want him to be a cobbler. I didn't want him to be anything but a priest."

Widely published stories that Stalin grew up among the Tiflis *kintos*—vagabond street-hawkers—from whom he is supposed to have acquired his capacity for coarseness and cynical wit, are extremely dubious. For Stalin won a scholarship to a college upon his graduation from the elementary school. That his was a hard adolescence of poverty and adversity is beyond doubt. His father died when he was eleven. His mother became a dressmaker. Having been left penniless, she worked at her sewing until late in the night, to earn a bare livelihood and to save a little for the religious education of her son.

V

Stalin's mother realized the first stage of her ambition. Soso was admitted to the theological seminary in Tiflis, where she and her son moved in 1893 from Gori. Little did she dream of what that cloistered, regimented institution harbored in its inner depths. Little did she perceive the western winds blowing in this eastern capital. Tiflis is a city of many educational institutions. It has a university, it has fine libraries and museums. Architecturally it resembles Palermo or Naples. It has been said that proportionately Georgia has more men of letters, journalists, poets, and dramatists, than any other country in the world. Tiflis contained the flower of the race. The theological seminary was a stronghold of new and exciting theories, a battlefield for nationalist and internationalist propagandists. Tiflis already had Marxist circles. Subversive leaflets were secretly in circulation. Under the tyranny of tsarist power, the first breaths of ideological rebellion were drifting in the air.

Into this hotbed of resurrection and insurrection the young Djugashvili came to receive his baptism for priesthood. He brought with him a gift for speech, a natural inquisitiveness, a smattering of knowledge, a quick temper, and a heritage of privation and fear. He was fourteen. In the southern climate of Georgia men and women mature early. Under the autocratic rule of the Romanovs they matured even earlier. Stalin imbibed the socialist doctrines, studied Karl Marx, and became one of the leaders of the secret Marxist band in the seminary. Soon, at the age of seventeen, he established connections with the Tiflis Social Democratic groups. He attended "underground" meetings, and engaged in such activities as distributing revolutionary proclamations and pamphlets.

"It is difficult to describe the process," said Stalin when asked thirty years later why he became a socialist. "First, one became convinced that existing conditions were wrong and unjust. Then one resolved to do the best one could to remedy them. . . . Russian capitalism was the most atrocious and bestial in the world. The tsar's government was also the most corrupt, cruel, and inefficient."

"I became a Marxist," he declared on a subsequent occasion, "thanks, one may say, to my social position—my father was an operative in a shoe factory, and my mother, too, was a worker—and also because there was a stir of revolt in the milieu around me, which was of the same social level as my parents, and, finally, because of Jesuitic repression and the martinet intolerance of the Orthodox Church seminary where I spent some years."

The years that the young Stalin spent in the seminary passed under the shadow of the great massacres in neighboring Turkey. During 1894–1896, about one hundred thousand Armenians lost their lives. Tiflis was the seat of a powerful clandestine Armenian society. The massacres rocked the public opinion of the western world. Lord Rosebery proposed to the governments of Russia and France to employ force against the sultan. The tsar's government replied that it "would not join in any coercive measures."

This was the international setting of the moment. The immediate vista as seen from Tiflis was more painful. Thousands of Armenian refugees trickled across the Turkish border into the Caucasus. The authorities received them none too kindly. The tsar's government was accused of abetting the massacres.

The young Armenians were turning from nationalism to internationalism.

"My whole atmosphere," observed Stalin, "was saturated with hatred of tsarist oppression, and I threw myself wholeheartedly into revolutionary work."

VI

The espionage system in the seminary was well established. The monastic inspectors kept a watchful eye on the "reliability" of their wards. Stalin was under suspicion. Surreptitiously and voraciously he read books on sociology, natural sciences, and the labor movement. The wakeful school officers searched his room, and discovered a book by Karl Marx. He was promptly expelled from the seminary, at the age of eighteen. To his mother, this spelled disaster. What would become of all her dreams? What would become of her son?

To be sure, Ekaterina Djugashvili had had her fears. The mysterious absences of her boy, his strange associates, his concealment of illegal literature, boded nothing but trouble. Yet her son never discussed politics at home. It was simply inconceivable that he would turn into an enemy of the mighty monarchy.

Stalin was now set loose in the world. The career his mother had planned for him was interrupted. His own career was still to be determined by the uncharted course of history. As so many youths of his day, Stalin turned to tutoring and then to clerical work. He became a bookkeeper in the daytime. At night he was pursuing a new vocation, that of revolutionist.

It was but five years later that Lenin laid the foundations for that modern phenomenon, the class of professional revolutionists. But already in a hundred obscure and scattered localities young men and women were subconsciously training themselves for the day of decisive battle. A thousand miles away, on the fringe of the Ukrainian steppes, another young man, but two months older than Djugashvili, also expelled from a tsarist high school, was preparing himself for the same task. His name was to be written into the records of the revolution as Trotsky. Somewhere in Siberia a bald-headed exile by the name of Ulyanov was studying English and translating Sidney Webb into Russian. Ulyanov was to become Lenin, and Sidney Webb—Lord Passfield!

In 1898 Stalin became a member of the Tiflis Social Democratic circle, devoting himself regularly to propagandist work. Circles like this one were to be found in the main centers of the country. But the national labor party organization was still to arise. That very year is memorable in the annals of the Soviet régime. It is the beginning of the Soviet "calendar." It was in March, 1898, that nine representatives of secret Marxist groups met in the city of Minsk, and held an "underground" conference, to go down in Russian history as the First Congress of the Russian Social Democratic Labor Party, the mother organization of the Bolshevist movement. To this day the congresses of the Bolshevist Party are dated and numbered from that Minsk conclave.

"Fifty years ago there swept over Europe the awakening storm of the Revolution of 1848," began the manifesto of the new party, written by Peter

Struve, who two decades later was to become a minister under the White general, Wrangel. "For the first time there has appeared on the scene, as a major historical force, the modern working class. . . . The Russian working class will carry on its powerful shoulders the burden of winning political freedom. This is necessary, but it is only the first step toward the realization of the great historical mission of the proletariat: the creation of a social order in which there shall be no place for the exploitation of man by man. The Russian proletariat will throw off the yoke of autocracy in order to continue with increased energy the battle against capitalism and the bourgeoisie until the complete victory of socialism."

VII

In the Caucasus, capitalism came with a rush. The forces of the proletariat were multiplying rapidly. The opportunities for employment attracted a number of advanced workingmen from St. Petersburg and Moscow. Among these arrivals was one Michael Kalinin, who found a job in the railway shops as a joiner. Twenty-one years later he became president of the Soviet Union. Another immigrant was one Sergei Alliluiev, a locksmith, the son of Central Russian serfs, who was to become an ardent Bolshevik and . . . Stalin's father-in-law.

Workingmen's circles appeared in Tiflis. A group of intellectuals, including seminary students, acted as their mentors. The manifesto of the First Congress struck not only a new but a timely note as well. The Stalins were arriving on the scene from one side, the proletarians were coming from the other. The manifesto was the link in a common faith. It was a new gospel, requiring dissemination and interpretation. Stalin carried this gospel to the railwaymen, the tobacco and leather factories, and to the artizans of the city. The congress adopted a set of eleven resolutions, and established a central committee as the supreme organ of the party. Did the youthful Stalin dream then that twenty-two years later, as the secretary-general of this Central Committee, he would be dominating the entire state of Russia?

For three-quarters of a century Russia had been in the grip of romanticist revolutionists. They had vision and had courage, they wrote brilliant essays and manufactured deadly bombs. But they had no roots in the soil, no physical mass to build upon. Theirs were imponderable arms. At last a concrete, a practical way to victory was mapped out. No more desultory warfare, no more dramatic assassinations. Such was the message of the first labor party. Instead, it outlined the strategy and tactics of an effective political and economic movement. The army was there—the proletariat. It needed only organization and formation. Stalin was among the first to enlist, to seize the implications and possibilities of the new program, to extract the real from the illusory, and to build brick by brick the cornerstone of an incredible foundation for a new crusade of social zealots.

Already Lenin was championing in the depths the need for a change in the method of mass organization. He advanced the point that the struggle for the economic improvement of the workers' condition was not an end in itself but a means for the development of a revolutionary party. The labor movement was at the time the battlefield of two elements: the "old school" was advocating pure propaganda by literature and speech; the "young school" stood for street warfare, mass action. Up to that time the method had been for intellectuals to select and enlighten individual workers in the theories of Marxism. Revolutionary work now took on new forms. Leaflets printed on secret presses were distributed among the people. Posters calling for the overthrow of the government appeared on the walls in the morning. Political demonstrations in the streets, planned and organized beforehand, became common occurrences in the big cities of the country.

Stalin's first indirect contact with Lenin belongs to this period. It was in 1900 that there arrived in Tiflis from exile a close associate of Lenin, who had served together with him a term of banishment in Siberia. This emissary, Kurnatovsky, was impregnated with Lenin's militant ideas, and propagated them in Transcaucasia. Stalin became one of his loyal disciples, and was able to imbibe Bolshevism in its incipient stage.

VIII

What sort of person was Stalin at the age of twenty, at the threshold of his career? Yenukidze, now the secretary of the Soviet Executive Committee, but at that time a young revolutionist in Baku was sent on a mission to Tiflis to secure two compositors, type, and a little money to set up a secret printing press. At first the Tiflis Committee was willing to give the necessary supplies only on condition of its retaining control of all the publications of the proposed Baku printing establishment. Yenukidze returned with this message, and was sent back to Tiflis with these instructions: "Find Soso Djugashvili there, he is a good fellow, tell him everything, and he will help."

The meeting took place in a saloon near the Tiflis railroad station. Soso was there with another comrade. The conversation was short, and Yenukidze got what he wanted.

"I see quite clearly before me young Soso Djugashvili at Tiflis," writes Yenukidze, "where I had my first business interview with him. Stalin even then, as now, was not distinguished by talkativeness. Brevity, clarity, accuracy were his distinctive qualities. . . . The natural simplicity of his speech and address, his absolute carelessness of his own private comfort, his inner hardness and complete absence of vanity, the fact that already he was politically educated, made this young revolutionary an authority among the Tiflis workers, who looked upon him as one of themselves.

" 'Our Soso,' the workers spoke of him. It is well known that for intellectuals active in labor circles the most difficult thing was to find 'a common language with the workers.' In this regard Stalin was and remains to this day a rare exception. He has always been remarkably capable of explaining to workingmen the most complicated things and events in a clear, simple, and convincing manner. He was just as able to find the 'tongue' of the peasants with whom he frequently came in touch in the revolutionary work in Georgia.

"He never scattered himself. All his actions,

meetings, friendships were directed at a definite aim, which at that time was the laying of a solid foundation for an illegal party organization in every district in which he was active.

"Stalin never sought personal popularity. The circle of his persistent activity he limited exclusively to the workingmen and that of his underground coworkers. That is why the advanced workers and professional revolutionists knew him well and rated highly his qualities as an organizer and revolutionist."

IX

These were years of passionate revolutionary activity. An affiliate committee of the national Social Democratic Party was formed in Tiflis in 1900. At the age of twenty-one, Stalin was a founder member. He had his hands full. Tiflis was swept by a series of strikes, of an economic character, in 1900 and 1901. With the aid of Stalin's committee, a political demonstration of workingmen and revolutionists was staged in the center of the city in May, 1901, within a short distance from the palace of the viceroy, where Stalin's aged mother has been residing for the last five years. The police then undertook a stern campaign against the revolutionists. The Tiflis committee was disrupted. Stalin's home was raided and searched. He had learned that there were orders from the Okhrana for his arrest, and was not to be found.

At this time Lenin was already abroad, acting as one of the editors of the Iskra (the Spark). This militant journal carried on its title-page the legend:

"From a spark a flame will rise." In its columns, Lenin was erecting the scaffolding of his grandiose scheme. The Iskra was smuggled into Russia through every port, across every frontier, from Persia to Archangel. Its influence was so potent that it had secret followers throughout the country. Stalin was one of them.

At the end of 1901, Stalin, under an assumed name went to Batum, on the Black Sea. Together with another socialist, the workingman, Kandelaki, he formed here the first local committee of the Social Democratic Party. He inspired and led from behind the scenes the strikes in the plants of Rothschild and Mantashev. The following February he organized a great political street demonstration of workers. There ensued, as usual, repressive measures and widespread raids. Stalin was caught in the drag-net, arrested and imprisoned. It is the test of a good conspirator not to be found "with the goods." Stalin was a model in this respect. He was transferred from Batum to Kutais. There it appeared that the prosecutor lacked evidence. The case was dropped, and Stalin was set free. He returned to Tiflis and became an active member of the committee conducting the railwaymen's strike movement. Finding himself under suspicion, he came back to Batum. Here he was arrested once more, in March, 1902, accused of participation in the activities of the Tiflis Committee, and lodged in jail where he was destined to spend nearly two years of his life.

While Stalin was behind bars, his friend Alliluiev moved from Tiflis to Baku where he was employed as a machinist. Alliluiev had married a Georgian woman. In September, 1902, she gave birth to a daughter who was named Nadejda—the Russian for Hope. Stalin was almost twenty-two then. After the revolution, Nadejda or Nadya came into Stalin's life to stay.

When the gates of the Batum prison were locked behind the twenty-two-year-old tall and slim Joseph Djugashvili, a life had been cast into a mold, and the ex-seminary student was admitted into an order which was as rigid as it was fearful. Cradled in an environment of terror, nursed on repression and intolerance, the son of the Gori shoemaker was thrown into the "underworld" of revolutionary conspiracy. During the following sixteen years he would operate under a series of aliases. Soso would become Koba, and then David, Nizheradze, Ivanovitch, Chizhikov, Vasiliev, and, finally, Stalin—the Russian for "the man of steel."

He would become a legend. He would wear a mask. He would develop into full manhood as a hunted "subterranean" inhabitant. Some day a revolution would come that would force him to show his fist and reveal his voice, but seldom his face, never his inner soul. Unable to discard the mysterious garb of a lifetime, he would long remain a "man of mystery."

Chapter Two

THE CRADLE OF BOLSHEVISM

I

THE Land of Faith . . . The Land of Despair . . . Eurasia.*

An immeasurable plain which is neither Europe nor Asia, a world conceived outside geographical boundaries—the Union of Socialist Soviet Republics—which recognizes no arbitrary national frontiers; where the Orient and the Occident are interlocked, where the surge of the Arctic tundra and the Mediterranean steppe overlaps—this is Russia, the sixth continent, the cradle of Bolshevism.

Here a million wooden villages have produced a score of brick and stone cities. Here arrogance and humility, cruelty and penitence, soulfulness and depravity, march together. Here creative impulses are strangled at birth by destructive instincts; energy is dissipated in contemplation, organic growth corroded by gnawing yearning. Here the heart demolishes what the mind originates. Here a straight line is the longest distance between two points.

A land over which time has no power. A land of a few dazzling ideas and a million stillborn ones. A land of a few passing moments and a myriad of

* This chapter is an outline of the origins of Bolshevism, as distinct from socialism. As far as the author knows, it is the first attempt in English at an historical survey and interpretation of Leninism—the creed of Stalin.

immovable eternities. A world which faces simultaneously the rising sun and the setting sun.

Faith, blind and pitiful, is burned into its flat bosom. Faith, the soul of despair. That is its cross. It is seared into its messianic soil, branded into its primitive heart. It is fixed in the relics of its ancient and contemporary saints. A dreary land where ikons supply color, blood furnishes visions. A land where the cold mysticism of the North drains itself into the landlocked Black and Caspian seas, where the warm imagination of the East wastes itself across interminable flatness.

An immense sponge for ideas which are absorbed and amalgamated in its depths. A land without rock bottom. To it came the Christians, the Moslems, and the Jews to peddle their creeds, and they all established themselves. All the utopias of the world were eagerly imbibed there. All the philosophies dropped their seeds in its loam. They bore fantastic fruits. English merchants brought industry to its doors. Chinese traders built a city in its heart, in the center of Moscow.

A land where the machine is a faith and faith is a machine; where politics is despair and despair is politics—this is the cradle of Bolshevism.

II

Bolshevism was ushered into the world by Lenin in 1903. It reached out for Stalin and converted him. In it he found his absolute faith. Stalin's career was set. The new creed would shape his life, and he in turn would shape its destiny.

The primary impulse of Bolshevism, as distinct from socialism, is the will to revolution. This Stalin possessed. The primary premise of Bolshevism, as distinct from socialism, is the Leninist interpretation of the dictatorship of the proletariat, the theory of seizure of power. This Stalin accepted.

Bolshevism is indigenous to Russia. What distinguishes Bolshevism from socialism is what distinguishes Eurasia from the West. Bolshevism is a western idea that has emerged as a challenge to the world thanks to the Russian armor with which it is clothed. The confusion that Bolshevism evokes as a social force is due to the obscurity of the sources from which it drew its life-blood in the West and the even greater obscurity of the powers which molded it in the East.

Bolshevism is not an accident. It is not without reason that the Soviet historians open their accounts of communism with Thomas More. The spiritual godfathers of Bolshevism in the sixteenth century are as amazing as that century itself: More, Calvin, Loyola, and Ivan the Terrible—all contemporaries.

One of the Soviet writers hails Thomas More as the first communist "at the break-up of the feudal order in England." To be sure, More in his "Utopia" did not favor revolution. He merely analyzed the causes and remedies for economic inequality. Yet to More the modern state was a conspiracy of the rich, pursuing private gain under the disguise of public weal. And More was the first to suggest a universal organization of communist economy in which all the means of production would be publicly owned.

Shortly after the death of Lenin, in 1924, the dean

of Bolshevist historians, Professor Pokrovsky, delivered a lecture at the Communist Academy in Moscow in which he compared Lenin to the revolutionary leaders of the past, and found him most closely related to "Calvin—the originator of Puritanism and militant Protestantism." Said Pokrovsky:

"He created for the first half of that century a militant doctrine, a sort of Protestant Leninism, the militant doctrine of Calvinism. But, in addition, his state structure was interesting. It greatly suggests the structure of our own Soviet state: two rows of institutions—on the one hand, civil institutions, but these are in fact subordinate to the church institutions, the consistory and the highest church assembly, which have legally no rights, but which in actuality direct the entire administration."

While the Bolshevist Party in its relation to the government greatly resembles the Calvinist pattern, the internal structure of that party is a replica of Loyola's Jesuit Society. Loyola conceived the church to be in a state of war, and Lenin considered society to be in a state of war. Loyola built his organization upon the principles of military discipline, of total abnegation on the part of those who joined his society, of an intricate system of espionage from which not even the supreme general was exempt. His teachings of obedience and his hierarchical order are closely reproduced within the Bolshevist Party. The Jesuit ethics of the end justifying the means recur frequently in the catechism of Leninism.

At the opposite pole of sixteenth-century civilization, in Muscovy, Ivan the Terrible, who has not been sufficiently studied in the West, was heading another social revolution, described by a Soviet historian as "military-autocratic communism." Ivan the Terrible, incidentally, was one of the most educated men of his time. Ivan organized and led a class war of the peasantry and new gentry against the established power of the boyars and princelings. He patronized the poor and persecuted the rich. He was the champion of the lower classes, but he was a Russian reformer, and carried into effect his policy of centralizing the state, distributing the land, fostering education and industry, by methods which suggest the mechanics of Bolshevism.

III

Lenin did not drop from the skies upon the soil of an elemental labor movement, declares Pokrovsky. "Lenin was a man who was able to link this labor movement with the immense revolutionary current sweeping onward not from the middle of the nineteenth century but from the eighteenth century." Lenin was in one aspect a direct descendant of the frustrated forces in the French Revolution. He was consciously a student and follower of the Jacobins, and especially of Babeuf, who was the first to attempt a communist uprising for the purpose of setting up a dictatorship of the poor.

The relation between Babeuf and Bolshevism is intimate. With minor changes, many of Babeuf's proclamations could be substituted for Lenin's, and escape detection. "The French Revolution is only the forerunner of another, a greater, a more majestic revolution which will be the last." How much this statement of Babeuf's suggests Lenin's utterances in the days following the overthrow of tsarism!

"Nature has given to every man the right to the enjoyment of an equal share in all property," began one of Babeuf's manifestoes in which he called for the overthrow of the government of "starvers, bloodsuckers, tyrants, hangmen, rogues, and mountebanks." What an assortment of Bolshevist epithets! And here are some of his principles:

"Only by stern discipline, obstinate work, merciless battling with the plunderers will we achieve true equality. It is our duty to set up a dictatorship of the poor. . . ."

"The earth belongs to no one. We demand common exploitation of the fruits of the earth. These fruits belong to everybody. . . ."

"We declare that we can no longer tolerate that the vast majority of the people should toil in the sweat of their brow creating luxury for an insignificant minority. . . ."

"Down with the revolting differences between the rich and the poor, between the strong and the weak, between the masters and the servants, between the rulers and the ruled."

The idea of a conspirative society to bring about the overthrow of capitalism and the establishment of a communist order was first launched by Babeuf. In 1795 he organized the League of the Just, a secret organization which soon became very powerful. He attempted an armed uprising. It failed, and he was executed. But his League survived him for fifty years, until Marx came to pick up its threads and weave them into his Communist Manifesto.

The legitimate heir to Babeuf was August Blanqui, one of the extraordinary characters of the nineteenth century, whose Society of Seasons had numerous conspirative branches throughout France. Blanqui had been condemned to death three times, he had spent thirty-four years of his life in prisons, had been identified with the revolutions of 1830, 1848, and 1871, and always aimed at changing not the political but the economic order. Blanqui, like Babeuf, conceived of revolution as an insurrection on the part of well-organized and armed plotters. Both Blanqui and Babeuf lacked an appreciation of the rôle of the proletariat in the achievement of their ends. Lenin was more than once accused of Blanquism, which became a synonym for revolutionary adventuring. But he never seriously repudiated the charge.

IV

The first western Bolshevik, who profoundly influenced Karl Marx, was Wilhelm Weitling, a German rover, the son of a poor workingman, and a person of enormous erudition. Lenin studied Weitling's writings in Switzerland. The communism of Weitling was class hatred, and it was he who originated the idea of the class struggle which Marx later elaborated into a scientific doctrine that remains to this day the cornerstone of socialism. But Weitling also anticipated Lenin in many of the ethics of Bolshevism.

Discontent among the masses, according to Weitling, must be increased "until the sense of indignation will break out in a whole series of revolutions and finally lead to the full liberation of the people." He had a plan to organize all the dark forces of society, thieves, ex-criminals, into a partizan army in order to cause the downfall of capitalism. When he was accused of unethical principles, he replied ironically:

"What does it matter? How is my principle wrong if the aim is good If strong poison is required to cure a sickness, then no weak application will avail."

"Everything will be delivered to the destructive fire," he declared. "Then we will proclaim a morality which no one has ever dared to preach anywhere, and which will make impossible the existence of a government based on selfishness; a morality which will transform bloody street riots into ceaseless partizan warfare, and which will destroy all exploitation of the labor of the poor, and which no soldiers and police in the world will be able to stop."

"The houses of the rich should be turned over to the poor. A provisional government consisting of loyal communists should be set up. The proletariat and artizans should be armed. All prisoners should be set free. Anyone fighting the communist principles should be shot."

Weitling also forestalled Lenin in his devastating criticism of modern democracy and parliamentary government.

"Let anyone try to write in favor of the poorer classes, and he will discover what freedom of the press means under the domination of a moneyed system," wrote Weitling. And again:

"What is the use of our having the right to ballot for this or that candidate? The results of the elections will always be the same. It will always appear that right was on the side of the rich, and that the lot of the poor will always be that of a class deprived of any rights."

Stalin has declared that it is impossible to understand Bolshevism without appreciating the major part which the dictatorship of the proletariat plays in it.

Lenin drew this idea from Marx the revolutionist, and not from Marx the sociologist from whom he inherited socialism as a science of the economic evolution of mankind. He found the idea in the Communist Manifesto and its literal expression in Marx's notes, and not in his major works. He developed it into a system in peculiarly Russian conditions, which achieved its final form under Stalin. Lenin also took from the casual observations of Marx such statements as "insurrection is an art, fully as much as the art of war or any other," and expanded them into pillars of Bolshevism. One of Lenin's favorite quotations from Marx, which has been reiterated and elaborated thousands of times by Bolshevist writers, is:

"The Terror of 1793 was nothing but a plebeian method of dealing summarily with absolutism and counter-revolution."

Marx was not only the father of modern socialism, but also a colorful rebel and prolific journalist. This western thinker provided a veritable arsenal of epigrams and formulas to support and justify in theory Bolshevism in action.

V

The ideas that came from Western Europe into Eurasia were laden with dynamite. Here they were received with the eagerness of savages, fanned with the intensity of fire-worshipers, cherished with the greed of treasure-hunters, and handed down to posterity with messianic ecstasy. Fine lines became blurred, fine thoughts became grotesque. What was faith in the West became militant faith here, and what was despair in Europe turned into frenzy in Eurasia.

Long before the French Revolution, the roots of Bolshevism budded in Russia. In the seventeenth century Stenka Razin, to whom the Soviet government has dedicated a monument, led a bloody rebellion of Cossacks and peasants against the landlords and the government in the name of absolute equality. In the following century, another rebel, Pugachov, raised a sweeping revolt with the promise of deliverance from serfdom and the destruction of the feudal yoke. These risings were accompanied by outbursts of monstrous ferocity, and left deep traces in the lore and hearts of the people.

Under the influence of the utopian socialism which in the West followed the French Revolution, and of which Fourier, St.-Simon, and Robert Owen were the prophets, the first revolutionary attempt to overthrow the monarchy occurred in Russia in December, 1825. It was the work of a group of liberal nobles and officers whom history remembers as the Decembrists. But how did their program reflect the utopian tendencies prevailing in the West? They already then advanced the doctrine of the nationalization of the land, as a concomitant of their plan to set up a democratic republic. The nationalization of the land! How far Europe was from such a thought as a practical measure. And how revolutionary it sounded nearly a hundred years later when Lenin promulgated the Soviet decree to that effect.

When the theory of the division of society into two classes first became current in the West, Bakunin, the great revolutionist who was later to become the father of anarchism, quickly seized upon it to define the world as separated into two enemy camps. "On the one side is revolution, on the other side is counter-revolution." This primitive simplification was typically Russian and characteristically Bolshevist. Lenin resorted to it on numberless occasions. Having gathered from Weitling that the parliamentary form of government was not advanced enough to provide economic equality, Bakunin, the flamboyant, declared that "European experience showed that the parliamentary system was not satisfactory," and that for Russia, more than anywhere else, a dictatorship was necessary. When one considers that Russia was then smarting under the severe autocracy of Nicholas I and that Europe was still struggling to achieve political democracy, one perceives the audacity involved in this leap of Russian imagination.

This towering rebel, who left a profound imprint upon his country, was so devoted to the idea of liberty that he could conceive of it only as absolute, unqualified, unlimited liberty. How short is the step from absolute liberty to absolute denial of it.

"I had only one mate—faith, and I said to myself that faith would overcome mountains, destroy barriers, conquer the unconquerable and create the impossible," wrote Bakunin in his memorable "Confession."

"Russia will never be the land of the golden mean," observed his friend Alexander Herzen, the brilliant essayist and revolutionary thinker who deserted his homeland and spent his active life in France and Great Britain.

Herzen had only one hope for Russia—the western influence. "Only the mighty thought of the West," he wrote, "is capable of fertilizing the dormant seeds in the patriarchal Slavic order of things.

"To become a duchy, Russia needed the Norsemen.

"To become a state—the Mongols.

"Europeism developed the Muscovite kingdom into a colossal empire.

"But in spite of all their receptivity, did not the Slavs show everywhere their complete unfitness to develop a modern European state structure, and do they not constantly fall into desperate despotism or insoluble disorder?"

The recognized literary precursor of Bolshevism was Chernishevsky, Lenin's favorite author.

"Who would be interested in pursuing propaganda that is not backed by bayonets?" asked Chernishevsky.

"Revolution is not a gala promenade," is the phrase which Lenin culled from his works repeatedly, and hammered into the philosophy and vocabulary of Bolshevism.

VI

Seventeen years before Stalin was born, the stem of Bolshevism sprouted from the soil of Russia. The essence of the creed which Stalin was to embrace at the completion of his period of adolescence was first formulated in 1862 by a remarkable revolutionist, Zaichnevsky, who organized and led a secret society.

"The first Bolshevist document in our history," writes Pokrovsky, is "The Young Russia," the proclamation of Zaichnevsky. "In it you will find such things as socialized factories, nationalized industry, the public ownership of shops, the nationalization of commerce, the complete and unconditional equality of women—a whole series . . . of flashes into the future, of extraordinary interest. . . . This scheme, you will perceive, greatly suggests that which we followed: the revolutionary party which seizes the power of the state, retains it in its hands until the new order has driven deep roots into the soil. It is not a petty, temporary, revolutionary government for a few weeks, but a firm and durable dictatorship."

How did Zaichnevsky propose to achieve this program?

"With complete faith in ourselves," reads his manifesto, "in our powers, in the sympathy of the people toward us, in the glorious future of Russia, which is fated to be the first to bring socialism into life, we shall issue one cry: 'Pick up your axes! and . . . attack the imperial party, without mercy, even as it has no mercy for us. Kill them in the public squares should this vile rabble dare appear there, kill them in their homes, kill them in the narrow city alleys, kill them on the wide metropolitan streets, kill them in the villages and hamlets. . . .' "

Zaichnevsky saw but one way out from the existing political and economic order—"a revolution, a bloody, pitiless revolution which will change radically and without exception all the foundations of contemporary society, and destroy the advocates of the present order. We do not fear it, although we know that a river of blood will flow, that even innocent victims will suffer."

After describing the seizure of power, "The Young Russia" goes on to say:

"We . . . are firmly convinced that the revolutionary party which will stand at the helm of the government, once the movement is successful, must conserve the present centralization . . . in order to introduce with its aid new foundations of an economic and social order in the shortest possible time. It must seize the dictatorship in its hands, and stop at nothing. The elections to the national assembly must be carried out under the influence of the government, which shall take care there and then that no one be elected who favors the present order (if any such remain alive)."

This first Bolshevist document concluded with the words: "Long live the social and democratic Russian Republic!"

Zaichnevsky was still alive when Lenin appeared on the scene in the early nineties, and the future creator of Bolshevism came in contact with his disciples.

A contemporary of Zaichnevsky, and one of the constitutional forerunners of Bolshevism, Tkachev, presaged, according to Pokrovsky, Article Sixty-

Five of the Soviet Constitution when he wrote: "To the workers belong all the rights, and no others can possess rights of any importance."

"The road of peaceful reform, of peaceful progress," Tkachev taught, "is one of the most unrealizable utopias which was ever invented by mankind to appease its conscience and to put its mind to sleep."

Tkachev was a doctrinaire, and he advanced the theory that for the good of humanity all people above the age of twenty-five should be destroyed. His "men of the future," upon securing power, would enact their social reforms by means of simple decrees.

"Neither in the present nor in the future," wrote Tkachev, "can the people, left to their own resources, bring into existence the social revolution. Only we revolutionists can accomplish this. . . . The socialist ideals are alien to the people; they belong to the social philosophy of the revolutionary minority."

Lenin inherited from Zaichnevsky and Tkachev many of the precepts of his political system. The soviet scheme of legislation is also a development of Tkachev's elementary outline. But the last stone in the foundation of Bolshevism was yet to be hewn.

VII

Lenin took his organizational method from Nechayev, who formed the secret "Society of the Ax" in 1869. Nechayev, in his famous catechism, made the first attempt to carry out Tkachev's principle of a compact revolutionary minority leading the masses to revolt.

"Our task is implacable general destruction. Our

purpose is full liberty and happiness for the toilers," reads Nechayev's catechism. He built his society on a strict rank basis, none of the members being initiated into all the phases of the organization's activities. Unanimous election was a requisite of membership.

"A revolutionist is a doomed person. He has no private interests, affairs, sentiments, connections, no property, not even a name," we read in the catechism. "He hates public opinion. To him everything is moral that promotes the triumph of the revolution. Everything is immoral and criminal that prevents it."

Nechayev's revolutionist "in the depths of his being, not only by word but by action, is one who has severed every bond with the civil order, with the educated world, with all its laws, decencies, with all the generally accepted conventions and morality of this world. He is its ruthless enemy, and if he continues to live in it, it is only to better destroy it. . . ."

"All the tender and softening feelings of kinship, friendship, love, gratitude, and even honor itself, must be crushed in him by the single cold passion of the revolutionary cause. . . . He must be ready to perish himself and to destroy with his own hands everything that interferes with the success of its achievements, considering it necessary to impose upon the people from above such forms of a new organization of social relations as he would deem essential and expedient. . . ."

"The revolution will hallow everything equally in this struggle. And so, the field is open! Let the unconcealed rage of the people select the victims. Let all the honest, fresh heads arise to renew life after centuries of rape. Let the last days of the social parasites be darkened. There will be moans of fear and repentance in society, the rag-writers will be emitting lyrical groans. Must we pay attention to them? No! You must remain deeply indifferent to all these whinings and enter into no compromises with them who are doomed to perdition.

"This will be called terrorism! Let them give it a loud name! Let them, it makes no difference. We do not value their opinion. The present generation must itself give shape to a brutal force which does not spare itself, and proceed unhaltingly along the road of destruction. The healthy and unspoiled brain of youth must understand that it is much more human to slaughter and to strangle scores, hundreds, of the most hated people, than to participate with them in the systematic legal slaughters, tortures, and torments of millions of peasants, as is being done more or less directly by our functionaries, our scientists, our priests, our merchants. . . ."

When one of the members of Nechayev's group grew critical of its methods, the leader had him assassinated. The cause of the revolution transcended everything. Nechayev's code of ethics became one of the integral premises of Bolshevism.

VIII

What a chasm divides the revolutionists of the West and of Russia! Babeuf, Blanqui, and Weitling had their counterparts in Zaichnevsky, Tkachev, and Nechayev—the Russian Jacobins. They all had in common the will to revolution, the hatred of the established order, and the conspirative method of organization. Yet what a gulf between them! It is the gulf that separates Eurasia from Europe, and in it lies submerged the key to the psychology of Bolshevism.

Plekhanov, Lenin's master in Marxism, later disavowed by his disciple, once derisively described Bolshevism as follows:

"Down with the Romanovs! Long live our Committee!"

This observation caustically emphasized the obscure but vast heritage of Bolshevism. Lenin had assimilated the creeds of a boisterous revolutionary century, and distilled them into the formulas, maxims, and slogans that adorn the edifice of the dictatorship of the proletariat.

"The history of all countries bears witness to the fact that the working class by its own powers alone cannot achieve more than the trade-union consciousness," wrote Lenin in his "What to Do?" in 1902. "The working class is unable to develop a socialist consciousness of its own. It can be impregnated with it only from the outside."

Lenin simply applied the principles of the Russian Jacobins to the western theory of the class struggle. "Men must be trained who will devote to the revolution not only their free evenings, but their whole lives," he announced in the Iskra. And he elaborated it in his "Where to Begin?" as follows:

"Without ten leaders of talent—and talents are not born by the hundred—tested and trained in their task, schooled in it through long years, it is impossible in present-day society for any class to carry on any kind of energetic struggle. . . . I shall uphold this principle however much you may arouse the masses against my anti-democratic attitude."

The ethics of Bolshevism, as outlined by Lenin, have their roots in his immediate precursors. "We repudiate," said Lenin, when already in power, in the course of an address to young communists, "all morality that proceeds from supernatural ideas or ideas that are outside class conceptions. In our opinion morality is entirely subordinate to the interests of the class war; everything is moral that is necessary for the annihilation of the old exploiting social order and for the union of the proletariat. Our morality thus consists solely in close discipline and in conscious war against the exploiters. We do not believe in eternal principles of morality, and we will expose this deception. Communist morality is identical with the fight for the consolidation of the dictatorship of the proletariat."

Stalin's predecessor in the post of secretary of the Bolshevist Party, Preobrajensky, further elucidated this theory. He declared:

"Whereas, in a society in which there are no classes, lying is a disadvantage in itself, because it compels the members of the society to use their energy in discovering the truth, the case is quite different in a society based on classes. In the struggle of an exploited class against its enemies, lying and deceit are often very important weapons. . . . The workers' state, surrounded as it is on all sides by hostile capitalist countries, finds lying very necessary and useful in its foreign policy."

From this it is but a short and inevitable step to Lenin's following tenets. When he was accused of sheltering in the party expropriators and bandits, he retorted to A. Bogdanov:

"When the revolution comes, all these will be with us. On the barricades a safe-blower will be more useful than Plekhanov."

"The party is not a dormitory for noble maidens. We cannot approach our active members with a narrow bourgeois yardstick. Some scoundrel may be useful to us just because he is a scoundrel."

"Ours is a great household, and in such all kinds of rubbish come in handy."

"Revolution is a serious business. It cannot be made in snow-white gloves, with scrupulously clean hands."

These epigrams of Lenin's found their culmination in his war-cry:

"Let every kitchen-maid learn to run the government!"

But it was another winged phrase of his of that period—"Loot the loot!"—that unwittingly summed up a dark past. When certain Bolshevist writers attempted in later years to interpret it in a philosophical sense, Demyan Biedny, the Soviet poet laureate, wrote that Lenin meant what he said and not "some incomprehensible Greek," and that he embodied the Bolshevist program in those three words.

"Crack them on the snout—that is Bolshevism!" was the manner in which one of Lenin's veterans, Krasikov, the present commissar of justice of the Soviet government, worded the same thought.

Such are the official ethics of Bolshevism. But the

power that drives it springs from deeper sources. It is the almost mystical will to revolution.

"History moves at a terribly slow pace. It must be given a push." This utterance of Zheliabov's, one of the founders of the People's Freedom, expresses the mainspring of Bolshevism. It was the society with whose followers Lenin came in direct touch, in his early manhood, that introduced terrorism as a political weapon. One of its members was Lenin's brother who was executed for an attempt to assassinate Alexander III. Lenin was inspired by the same will, but he observed: "No, this is not the right road."

It was not a question whether the revolution was needed for the workers, but whether the workers were needed for the success of the revolution. This remark of Plekhanov's applied equally to the People's Freedom and to Lenin.

Lenin decided that the workers were needed for the revolution. For Lenin was moved by the same dynamic will of giving history a push. But he discarded the weapon of individual terrorism as impracticable. He surveyed the field in search of a more effective instrument. He discovered the proletariat. And he attached the current of western revolutionary theory to the Russian wagon.

IX

The world that had been nourished on Tolstoy, Turgenev and Chekhov knew of a Russia of saintly peasants, martyred intellectuals, and French-speaking gentlefolk. It did not know that this Russia was being swamped by the turbulent rise of a new class —the proletariat.

The era of revolutionary ferment was matched by an era of capitalist development in Russia. In one century Russia spanned the course of industrial progress which Western Europe had taken three centuries to complete.

At the end of the eighteenth century, Russia had virtually no industries. In 1891, it was the first country in Europe in the textile field, having 6,000,000 spindles, more than any European nation. In 1890, Russian factory workers numbered 1,424,000. In 1897, they totaled 2,098,000.

The growth of capitalism and of the proletariat was violent indeed.

Like that of the United States, the industrial expansion of Russia was on a large scale, concentrated in great plants, perhaps because of the vastness of the country and of the wealth of resources. In Western Europe, small factories were in the majority. In Russia, gigantic enterprises predominated. In advanced Germany, in 1895, but 10 per cent of the workers were employed in plants having more than 1,000 hands each. In Russia, 38.5 per cent of the proletariat worked in such establishments in 1902.

Russia led the Old World in large-scale strikes. In June, 1896, an unprecedented strike of textile workers, involving 35,000 men, broke out in St. Petersburg. Count Witte was then forced to enact a law limiting the work day. Such advanced legislation was at that time unknown in many progressive western countries. In 1897, the total number of strikers was 102,000. In 1899, it reached 130,000.

The student revolutionary movement—a characteristic Russian phenomenon—developed alongside the proletarian current. In February, 1899, 25,000 university students in the country went on strike. It was the first political demonstration of its kind in history. Three years later, occurred the great city-wide strike in Rostov, under socialist auspices. It is a landmark in the annals of the Russian labor movement. In 1903, nearly all of the Ukraine and the Caucasus were swept by a tide of strikes in which 250,000 men participated.

These figures are vital to an appreciation of the magnitude of the industrial revolution in Russia.

Because of its rise by leaps and bounds, because of its patronage by a despotic government, Russian capitalism had no deep roots in the soil. On the other hand, the rebellion against the machine on the part of the proletariat of semi-peasants was fresh, instinctive, and headstrong. Capitalism in Russia was that center of contradictions which is the manure of cultivated revolution. Internationally, this capitalism was similarly situated.

"It was lying on the frontier," Stalin wrote many years later, "between the East and the West, it combined two social régimes that are common both to the highly developed capitalist countries and to the colonies. It was the most important pillar of western imperialism which connected the financial capital of the West with the colonies in the East."

Viewed from within or without, it was the most explosive compound in the modern social order.

To this powder magazine came Lenin with his Spark.

X

Stalin was behind bars in Batum studying Marx and reading the smuggled Iskra when two great currents of history met in London in 1903, where forty-three Russian revolutionists assembled in conference and constituted the Second Congress of the Russian Social Democratic Labor Party. Here Bolshevism was christened, gaining its name by accident but its identity by a clash of arms.

The current of revolutionary thought and the current of capitalist development in Russia united and found their joint expression here. Yet no one could have dreamed at the time that out of the impact of the two streams a force would arise that was to change the face of the world, to deflect and perhaps completely alter the course of civilization.

The participants of the congress were temperamentally and intellectually incompatible. On the one hand, were the traditional socialists, imbued with western philosophy, with humanitarian ideas, carriers of nineteenth-century democratic sentimentalism, seekers of a place for Russia in the European scheme of things. On the other, were the young and impudent rebels, impatient for action, utterly contemptuous of the achievements of European culture, conspirators by nature, militants, to whom Marxism was a bludgeon with which to knock the old order unconscious.

Presiding over the conference was the suave and erudite Plekhanov, who sided now with one faction, now with the other. Perhaps the youngest delegate present was Trotsky. The brilliant Martov led the "soft" camp against the aggressive Lenin, who had groomed the "hard-boiled" contingent. Lenin came primed for battle, with a definite objective in his mind. He came to translate theory into organization, to formulate a synthesis of doctrinaire Marxism and practical revolutionary tactics. He did not come to talk revolution. He came to make it.

Lenin took the offensive, and his fixed ideas of organization became the issue that split the Russian socialist party into Bolshevism and Menshevism. "Give us an organization of revolutionists, and we will turn Russia upside down," he had written several months before the congress. He meant a highly centralized body of trained, professional revolutionists, in opposition to the diffuse and free democratic form of organization advocated by Martov. To Lenin democracy was not an aim but a means. He wanted a party built and controlled not from the bottom up but from the top down. He accepted the epithet of Jacobin flung at him. He mocked at the phrase of freedom: "Freedom is a great word, but under the banner of freedom of trade the most plunderous wars have been waged, under the banner of freedom of labor, the toilers have been robbed." He declared that the one who "is frightened by the dictatorship of the proletariat, and babbles about the absolute value of proletariat claims, is an opportunist."

In this stand, Lenin was supported by Plekhanov, who declared: "The success of the revolution is the highest law, and if this success dictated temporarily the limitation of democratic principles, it would be criminal not to limit them. It is my personal opinion that even universal suffrage must be regarded from this viewpoint. The revolutionary proletariat could limit the political rights of the higher classes even as these classes once limited their political rights."

Ramsay MacDonald, who had been raising funds for Russian revolutionists, and the English Fabians, like H. G. Wells and G. B. Shaw, who were so sympathetic to their Russian comrades, would have been horrified to learn what was transpiring at the congress. They to whom universal suffrage was but a dream were already talking of limiting it while the masses followed them in the name of universal suffrage! The western parliamentarians would have been shocked to discover that this assembly of Russian fighters for freedom had rejected a motion to incorporate in their program a clause calling for the abolition of capital punishment.

These Russian socialists adopted a platform which was a most radical departure from that of their European colleagues. "A necessary condition for the social revolution," read a plank submitted by Plekhanov and amended by Lenin, "is the dictatorship of the proletariat, that is, the conquest by the proletariat of such political power as would permit it to crush all resistance on the part of the exploiters."

Bolshevism emerged from the congress as a definite faction that was still to win its independence. A unique organization came into being.

XI

It is a far cry from the dictatorship of the proletariat to the dictatorship of the party.

The proletariat stands for the masses. The party stands for the leaders.

The proletariat comprises the entire conglomerate class of workers. The party signifies a monopoly of an arbitrary group of professional revolutionists.

Lenin spoke of the dictatorship of the proletariat, but he aimed at the dictatorship of *his* party.

This is the crux of Bolshevism, the touchstone of the Soviet Revolution, the compass of Stalin's career.

The autocracy dictated the conspirative method of organization to all the revolutionary parties in Russia. But the Bolshevist group was the most uncompromising enemy of the existing political as well as social order. It opposed absolutism with absolutist methods of combat, and tsarism thus helped shape the dictatorial form of organization within the Bolshevist Party.

"Having laid the foundations of our organization underground," writes Yakovleva, who, like Stalin, is one of the oldest conspirators of Bolshevism, "our party acquired in the conspirative environment and forged there those characteristic features which distinguish it from all other parties: . . . Iron discipline, a single will, an ability to understand and sense the interests and aspirations of the wide laboring masses and give them their proper expression.

"Our Russian underground system was probably the darkest and most oppressive illegal existence ever known in history. At times it did not leave any outlets for the party, and it was solidly walled in. Seldom did it have an opportunity to apply the elements of democracy. The forms of its organization were always founded upon the principle of centralization."

How did this principle operate? A few individuals would constitute themselves into a committee which gradually formed circles in factories and intermediary committees. The members of the latter would be selected from the top. "Before being put on a committee, the comrade had to prove first by actual experience his loyalty, agility, and ability to hold his tongue. Each of the intermediary organizations maintained contact with the highest committee through one member only."

So long as Bolshevism was struggling for power, its centralized system was a means to an end. But what would happen if it ever achieved power?

Under the slogan of the dictatorship of the proletariat, the dictatorship of one party would be installed.

Constructed as that party was by Lenin, it would become a dictatorship of the consistory of its chiefs.

When put in office, such a form of organization would lead to a dictatorship of the higher bureaucracy.

The dictatorship of the bureaucracy would create an abyss between the government and the masses it purported to lead.

To preserve the government, there would unavoidably arise a system of terror and arbitrary rule.

The dictatorship of the proletariat would naturally evolve into a dictatorship of the police power of the government.

When the revolution came and Bolshevism did seize the reins, it brought with it a framework of centralized authority that was more inhibited with fear, with the idea of power, than the absolutism which had nourished it so long.

XII

Thus was Bolshevism cradled. Thus did it appear on the stage of modern history, at the inauguration of a new century, summing up the social advances and retreats of a previous century, and carrying within it the seeds of a deep past and an even deeper future.

Stalin found faith and despair coordinated in a complete political creed. He had subconsciously embraced it in his youth. He now embraced it consciously in his manhood.

CHAPTER THREE

IN THE RED CRUCIBLE

I

BENEATH the surface Russia, there now flourished an amazing underground Russia. People from abroad, eminent observers, foreign correspondents, visited St. Petersburg and Moscow, the Caucasus and the Crimea, interviewed high personages and studied the deep "devotion" of the Slavic peasants to the Little Father. They saw glittering palaces, cabarets, gala opera performances.

In the bowels of this "potent" empire, a subterranean empire was coalescing. Here people lived on false passports, here wigs and artificial whiskers went with hidden printing presses and forged official seals. They who walked on the streets were unaware of the catacombs below. A thousand leagues from the visible Russia worked these miners of the revolution. When they emerged into the open, their identities changed according to the place, time, and danger signals. Now the police would arrest a man under one name, now they would search for him in vain under a new alias.

The channels of underground Russia penetrated everywhere. Prison walls and bars did not stop revolutionary means of communication. Was not chemical ink invented for such purposes? A hundred devious and surreptitious ways were resorted to for secret correspondence. Stalin early displayed unusual ingenuity and resourcefulness in the art of deceiving and misleading the tsarist authorities. He was imprisoned in Batum, but was in touch with the nerve-center in London.

The London Congress had included a delegate from the Tiflis organization. The struggle that went on there between the two wings reverberated in the Batum prison. In his cell, Stalin learned of the differences within the party. Temperamentally Stalin belonged to Lenin's camp. His official biographers assure us that Stalin at once turned Bolshevist. Yet there is some doubt as to this claim. While resolute in the face of action, in the midst of battle, Stalin has more than once displayed a vacillating attitude in matters of pure policy, of choosing direction. The records of the Okhrana of that period contain a significant report dated 1903, which reads:

"According to new information received from our agents, Djugashvili is known in the organization under the sobriquet of 'Soso' or 'Koba.' He has been active since 1902 in the Social Democratic Party organization, first as a Menshevik and then as a Bolshevik, in the capacity of a propagandist and leader of the first district—that of the railwaymen."

Trotsky, from his place of exile, accused Stalin, on the basis of his failure to refute this statement, of having once been a Menshevik, than which nothing more damnable can be said of any member of the ruling party in the Soviet Union. It is probable that Stalin failed to distinguish at first between the two groups. It is even more likely that the young Stalin was still under the influence of the demigods who headed the Menshevist wing, and not sufficiently impressed by the reputation of the relatively new Lenin. In his later life, Stalin has but too often shown a proclivity for self-effacement, a ready acceptance of intellectual leadership, and an inability to adjust himself theoretically to a problem in short order.

II

If Stalin did not go into exile as a confirmed Leninist, he returned from it in that frame of mind. And he remained in Siberia for a singularly brief period. It was at the close of 1903 that he was dispatched to serve a three-year sentence of exile in a village in the Irkutsk Province. He hardly had time to reach his destination when he made his escape in January, 1904. But he had time enough to receive his first direct letter from Lenin, who was abroad. Let Stalin himself recite this episode:

"I came to know Lenin in 1903. This acquaintance, however, was not personal, but by correspondence. But it made upon me an unforgetable impression which did not leave me throughout the entire period of my party activity.

"My acquaintance with the revolutionary activity of Lenin at the end of the nineties, and especially since 1901, after the appearance of the Iskra, convinced me that we were dealing with an extraordinary person. I saw in him then not a simple leader of the party, but its actual founder. For he alone understood the inner being and immediate needs of our party. When I compared him with the other leaders, it seemed to me that his brothers-in-arms, Plekhanov, Martov, Axelrod and the others, were a head lower than Lenin, that Lenin in comparison with them was not just one of the leaders, but a leader of a higher type, a mountain eagle, who did not know fear in the struggle and who boldly led the party forward over the unexplored paths of the Russian revolutionary movement.

"This impression was so deeply implanted in my soul that I felt the necessity of writing about him to one of my nearest friends who was then a refugee abroad, requesting his opinion. Sometime afterward, when I was already in exile in Siberia—it was at the end of 1903—I received an enthusiastic reply from Lenin, to whom, it appeared, my friend had shown my note. Lenin's letter was comparatively short, but it offered a daring, fearless criticism of the practical policy of our party, and a remarkably clear and concentrated exposition of the entire plan of the party's activity for the nearest period. Only Lenin was capable of writing of the most confused things with such simplicity, condensation, and daring that each phrase did not speak, it shot. This simple and daring letter strengthened me even more in the belief that we had in Lenin's personality the mountain eagle of our party. I cannot forgive myself for burning up that letter of Lenin's as well as many others, just from the habit of an old underground worker."

Stalin made his way from Siberia to Baku, the great oil center, a hotbed of revolutionary activity. In this Tatar city he was one of the Marxist teachers of the Moslem circle "Hummet," which was the pioneer band of the labor and emancipation movement among the Mohammedan population. He organized many clandestine revolutionary committees and groups, and taught his followers, in addition to the elements of socialism, how to carry on conspirative activity, how to recruit and form the workers into circles, and how to establish underground communication.

The controversy between the Mensheviks and Bolsheviks was waxing warm. The Mensheviks advocated the policies of struggling for economic improvement and political freedom. The Bolsheviks argued for the overthrow of the whole bourgeois order together with the autocracy.

Stalin hammered this idea into the minds of his audiences. His favorite phrase in Baku was:

"The working class must win control of the state, for only in that way can it achieve its liberation."

III

One night there took place in Baku a heated debate at which Stalin was one of the spokesmen of the Bolshevist side. The atmosphere was surcharged with the conflict. One of Stalin's followers, Gazmamed, pulled out his dagger and rushed at the Menshevist speakers. Bloodshed was averted, but feeling ran high.

Throughout Russia the contest between the two factions now entered upon a period of bitter clashes. Nominally, the party was still united. Actually, the Bolsheviks and Mensheviks maintained independent central organizations. Each strove to win the largest following. The Caucasus was one of the strongholds of Menshevism. Stalin was associated here with

Kamenev, who was to become eventually one of the outstanding figures of the Soviet Revolution, in the United Bolshevist Committee of the Caucasus.

It was a period of great revolutionary events. The Russo-Japanese War was on. Stalin had laid the groundwork, together with many Leninist stalwarts, for the impending outbreak. In December, 1904, Baku gave the signal for the national upheaval. A general strike broke out, and in the riots and repression that ensued, the immense oil fields were set on fire and most of the works destroyed. That blaze lighted up the horizons of the vast country, and was reflected in Europe. In a sense, the event marked the début of the revolutionary proletariat of Russia on the national and international stage.

The following January, Father Gapon led the masses of the capital to the Winter Palace. Bloody Sunday came. The Socialist-Revolutionary Party was carrying out one terrorist act after another, assassinating high ministers and governors. The tsar's uncle, Grand Duke Sergei, had been blown to bits in Moscow. It all culminated in the first national general strike in the history of the world, in the formation of Soviets in St. Petersburg and other centers, in the famous October Manifesto of the tsar granting liberty and a constitution, and, finally, in the ferocious suppression of the gained freedom and in thousands of executions.

This memorable year passed under the aegis of Menshevism. Lenin and his fierce partizans were on the outside of the great popular movement. The Bolsheviks condemned the Menshevist fraternization with the liberal elements. They were not interested in democracy under capitalist auspices. They were more eager to overthrow capitalism than to subvert the autocracy. The downfall of the latter was desirable only as a step forward. Moreover, the Leninists were too engrossed in their battle against the Mensheviks, and too inexperienced to lead the great struggle of the people. Also, it was a period of beautiful speeches, of dramatic gestures, and Lenin with his Stalins and Kamenevs were not cut out for histrionic rôles. The authority of the party was great, and the Bolsheviks were in the minority in the Central Committee, unable to avail themselves of its prestige.

In the Caucasus, the revolution of 1905 assumed a climax of its own. An independent socialist republic arose in the Guria district. It was controlled by the Mensheviks. Stalin was at that time in charge of the local Bolshevist faction. He was active as the editor-in-chief of the illegal Bolshevist magazine, "The Struggle of the Proletariat." He persistently advanced the Bolshevist fighting slogans of the time, but the masses were largely in the Menshevist flock. He wrote a pamphlet, in his native language, under the title of "Briefly on the Differences in the Party." The climax of the revolutionary year found him in Tiflis, in the midst of this controversial activity, even as it found Lenin in Finland, leading a critical and dialectical battle against his comrades.

Neither Stalin nor Bolshevism emerged from the revolution of 1905 with flying colors. Lenin virtually sabotaged the Soviets, for of what use were Soviets under Menshevist control? It must be said that Lenin later confessed his error, although the mountains of apologetic literature issued by the Bolshevist Party in recent years on its policy in 1905 contain no mention of it. Lenin and his disciples thought in terms of insurrection and not mass movement. The masses were incapable of attaining the true objectives, for their leadership was wrong, for only the Bolsheviks possessed the correct map showing the road to the ultimate remaking of the world. And so it came to pass that the brilliant and independent Trotsky organized, inspired, and led the St. Petersburg Soviet of 1905, because of his faith in the creative abilities of the awakening common people, while Lenin and Stalin and their associates engaged in partizan politics and plotted adventurous uprisings, such as the disastrous Moscow revolt in December, 1905.

On the face of it, in our times, history has justified the pragmatical Lenin and Stalin. Whether it has justified it because of the incurable blindness of tsarism, or because of the inherent incapacity of the Russian intelligentsia for organic growth into statehood, whether it has justified it temporarily or permanently, the distant future will determine.

IV

Stalin found himself in the crucible of revolutionary action, theoretical conflict, and partizan politics. And as usual it was the aspect of partizanship which dominated the period and the career of the man. Was it not necessary to settle first of all whether Bolshevist or Menshevist policy was right? Stalin had no doubts. The Mensheviks were of the opinion then, as they are now, that Russia was not ripe for socialism, that the revolution was essentially bourgeois in character, that the best to be expected from it was a republic on the western pattern, that in such a free government the labor party would participate in parliament as a legitimate opposition fighting for socialist ideas and the betterment of the condition of the working class. Not so the Bolsheviks. To Stalin, the trend of the revolution was of paramount importance. Did not Lenin teach that in Russia a democratic revolution should be a prelude to socialism, and that the social revolution would come the sooner the more radical the scope of the democratic revolution was?

Twenty-five years ago this academic discussion would probably have brought a smile to the face of any European or American student of politics. Was the autocracy not enthroned? Was the revolutionary movement not weak and young to permit inner squabbles as to the ultimate division of spoils? Yet such is Leninism, and the completeness with which Stalin embraced it at that time is a key to his power today. The Soviet Revolution still draws its sap from the roots of those discussions, and the principles of its guidance are defined in the light of the early gospels.

From his refuge in Switzerland, Lenin wrote in March, 1905, six months before the climax of the general strike: "After the gigantic experience of Europe, after the unprecedented burst of energy on the part of the labor class in Russia, we shall be able to fan as never before the blaze of revolutionary light before the dark and crushed masses. We shall succeed in realizing with unequaled completeness all the democratic reforms, our entire minimum program, thanks to the fact that we stand on the shoulders of a row of revolutionary generations in Europe. We shall succeed in making the Russian revolution not a movement of several months, but of many years, leading not merely to minor concessions on the part of the ruling powers, but to the fullest downfall of these powers. And if we succeed in that, then . . . then the revolutionary conflagration will set Europe on fire and the European workingman, worn out by capitalist oppression, will rise in his turn and show us 'how it is done.' Then the revolutionary flow in Europe will in turn inspire Russia, and the epoch of several revolutionary years will become an epoch of several revolutionary decades."

This was not a tactical program, but a faith. It was addressed to the Russia of 1905, and not of 1917. The despair of the World War was absent. The ground for world revolution was not yet sufficiently cultivated. Yet it is remarkable that in this internationalist pronunciamento Lenin spoke of Europe and Russia as two separate and contrasting entities. Here was Lenin's true self speaking. Russia was not Europe. And only in Russia was it possible for a revolutionary party to look so far ahead as to miss its immediate opportunities.

V

Stalin emerged as the undisputed leader of the Bolshevist faction in the Caucasus. According to the testimony of his associates, Yenukidze and Ordjonikidze, he "literally bore on his own shoulders the entire brunt of the battle with the Mensheviks." He was the organizational leader and the philosophical exponent of the movement. The Bolshevist press was largely in his hands. He addressed numerous conferences and meetings. He gave no quarter to the "half-measure" creed of the Mensheviks, and gained the reputation among the latter as the "most odious Bolshevik" in the country.

"The Bolshevist newspapers of the period in Tiflis were largely founded on Stalin," writes Yenukidze. "In addition to numerous revolutionary articles, on questions of historical materialism, the labor movement, the trade-union question, Stalin wrote a lot on the national problem. Incidentally, in this question he undoubtedly, with the exception of Lenin, is the leading theoretician of our party. In a word, Stalin was the ideological and practical guide of our organizations in Transcaucasia. In order to take care of this enormous task, it was necessary to work incessantly, to be swallowed up by it entirely, and constantly to replenish one's knowledge. Stalin actually gave all of himself to the work. For him, outside of the revolutionary activity, there was no life, nothing existed. When he did not attend meetings and conduct circles, he spent all his time in a little room piled with books and newspapers, or in the editorial office of a Bolshevist journal which was just as 'spacious.' "

In the summer of 1905, it was decided that the Bolsheviks should, on their own initiative, call a general strike in Baku. Stalin went there as a representative of the central committee to supervise the work. Later in the year, he spent some time among the rebels of the so-called "Gurian Republic." He carried on effective Bolshevist propaganda among the peasants there. The year was marked by a general strike in Tiflis, preparations for an uprising, organization of military detachments of revolutionists. In all these activities, Stalin had a direct hand. The importance of winning the masses over to the Leninist slogans was to Stalin transcendental. The proletariat was the only weapon for a successful revolution, and it had to be saved from itself, from its friendly enemies.

In December, 1905, a Bolshevist national conference was held in Tammerfors, Finland, where Lenin was in hiding. Stalin went there as a delegate from Transcaucasia. Here he met for the first time his master. His description of this event reveals Stalin as well as Lenin:

"I first met him in December, 1905, at the Bolshevist Conference in Tammerfors, Finland. I had hoped to see the mountain eagle of our party, a great man, great not only politically but, if you please, physically, for Lenin had assumed in my imagination the shape of a giant, a statuesque and imposing figure. How disappointed I was when I beheld a person of most ordinary appearance, in height below medium, in no way different from the common run of people.

"It is customary for a 'great man' to come late to meetings, so that the assembled audience would await his appearance with bated breath, and so that before the 'great man' came out the listeners could utter warnings: 'Sh . . . quiet . . . he is coming.' This ritual did not seem unnecessary to me, as it was impressive, inspiring respect. It was therefore with great disappointment that I learned that Lenin had appeared at the meeting ahead of the delegates and had gone to a corner where he conducted a conversation, a most ordinary conversation, with the most ordinary delegates of the conference. I will not conceal that at the time it seemed to me in the nature of an infraction of some necessary rules.

"Only later did I understand that this simplicity, modesty of Lenin's, this seeking to remain unnoticed or at least not to strike the eye and not to emphasize his high position, was one of the strongest features in Lenin, in the character of this new leader of the masses of plain and lowly humanity.

"Two of Lenin's speeches at this conference were remarkable. They dealt with the current situation and the agricultural question. Unfortunately they have not been preserved. These were inspiring speeches which caused a storm of enthusiasm among all the listeners. The unusual force of persuasion, the simplicity and clarity of the argumentation, the brief and easily understandable phrases, the absence of posing, the absence of dizzying gestures and affected phrases intended to make an impression, all these advantageously distinguished Lenin's speech from those of the usual 'parliamentary' orators.

"But it was not this phase of Lenin's speeches that fascinated me then. I was fascinated by his insuperable force of logic, which somewhat dryly but solidly took possession of the audience, electrifying it gradually and then capturing it completely. I remember many of the delegates remarking that the logic of Lenin's speeches resembled all-powerful tentacles which gripped one like pincers and from which there was no escape; that one had either to surrender to him or to face utter failure."

VI

The collapse of the revolution of 1905 led to conciliatory attempts in the Bolshevist and Menshevist camps. Although the opportunity had been missed to overthrow the monarchy, certain victories had been won, such as the Duma, the right of workers to organize trade unions, and freedom of press and assembly which was at the time still respected by the authorities. The two factions now decided to unite on the basis of the election of a new Central Committee. In April, 1906, a "united" congress of the party was held in Stockholm.

It was the first time that Stalin was a delegate to a national convention, a high distinction. It was the period of the election campaign to the first Duma. The Bolshevists stood for a boycott. They lost out. Stalin returned to Tiflis to edit a daily paper, Dro. He waged a bitter campaign against the anarchist and syndicalist elements then active in Georgia, and wrote a series of articles on "Anarchism and Socialism."

The following year, another party congress met in the Brotherhood Church in London. There were three hundred delegates present, representing about one hundred and fifty thousand organized members. The Bolsheviks and the Mensheviks were about evenly divided. Stalin attended under the name of Ivanovitch. The delegates were mostly without money, and the treasury of the party was empty. It was Maxim Gorki who saved the situation by securing a loan from an Englishman sympathetic to Russian freedom. The lender, however, insisted on getting the signatures of all the delegates to the strange promissory note. This note was not redeemed until after the Soviet Revolution. All the labors and resolutions of the London Congress were reduced to naught by the action of the tsar's government a month later, when the Duma was dissolved, the legal labor press shut down, stern repressions were inaugurated throughout the country, and the various revolutionary parties wrecked for many years to come by sweeping arrests and exiles.

"I met Lenin for the second time, in 1906, at the Stockholm Congress of our party," narrates Stalin. "It is known that at this convention the Bolsheviks remained in the minority, and suffered defeat. I then saw Lenin for the first time in the rôle of a beaten person. In no respect did he resemble those leaders who whine and pine away at reverses. On the contrary, defeat turned Lenin into a ball of energy, inspiring his followers to new battles, to future victory. I am speaking of Lenin's defeat. But what kind of defeat was it? It was enough to look at his opponents, the victors of the Stockholm Convention—Plekhanov, Axelrod, Martov, and the others. They little resembled real victors, for Lenin in his merciless criticism of Menshevism left them no room to turn about. I recall how we, the delegates, of the Bolshevist faction, assembled in a cluster and asked Lenin's advice. In the conversation of some of our people, one could detect fatigue, dejection. I recall how Lenin, answering one such comrade, hissed through his teeth: 'Do not whine, comrades, we will certainly win, we are in the right.'

"Lenin spoke to us then, giving expression to his hatred for whining intellectuals, to faith in our own strength, faith in victory. One felt that the defeat of the Bolsheviks was temporary, that the Bolsheviks must win in the near future.

"At the following congress in 1907 in London, the Bolsheviks came out victorious. Here I saw Lenin for the first time in the rôle of victor. Usually, victory turns the heads of certain leaders, making them haughty and presumptuous. More frequently, in such cases, do the victors celebrate their victory and rest on their laurels. Lenin in no manner resembled such leaders. Quite the opposite, after victory he became especially watchful and alert. I recall how Lenin persistently urged the delegates: First of all, do not be carried away by victory and do not become grandiloquent; second, solidify your victory; third, finish your enemy, for he is only beaten but still far from dead."

VII

In the eventful four years that had elapsed, Stalin forged on imperceptibly to the front ranks of his party. Yet outwardly there was nothing to mark him as a man of promise, a man of destiny. The party had scores of brilliant generals, forceful orators, deep students of socialism, writers of distinction, deadly dialecticians. In the verbal duels at the Stockholm and London meetings, Stalin took no part. He was not elected to the general staff, the Central Committee, at either of the congresses. He remained a captain, in charge of a field detachment. Possibly his command of the Russian language was deficient. Possibly his conspirative work had trained him to stay in the background. And perhaps it was a lack of original ideas that made Stalin, in a day of searching for new paths, just another delegate. But if he then lacked in the art of self-advancement, he did not lack the capacity of absorption. Like so many of the Bolshevist leaders, he was wax in the hands of Lenin. He was molded to an amazing degree by the personality of his master. And like so many of Lenin's satellites, he emitted no light of his own.

CHAPTER FOUR

BANDIT OR REVOLUTIONIST?

I

THE revolution was prostrate. Lenin was conscious of defeat. But the Bolshevist army had not been raised for retreat. Its ranks included men whose ideological equipment was scant, but whose temperamental armor was inflexible. There had been bloodshed, conflagrations, there had been "republics," Soviets, and "parliaments." All of that had penetrated deep into the veins of the fierce warriors. The thought of surrender except on the actual battlefield was foreign to them. The will for vengeance was not to be side-tracked. That was the psychology of the Bolshevist ranks. But the Bolshevist leadership was contaminated with it, too. It not merely abetted it. It inspired and nourished it.

From the arsenal of revolutionary communism of the past, Lenin and Stalin pulled out the slogans and theories to fit the moment. Partizan warfare, a forlorn hope, a dubious adventure at best, was elevated to a philosophical plane, was blessed with quotations from Marx and other sacred gospels.

The desultory revolutionary fighting assumed two distinct forms. There was a wave of assassination of cruel officials. This Bolshevism never countenanced as an effective weapon. Then there was the widespread method of staging raids on public or private persons or institutions. This was "expropriation"—confiscation of wealth—which was interpreted as a justifiable means of combating the capitalist order.

"We consider that acts of violence are admissible for the purpose of seizing funds belonging to the enemy, the autocracy, when these funds are turned over for use in organizing insurrections," read the resolution of a group of Bolsheviks, with which both Lenin and Stalin were identified, at the "United" Congress held in Stockholm in 1906. It is clear that such a statement was comprehensive enough to permit individual adventurers to organize revolutionary bands for raids and robbery, so long as they turned over some of the seized treasure to the party.

That was precisely the condition prevailing in many parts of Russia during 1906 and 1907. The resolution of the Bolshevist faction, however, made the reservation that all "partizan attacks be under the control of the party."

The Mensheviks and other revolutionists denounced this policy as one of anarchism, Blanquism, as leading to the demoralization of the masses. Lenin was represented as the chieftain of a band of highwaymen. In the Caucasus, Stalin was the head, the chief of staff, of the "fighting organization" of his party.

"When I hear Social Democrats declare proudly and smugly, 'We are not anarchists, not thieves, not robbers, we are above it, we reject partizan warfare!' —I ask: Do these people understand what they are talking about?" Thus Lenin in his article on "Partizan Warfare" in September, 1906.

To Lenin, as well as to Stalin, it was impossible to

apply a yardstick of "principles" or ethics to the methods of civil warfare. He elaborated this viewpoint, and declared that to him it was all a question of technique, of expedience, that the partizan raids were an answer of the lower strata to the challenge of reaction, and as such were inevitable. Having started from the premises that a state of civil warfare existed—events proved that he was wrong—having stated that partizan violence was spontaneous, he found it logical Bolshevism to justify it, to goad it on, and to clothe it in the phraseology of orthodox Marxism.

II

In the home town of Stalin, from the hot soil of the Caucasus, under the severe training and care of Stalin's own hand, blossomed forth the highest expression of revolutionary banditism or partizan warfare—depending upon the viewpoint of the reader.

It is a chapter still largely wrapped in darkness. But every ray of light cast upon it is of the utmost value in penetrating the soul of Bolshevism. Stalin himself and all the innumerable historians of Bolshevism have perpetuated the mystery surrounding the episode, and in that way emphasized its doubtful character. The "Tiflis affair" is banned from the annals of the revolution, and only a few obscure Bolshevist sources are available to help illuminate it.

In the town of Gori, Stalin had for one of his playmates a boy by the name of Petrosian, the son of a well-to-do Armenian merchant. He was to become the armor-bearer of Stalin in later years. Lacking the education and mental abilities of S

Petrosian shared with his older comrade an uncanny aptitude for conspirative work. Petrosian was also endowed with extraordinary courage. He had been expelled from school for offending the religious sentiments of his teacher. His family had moved to Tiflis, and engaged Stalin to become his tutor. But Stalin was already a member of the party, and he converted his pupil. Petrosian became Stalin's right-hand man. He was entrusted with dangerous missions, with technical jobs. Speaking Russian poorly, he once, starting on a party errand, mispronounced "komu"—the Russian word meaning "to whom"—as "kamo."

"Eh, you Kamo, Kamo!" laughed Stalin.

The name Kamo stuck to Petrosian. Kamo became a legendary hero of the revolution, a Robin Hood of Bolshevism. During the years that followed, he managed under Stalin all the secret affairs, from transporting arms and illegal literature to securing forged passports. He gained a reputation for amazing inventiveness. He would change his disguise frequently. Now he would dress as an officer, now he would turn into a street hawker. Kamo was the most elusive person in Tiflis, and yet he paraded in the center of the town, his appearance changed beyond recognition.

Toward the close of 1906, there came into being in Tiflis the Bolshevist partizan organization. Its objective was the securing of funds and arms. Its brains were those of Stalin, its hand that of Kamo.

The group of warriors was small but select.

"Kamo was able to assemble from the ranks," writes Lepeshinsky, the communist historian, in his introduction to the memoirs of Kamo's widow, the only extant official document on the "Tiflis affair," "the best of the adventurers, of the elements inclined to banditism, and to lead them toward the light by welding them into well-disciplined bands animated by the revolutionary spirit."

The partizan squad selected Kutais as its testing ground. Here the first raid of consequence was carried out. It netted fifteen thousand rubles, not an insignificant sum in the condition of the Bolshevist treasury at the time. The police sought Kamo, but all efforts to apprehend him were in vain.

Kamo was now ready for the great achievement of his career.

III

In Finland, in a little villa, the generalissimo of the Bolshevist forces was still watching the dying embers of the extinguished revolution. In a few months he would go abroad, to stay there for ten years, until the second revolution came. The financial position of the party was most deplorable. The adventure in Moscow lost for the Bolsheviks all their moneyed friends. The situation was desperate. There were no means to acquire the grease for oiling the creaking chariot of the Bolshevist machine.

Stalin dispatched Kamo to Finland. What Stalin could not achieve by correspondence, Kamo could by his magnetic personality. Had he not earned the gratitude of the party by the Kutais raid? Let Lenin himself behold the culprit. And it must be said that Kamo was an idealist, personal gain was remote from his mind. His habits were ascetic. His enthusiasm contagious.

What a strange pilgrimage! To the prophet of the materialistic philosophy of history came this "Caucasian robber"—as Lenin jestingly described Kamo.

He went away not with a load of Marxist quotations, but in quest of a transport of arms and dynamite. Lenin sent Kamo abroad, to Litvinov, the present commissar of foreign affairs. In his reminiscences, Litvinov describes in detail the amazing mission. He was able to purchase the arms and secure a boat which was to leave from a Bulgarian port with false consignment papers. Kamo was on board, in charge of the precious cargo. The boat was wrecked off the Roumanian coast. Kamo escaped and made his way to Berlin. His associate, Luter, tells of an argument in Kamo's presence with a Caucasian Menshevik. Kamo broke in with the remark: "Why argue with him. Let me cut his throat."

Kamo returned to the Caucasus.

IV

At ten o'clock in the morning of June 23, 1907, the city of Tiflis was rocked by a series of explosions. When the smoke had cleared away, an appalling scene was revealed. Around the central Pushkin Park scores of bodies were swimming in pools of blood. Many were writhing in pain. The harvest totalled fifty dead and wounded.

What had happened? A few minutes before, two carriages accompanied by two policemen and surrounded by five armed Cossacks on horseback, had left the post office on the way to the state bank. In one of the carriages was the bank cashier, in the other the bookkeeper. They were transporting 250,-000 rubles.

The streets were crowded with people. No one noticed a group of men sitting in a café on the sidewalk. Seven of the associates of this group were posted in different places. Among them were two women. Concealed about them were half a dozen deadly bombs. A dashingly dressed officer was riding about in the neighborhood, attempting to warn bystanders away. That was Kamo.

As the procession carrying the money turned the nearest corner, a woman on watch appeared with an open newspaper. This was the signal. Within a few moments two bombs were launched at the carriages. In another instant, two more were thrown. There were two and then two more explosions. For a mile around the window panes were shattered. The two policemen and one of the Cossacks were stretched on the street. The horses broke through the cavalry guard and swept on madly. They carried the coveted treasure.

At this critical moment, one of Kamo's men, without losing his head, made a dash for the carriage, and launched his bomb. He was knocked to the ground by the detonation. A comrade of his, however, was on the job. He seized the bag with the money.

The confusion and panic that ensued made it impossible for the authorities in their investigation to establish all the facts. These, however, we now have on the good authority of Mrs. Kamo.

Kamo drove through the death scene a few moments after the explosion. He was shooting into air, and swearing loudly, to give the impression that he was pursuing the perpetrators of the act. On the way he picked up his wounded comrade. All the participants in the bloody affair disappeared. No trace was found of the money in Tiflis. When the officials and troops arrived on the scene, the field was deserted. Afterward, the city was surrounded and numerous searches instituted, but all in vain. The money was hidden in a place that defied any suspicion. It was upholstered in a couch belonging to the manager of the Tiflis Observatory.

Such was the most celebrated act of Lenin's "Partizan Warfare." It was regarded as a ghastly affair, especially because of the death and injury it inflicted upon scores of innocent people. But technically it was a perfect achievement. Kamo had reason to be gratified with his success. Stalin had reason to be gratified with the craftsmanship of his disciple. And would not the Bolshevist generals be gratified with such an ample treasury?

Apparently, in the headquarters abroad, the Tiflis act launched a bomb, too. Many Bolsheviks were horrified by the bloody adventure. It had occurred, it should be noted, soon after the London Congress, which had expressly forbidden such terrorist action. But Lenin circumvented the prohibition by creating a secret Bolshevist center to maintain relations with the revolutionary partizans.

We know that the money reached the hands of Lenin and Krassin. It was in large bills, mostly five-hundred-ruble notes, and Litvinov received his first valuable training in international affairs when he was entrusted with the job of exchanging the money into foreign exchange. He was arrested in Paris in the course of the operation.

Semashko, now commissar of health, was seized in Switzerland. "I was arrested in Geneva, in 1907," he writes. "It was the most absurd event in my life. I was put in jail on account of a misunderstanding. They connected me with the famous Tiflis expropriation of 1907." Declaring that he was one of those Bolsheviks who had in principle opposed such methods, Semashko reveals that the cause for his arrest was his receipt of a letter from a woman involved in changing the Tiflis money abroad.

The failure to convert all of the looted hoard, the fear of further arrests and of an open scandal that would disrupt the Bolshevist ranks, compelled Lenin to come to the decision to destroy the remaining "scraps of paper."

V

The reverberations of the Tiflis affair in revolutionary and party circles nearly upset Stalin's whole career.

Bolshevism had been reared on discipline. And now Lenin and his Caucasian lieutenant had violated the first dictates of their platform.

The Social Democratic leadership demanded vengeance. In the prevailing circumstances of general decline, Lenin could not think of picking up the gauntlet in defense of Stalin. The Caucasian regional committee investigated the Tiflis raid. Stalin's leading share in it was exposed. A tribunal was set up to pass judgment.

Stalin and several of his associates were expelled from the party.

To be sure, Lenin had his own secret Bolshevist center, and he had no intention of making the excommunication of Stalin effective and genuine. Nevertheless, it is an extraordinary blot on the career of the man who holds so high and sacred the tradition of an inviolate record as a member of the party.

Small wonder that the invulnerable Stalin is most vulnerable when the "Tiflis affair" is brought up. His customary silence is deepened in this connection. In his politico-biographical sketch of Stalin, published in Paris, in August, 1930, Trotsky from his place of exile in Turkey struck at his enemy in this direction. Trotsky, it is true, drew his own conclusions from the episode, but none the less he afforded an insight into Stalin's personality. Wrote Trotsky:

"In 1907, Stalin participated in the expropriation of the Tiflis bank. The Mensheviks were indignant at this adventurous method of Bolshevism. The fact of his participation in a daring although but partial attack on the enemy does credit to the revolutionary resoluteness of Stalin. However, one cannot but be amazed that this fact has been, in cowardly fashion, removed from all the official biographies of Stalin. Is that done in the name of bureaucratic respectability? We think that that is not the case. Rather is it due to political consideration. For if participation in an expropriation cannot in itself compromise a revolutionist in the eyes of other revolutionists, the false political estimate of the situation of that period does compromise Stalin as a political thinker. Isolated blows at institutions, including treasuries, of the enemy are compatible only with mass risings, with a revolutionary tide. When, however, the masses are on the retreat, private, isolated partizan attacks inevitably degenerate into adventures, and lead to the demoralization of the party. In 1907, the revolution was receding, and such expropriations became adventures. Stalin showed at that time, at least, that he could not distinguish between the ebb and flow of revolution."

VI

The surge of the successful revolution ten years later washed away the stain on Stalin's past. And fifteen years later, garbed in the vestments of august authority, Stalin, the impeccable revolutionist, was admitted to the Bolshevist hall of fame.

As to Kamo, his memory is revered in the Soviet Union as that of a "hero of the revolution." After many more incredible adventures, Kamo lived to see the revolution and to head the Baku Cheka. He died as a result of an accident. He was run over by an automobile. When Stalin learned the news, he wired the head of the Tiflis Cheka: "Have the chauffeur shot!" The innocent chauffeur, a member of the party and of the trade union, was executed without trial.

In Tiflis today a street, a hospital, a steamboat and . . . nurseries bear the name that Stalin once jestingly bestowed upon his faithful comrade in arms.

CHAPTER FIVE

IN THE SHADOWS OF DEFEAT

I

THE Tiflis bombs necessitated a change of residence for Stalin. Moreover, Bolshevism was on the wane in Georgia. The Bolsheviks were unable to elect a single deputy to the Duma while the Menshevist representation there was unusually large. The Bolshevist organization deteriorated into a narrow circle, and its center of activity was therefore transferred to Baku. There Stalin went, too. Once more the conflict with the Mensheviks flared up. The "united" front had virtually collapsed, and the issue between the two factions became one of survival. Stalin directed a campaign of boring from within the Baku organization, with the result that in two months the Bolsheviks captured control by means of securing a majority in the local committee. Was it an honest majority? Not according to the Mensheviks who would not submit, and accused Stalin of treachery and splitting the labor ranks. That Stalin employed rough methods is evidenced by his official biographer, who speaks of his "squeezing out the Mensheviks from the workingmen's districts in the city."

An independent Bolshevist union of oil workers was set up as a result of Stalin's hidden machinations. "The leading rôle in it was played by Djaparidze," writes one of its organizers, Stopani.

"Comrade Koba [Stalin] played a lesser part, as he devoted most of his energies to party work of which he was the guide." There developed differences among the Baku Bolsheviks on the question of the relations between the labor unions and the party organization. The methods championed by Stalin for subordinating the former to the latter earned him in the controversy the position of a Left extremist.

At the same time, Stalin was in charge of the Bolshevist publication, the Baku Worker. He achieved a notable success in the fall of 1907 in connection with the move for the signing of a collective agreement between the oil workers and producers. A conference was scheduled to be held with the oil interests. Should the Bolshevist organization participate in the conference or boycott it? Here was a test for a practical politician. Stalin advanced the proposition that the workers should attend the conference on certain conditions. These required the owners to recognize the trade unions and to guarantee free elections of delegates and a free press. Stalin won. There followed the strange spectacle of a labor "parliament" in session in Baku at a time when reaction was rampant in the rest of Russia. After functioning for a couple of weeks, the Baku "parliament" was dispersed and many of its members arrested. Although Stalin had kept himself in the background, the widespread raids resulted in his seizure, too. He was put in the Bayilov Prison. But he at least had the comfort of knowing that he had imposed Bolshevism upon labor in the great oil center. "From that time on Baku became a citadel of Bolshevism," runs the official account.

Stalin was arrested as a member of the Baku strike committee and charged with fomenting revolution. He spent eight months in prison. But the authorities lacked evidence to justify an indictment and trial. He was then given an administrative sentence of exile for a term of three years to Solvychegodsk, in the north of European Russia.

II

Easter Sunday was dawning upon the Bayilov Prison in Baku. The political inmates were in rebellion. Groups of men were rushing from cell to cell, urging their comrades to join in the outbreak. An armed band hammered at the door of Stalin's cell. But Stalin would not participate. He bolted the door. He was threatened by the rioters at the point of a gun, but refused to join.

In the morning, order was restored. The First Company of the brutal Selyansk Regiment had been called out to quell the rebels. The soldiers were lined up in two rows, and commanded to use their rifle-butts. All the political prisoners were forced, in single file, to run the gantlet of the punitive company. Stalin, holding his head erect, with a book under his arm, proudly marched under the rain of blows.

This picture of Stalin as a heroic figure was drawn by a political enemy of his, Semyon Verestchak, a fellow prisoner of his in Baku. "One day," he writes, "a new face appeared in the Bolshevist camp. I inquired who the comrade was, and in great secrecy was told: 'It is Koba [Stalin].' "

The Bayilov Prison was the central jail from

which the political prisoners of the entire Caucasus were distributed all over Siberia and other northern zones of exile. Built to accommodate four hundred inmates, it was now crowded with fifteen hundred men and women. Within its walls, however, the régime was relatively lax for the political convicts.

"It was a training school for professional revolutionists, a kind of propagandist institute, a militant academy," relates Verestchak. "Koba stood out among the various circles as a Marxist student. He wore a blue satin smock, with a wide-open collar, without a belt. His head was bare. A bashlik—a sort of detached hood with two tapering scarfs—was thrown across his shoulders. He always carried a book. Of more than medium height, he walked with a slow catlike tread. He was slender, with pointed face, pockmarked skin, sharp nose, and small eyes looking out from under a narrow forehead, slightly indented. He spoke little and sought no company.

"The Stalin of these days was defiant; he submitted to no regulations. The political prisoners at Baku endeavored to segregate themselves as much as possible from the criminal convicts. The younger political prisoners were punished if they infringed upon this unwritten law. Openly flouting the custom, Koba was constantly to be seen in the company of bandits, swindlers, and thieves. He chose as his cellmates the Sokvadelidze brothers, one a counterfeiter, the other a well-known Bolshevik. Active people, people who did things, attracted him."

Stalin never engaged in any arguments with individuals. "He always challenged his opponents to an 'organized debate.' These debates were held almost on a scheduled program. They were on such issues as the agrarian question, and the tactics of revolution, or on philosophical topics. The arguments on the agrarian problem were especially heated and sometimes ended in blows. I remember such a discussion in which Koba took part. His comrade Ordjonikidze came to the defense of his thesis, and wound up by striking his opponent in the face. He was severely beaten up by the Socialist-Revolutionists.

"Koba's appearance and mannerisms did not conduce to ease at these debates. He lacked wit and expressed his thoughts somewhat dryly. The mechanical precision of his memory, however, amazed everybody. He had apparently learned by heart all of Marx's 'Capital.' Marxism was his element, and in it he was invincible. There was no power that could dislodge him from a position once he had taken it. He was able to quote a corresponding formula from Marx for every phenomenon. This created a strong impression on the young and unenlightened members of the party.

"Koba generally enjoyed in the Caucasus the reputation of a second Lenin. He was regarded as the leading Marxist expert. Hence his very special hatred for Menshevism. In his opinion, anyone who professed Marxism but who did not interpret it in the Bolshevist light was a scoundrel.

"He always actively supported the ringleaders in jail, and this made him a good fellow in the eyes of the prison public.

"At a time when the whole prison was upset, sleepless, tense, in expectation of a night execution, Koba would calmly compose himself in slumber or else study Esperanto, which he regarded as the future language of the Socialist International."

Several months before his imprisonment Stalin married a Georgian girl, a member of the party, also an active Bolshevik, of whom very little is known. It was his first marriage. In 1908, while he was in the Baku jail, his wife gave birth to a son who was named Jacob—more popularly known as Yasha. The boy spent the greater part of his childhood away from his father, who was being driven from prison to exile and from exile to prison.

III

Stalin escaped in July, 1909, from his place of exile, and made his way to St. Petersburg, but a few hundred miles away. Here he remained in hiding in the apartment of Savchenko, the chief supply officer of a cavalry guard regiment. He returned to Baku a month later, to resume his underground career. But his freedom did not last long.

This was the period of the strong-arm reign of Premier Stolypin, a period of darkest reaction and greatest demoralization in revolutionary ranks. Many prominent leaders had become disillusioned, given up their underground activity, and taken up private careers. The longing for "peace" and comfort overcame large numbers of revolutionists. The Bolshevist Party did not escape the general trend. Moreover, it split into numerous factions, and was passing through one crisis after another. There were those who were for "liquidating" the old conspirative methods and who favored activity within the restricted legal conditions. Stalin was and is essentially a person of dominating will on the offensive, when the tide is rising, and of impatience and reticence on the defensive, when it recedes. His rôle during the depression was hardly in keeping with his later professions.

In January, 1910, the Central Committee, elected three years before in London, held its last plenary session in Paris. Two of its members were sent back to Russia to assemble the scattered forces and reconstitute the Home Bureau of the Central Committee from representatives of both factions. This bureau was to consist of five men. Lenin empowered the prominent Moscow Bolshevik, Nogin, to draft Stalin. In order to get his acceptance to serve, Nogin made a special trip to Baku. This was an unusual procedure, in view of the importance of Nogin then and the relative unimportance of Stalin. Nogin's associate Germanov writes: "Both of us knew Stalin personally, as one of the best and most active Baku workers. Nogin went to Baku to come to an agreement with him, but for a number of reasons, Stalin would not assume the duties of a member of the Central Committee."

This was an unprecedented act on the part of an officer of the most disciplined party in the world. Stalin had not forgotten his treatment as a result of the Tiflis affair. His attitude of aloofness caused Lenin to send Nogin on a special mission to come to an "agreement" with Stalin. Yet the Bolshevist vocabulary has no such word. It knows only obedience. But Stalin knew his price, and he turned down the offer to become affiliated with the supreme organ, the Central Committee!

Stalin was arrested again as a fugitive from exile in March, 1910. This time his sentence was increased from three to five years, but instead of the customary transfer to a worse and more isolated section, he was returned to Solvychegodsk. Here he developed considerable activity, and entered into a literary controversy with Jordania, the eminent leader of the Georgian Mensheviks, on the question of the hegemony of the proletariat in the future social revolution. But Stalin did not confine himself to theoretical work; he helped organize a socialist group among the residents of Solvychegodsk. He even managed to deliver lectures, as the police surveillance was not strict. From among the other exiles in the district he recruited men that seemed to him born conspirators, and trained them in the art of underground operation.

IV

Stalin had no patience with the hair-splitting squabbles and acrimonious polemics that racked the entire socialist labor movement in Russia during this period. Yet the same Stalin, when in power, displayed an amazing capacity for theoretical hair-splitting against Trotsky, Zinoviev, Kamenev, Rykov, and Bukharin. A letter of his, dated January 24, 1911, written while in exile and intercepted by the police, has been preserved. It shows Stalin's attitude toward the differences in which Lenin and Trotsky were at the time involved, and which Stalin ably capitalized fifteen years later.

"We have, of course, heard," wrote Stalin, "of the 'tempest in a teapot' abroad: blocs of Lenin and Plekhanov on the one side; of Trotsky, Martov, Bogdanov, on the other. The attitude of the workingmen toward the first bloc is, as far as I know, favorable. But generally, the workingmen are beginning to look upon 'abroad' with an attitude of contempt, as if saying:

"'Let them scale the walls to their hearts' content; but the way we feel about it, he who has the interest of the movement at heart, should keep busy: as for the rest, it will all subside.'

"I think such an attitude is for the best."

Thirteen years later, speaking in the Kremlin, shortly after the death of Lenin, Stalin had this to say to the victorious proletariat:

"The period of 1909–1911, when the party, disrupted by the counter-revolution, had gone through a process of complete disintegration, was a period of lack of faith in the party, a period of wholesale desertion not only on the part of intellectuals but partly of workingmen, a period of negation of underground methods, a period of 'liquidation' and decay. Not only the Mensheviks but the Bolsheviks represented a whole series of factions and currents, largely removed from the labor movement. It is known that at that time the idea of completely 'liquidating' the conspirative work became fashionable, and it was advocated that the workingmen should be organized into a legal, liberal party under the Stolypin régime.

"Lenin was then the only person who did not become influenced by the general trend and who held high the banner of the party, collecting the divided and shattered forces with amazing patience and unexampled obstinacy, battling against everybody, against all anti-party currents within the labor movement, defending the old party system, with unusual bravery and with unprecedented persistence. It is a fact that Lenin emerged victorious from this conflict."

The Stalin of the Kremlin was able to forget the words of Stalin the exile, and his former carping criticism of Lenin's "tempest in a teapot" now became "that policy of truest principles which enabled Lenin to storm the impregnable positions of the enemy."

V

Stalin proved himself one of the most successful evaders of the tsar's exile and espionage system. There were others who had records of numerous escapes, but it is doubtful if there was another revolutionist of similar standing who managed to get off with such light sentences. The explanation lay in his uncanny method of conspirative activity. He was always able "to cover up his traces," and to make the impression upon the authorities of being an unimportant, obscure member of the party. This condition was to change soon. As he climbed higher to the top, he would be more easily detected. In the highest sanctum of Bolshevism there was soon to appear an agent of the Okhrana, and the tsar's government was to know of every move, contemplated and made, by Lenin's group.

Stalin was now thirty-one. He had been identified for fourteen years with the Caucasian revolutionary movement. He was now ready to abandon his native field, and continue his strange career on the national scene, but still deep underground. At the invitation of the Central Committee, Stalin perpetrated his periodic escape in the spring of 1911 and made St. Petersburg his headquarters. From this moment on, he devoted himself to all-Russian work, gradually losing his provincial interests and perspective.

This year marked the final rupture between the Mensheviks and the Bolsheviks. The irreconcilables, Lenin, Kamenev, and Zinoviev definitely decided to create an independent Bolshevist Party. With this policy, Stalin was in full accord. Preparations were under way for a clandestine national conference to be held abroad, in Prague. Under the name of Ivanov, Stalin took up his abode in a small hotel in the capital. From time to time, he visited, in various disguises, the main labor centers in the country, and carried out the difficult task of restoring the shattered units of the party. He quickly showed himself to be an organizer of the first order. At the same time, he contributed articles to Lenin's journal, the Social Democrat, in which he conveyed his impressions of the workers' fighting mood. To one such contribution which appeared in the September issue of the magazine, Lenin appended the following note:

"The correspondence of Koba deserves the greatest attention on the part of those to whom our party is precious. . . . It would be hard to imagine a better refutation of the views and hopes of our 'conciliators' and 'compromisers.'"

Shortly afterwards Stalin was seized in his St. Petersburg hotel room. After a few months in prison, he was returned once more to his former place of exile in the province of Vologda. This time he did not tarry long. Taking advantage of an early opportunity to escape, he was soon back on the job.

At the conference held in Prague in January, 1912, a Bolshevist Central Committee was formed, in violation of the party constitution which lodged this power in a congress only. The new committee was given the optional right to increase its membership by its own vote. In this manner, Stalin was soon joined to the Central Committee. By subsequent reelections, he has remained a member of that body uninterruptedly for the last nineteen years. The conference decided to take an active part in the election campaign to the Fourth Duma, and to attempt to establish a legal daily newspaper in St. Petersburg.

Stalin led a precarious existence in the capital. He was Lenin's plenipotentiary, it is true, but who could possibly know of it? Yet he found himself frequently shadowed, and he scented traps set for him in the most secret of hiding places. He did not know then that his fellow member of the Central Committee, Malinovsky, one of Lenin's most trusted lieutenants, was in the pay of the Okhrana.

Nevertheless, he was hopeful. "Things are going rather well," he wrote to Lenin in Paris on February 10, 1912. "I hope they will be going very well. The frame of mind of our crowd is reassuring." Indeed, he reported that he was able to locate many important party workers. He quoted a resolution adopted by a secret conference, which offered support to the Central Committee in its effort to unite all the elements and in its relentless struggle against the party-wreckers. That was great news for Lenin.

He emphasized the need for a daily paper, told of the preliminary work in connection with its establishment, and declared that only three thousand rubles were needed to launch it. He asked Lenin to let him know by telegraph whether the money would be forthcoming. Finally, Stalin explained that because of his not having permanent quarters and of his being extremely busy with party affairs, he was unable to live up to the undertaking of writing Lenin a daily report.

At this time, Stalin resumed his acquaintance with Alliluiev, the metal worker who had spent several years in the Caucasus during Stalin's early career. Alliluiev was now a foreman in an electrical station, his wife was a native of Georgia, and Stalin became a close friend of the family which included two daughters, Niura and Nadya, twelve and ten years old. Here he frequently found shelter for the night. Alliluiev tells of the hunted life of Stalin at this period. Sometimes, he would spend the night in the streets when he suspected that his quarters were being watched.

VI

Despite the renewed undermining operations of the indefatigable Bolshevist sappers, Russia was in the grip of a dead calm. Six years had passed since the collapse of the revolution of 1905. During these years the peasants had been subdued and partly appeased by Stolypin's agrarian reforms. The proletariat had been crushed, but it was given a sop in the form of the curtailed right to organize trade unions. The middle class was demoralized, but clung to constitutional ideas, the Draconic electoral laws notwithstanding. The intelligentsia had turned to pornography and mysticism. The revolutionary parties had been pulverized as a result of partizan politics and infinitesimal splits. The mailed clutch of tsardom was growing tighter and tighter. Icy winds were blowing from the Baltic to the Pacific.

And, then, suddenly a social earthquake rocked the fettered empire. A volley that was fired in remote Siberia echoed throughout the immense land and re-echoed around the world. In northern Siberia, a thousand miles from a railroad station, in the isolated Lena goldfields, in which British capital was heavily invested, the enslaved workers went out on strike without any political guidance. Their delegates were arrested. The entire body of toilers gathered and demanded their release. Without warning, the tsarist soldiers opened fire upon the strikers. Hundreds were shot down.

It happened on April 4, 1912. It was a week before the news reached civilization. The shock of the massacre was terrific. Within a few days a spontaneous tide of strikes swept nearly all the great industrial cities of Russia. In protest against the blood bath, 215,000 workers walked out without central leadership.

Two weeks later, on May 1, 300,000 men participated in the demonstration against the government. It was the first time since 1907 that there was a May First political strike in the country.

In 1910, in all of Russia, 4,000 men had taken part in political strikes; in 1911—8,000 men.

In 1912, after the "Lena Days," 850,000 men participated in similar strikes in the country.

The proletariat was on the march again. The autocracy was in confusion. Out of the ashes of a betrayed constitution and suppressed discontent, the blaze broke forth with monstrous power.

And Lenin alone was not unprepared for it. Certainly he was the first to rush into action. Stalin was in command in St. Petersburg. He was guiding the Bolshevist weekly Zvezda.

"The Lena Days were the result of the Stolypin régime of 'pacification,'" reads Stalin's own account of the period. "Petrifaction of public thought, general fatigue and apathy, need and despair among the workers, a sense of futility and fear reigning among the peasants, while the gang of police, landlords, and capitalists was jubilant—these are the characteristics of the Stolypin era of 'pacification.'

"The superficial observer might have thought that the day of revolution had been lost forever, that the period of constitutional development of Russia along the lines of Prussia had arrived. And certain old Bolsheviks, sympathizing at heart with preachings to that effect, were at that time leaving the ranks. The triumph of the knout and of darkness was complete.

"The Lena Days broke upon this malodorous morass like a hurricane, and revealed a new scene to everybody. It appeared that the Stolypin régime was not so solid. The Duma had aroused contempt in the masses, and the workers had stored up sufficient energy to throw themselves into battle for a new revolution.

"It was enough to shoot down workers in the depths of Siberia for Russia to be inundated by strikes and for the St. Petersburg proletariat to pour into the streets and wipe out, with one stroke, the impudent slogan of the braggart Minister Makarov that 'it has always been so and it will always remain so.'

"These were the first swallows of the approaching mighty movement. The rise of the new revolutionary current was at hand. On its waves was born the newspaper of the masses, the Pravda.

"It was in the middle of April, 1912, in the evening, at the home of Poletayev, that two Duma deputies, Poletayev and I. Pokrovsky, two writers, Olminsky and Baturin, and I, as a member of the Central Committee, met. On account of my illegal status, I lived as a 'hostage' with Deputy Poletayev, whose person and premises were 'inviolable.' We agreed as to the platform of the Pravda and made up the first issue.

"It was not an ordinary paper, but an organizational center for the consolidation of the underground hearths of the party. . . . In 1902, in his 'What to Do?' Lenin said: 'A newspaper should be not only a collective agitator, but a collective organizer.' And the Pravda became just such a paper."

The founding of the Pravda, in the prevailing conditions, was a great achievement. It was destined to play an immense rôle in paving the way for the ultimate triumph of Bolshevism. Published legally, under the severe eye of the censor, it could not conduct direct anti-government propaganda. Its open policy was primarily that of a popular labor paper ministering to the needs of the masses. Its popularity was instantaneous. Behind its fictitious editors was the hand of Stalin.

The government was now well informed of Stalin's activity, thanks to Malinovsky's association with the Pravda. A few days after the appearance of the newspaper, Stalin was caught by police agents. This time, after the customary prison period, the authorities exiled him to the distant Narym district, in Siberia. Here, in the village of Kolpashevo, his former prison mate in Baku, Verestchak, met him again. "He spent several days here," he writes, "before proceeding to the town of Narym. His arrival revived Bolshevist activity and was signalized by a series of escapes. Sverdlov made a start but was caught on the way. Then Lashevitch escaped, and finally Stalin himself."

Stalin returned late in the summer to his work in the capital, but this was his last escape.

VII

The irrepressible fugitive was back at his hazardous post. It was at the height of the election campaign to the vitiated Fourth Duma. Once in a while he even dared to show himself at the editorial offices of the Pravda, where it was always crowded. A staff writer on the paper, describing Stalin in the rôle of editor-in-chief on a day when the editors were impatiently waiting for some articles from Lenin, who was a constant contributor under various pseudonyms, observes:

"Stalin wields his director's baton calmly, with an ironic smile under his mustache. He issues instructions briefly but clearly."

Stalin remained in the capital about four months,

from September to the close of 1912. During his stay, the Pravda was repeatedly suppressed, only to reappear the following morning under a new title and new nominal editor. "It was the period of the pre-election struggle with the Mensheviks," writes Nicholas Krestinsky, then a St. Petersburg attorney and now Soviet ambassador to Germany. "The tendencies toward compromise were very strong among the workers, and it required great discipline and firmness to prevent a fusion with the Mensheviks at the polls. This task was performed by Stalin. It was he who also guided the Bolshevist delegation upon its formation in the Fourth Duma. It was Stalin who stamped that delegation with its Bolshevist individuality, and who with the aid of the Pravda created for it a supporting body among the workers of the capital."

There were thirteen Social Democrats in the new Duma. Six of these were Bolsheviks, nearly all workingmen, put up as puppets by Lenin's Central Committee. The speeches of these deputies were written in advance by Lenin, who was abroad, by Stalin and other Bolshevist intellectuals. Among the six was Malinovsky, the agent of the Okhrana, elected in Moscow with the connivance and aid of the police department. Three years later Malinovsky was exposed by the conservative president of the Duma, who had been shocked to learn of the Okhrana having a deputy in parliament. Malinovsky was caught and executed after the Soviet Revolution.

The Social Democrats at first formed one bloc in the Duma. It required a stern educational campaign on the part of Lenin to divorce the Bolsheviks from the ideas of cooperation with the Mensheviks. In this, Stalin rendered Lenin invaluable service. The Central Committee appointed him as the mentor of the Bolshevist deputies. It was customary upon the opening of the Duma for each party to come out with a declaration of its principles and program. This was a great opportunity for propaganda. But the Bolshevist representatives were still imbued with the heresy of conciliation, and were intellectually much inferior to their Menshevist colleagues. Here Stalin's hidden arm and inflexible will were taxed to the limit. In his report to the St. Petersburg committee of his party on his "parliamentary" activity, Stalin declared that for nine days and nine nights he had not left the quarters of the Bolshevist deputies, exorcising the spirit of compromise from their platform until he finally succeeded.

In the memoirs of Badayev, one of the six Bolshevist representatives and perhaps the one who took the most active part in the administration and protection of the Pravda, Stalin is represented as the chief engineer of the party in all matters of policy. It was Stalin who was responsible for the creation of the Bolshevist caucus. It was Stalin who framed the basic Bolshevist planks in the platform of the Social Democratic bloc. And again it was he who did not lose his head and did not yield an inch in the many all-night conferences that were marked by extreme passion.

"I would meet Stalin in the editorial office and in other places," writes Badayev. "Sometimes our meetings and conferences took place in my apartment where Stalin would come to hide after evading spies in every possible way. . . . The future proved that Stalin was altogether right when he was skeptical as to the possibility of a reconciliation between the Bolsheviks and the Mensheviks in the Social Democratic bloc. . . .

"Stalin raised the question of the necessity of calling a conference abroad of the Central Committee and the workers' deputies in the Duma, to prepare a plan of action for the Bolshevist delegation and to decide a whole series of questions bound up with our future activities. I fully approved of Stalin's suggestion, believing it was necessary for us, the deputies of the working class, to form close ties with the Central Committee from the very first day and to be guided directly by its orders."

Direct orders from the Central Committee meant, of course, orders from Lenin, conveyed through his mouthpiece Stalin. It was found inopportune to hold the proposed conference at that moment, and the meeting was postponed until the Christmas recess of the Duma. The intervening period enabled Stalin to go through a school of experience that proved invaluable in his later career. That Caucasian ex-seminarist, agitator, plotter, and student of Marx was rapidly developing into a type so foreign to Russia then but so familiar to America—into a political boss.

VIII

Stalin was now preparing to go abroad for a lengthy stay. He had been in Stockholm in 1906 and in London in 1907, but only for brief trips. He was now arranging that projected conference which was scheduled to take place at Krakow where Lenin had moved to be closer to the Russian border. Stalin had been especially invited by Lenin and his wife, Krupskaya, to visit with them and to spend some time in Austria. This was the first occasion Stalin had to come into intimate contact with his master, who in this manner also showed his recognition of his disciple's achievements.

In a letter written in invisible ink and dated December 6, 1912, Lenin took up with Stalin the question of his illegal passport needed for foreign travel. At the same time he urged upon Stalin the necessity for organizing a demonstration to commemorate the approaching anniversary of the Bloody Sunday, and outlined the slogans for a revolutionary leaflet for the occasion. A missive of December 23, from Lenin's amanuensis Krupskaya, reveals the financial plight of the Bolshevist chief as well as his guidance of the St. Petersburg affairs.

"We insist," writes Mrs. Lenin, "that the ones who come—you must not fail to be among them—should bring with them the most accurate and detailed statistics on the budget of the Pravda, both as to revenue and expense. When one is presented with summary figures, it is impossible to make head or tail of anything. It is necessary to analyze in the most minute fashion the cost of paper, composition, administration, contributors, the income from advertising, stand sales, subscriptions, etc., and then make the decisive conclusions. . . .

"Now, about the remuneration due to us. Two days ago we received word that 'tomorrow the money will be sent to you.' Then came your short note that it cannot be sent. The question is important, because without this payment we absolutely cannot exist even for the shortest period. And if it does not arrive, we shall have to leave Krakow, for there is no way of earning anything here. . . . If the Pravda is unable to pay, we shall have to liquidate the local affairs. Without exaggeration, we have written dozens of times urging a campaign for yearly and semi-yearly subscriptions. It is not utopian to collect a couple of thousand new subscribers and create a fund of several thousand rubles. This fund would enable us to enlarge the paper and keep afloat for a while. In reply, we have heard nothing. Why? Who is managing things? People who cannot understand such elementary things?" The letter then outlines a subscription campaign and promotion program that would have done justice to an American enterprise.

Stalin spent over two months in Krakow and Vienna. Between drinking beer and playing chess with Lenin, Stalin found time to devote himself to writing an exhaustive study on "Marxism and the National Question." The Krakow conference of the Bolshevist deputies and the Central Committee had ended on New Year's Day, and most of the delegates had departed. Stalin remained with Lenin for several weeks. Writing to Maxim Gorki early in February, Lenin said:

"I agree with you that it is time to take up seriously the national question. We have here with us a wonderful Georgian who has collected all the Austrian and other materials and has settled down to prepare a big article on the subject."

Stalin completed his work in Vienna. It was published in three instalments in a monthly journal, and later republished in many editions in book form. In his absence from St. Petersburg, the local Bolshevist chieftains thought it prudent to complain to Lenin against his policy. On February 8, 1913, Mrs. Lenin wrote to Podvoisky:

"We extremely regret to learn that you think Stalin exaggerates the rôle of the Pravda. In reality, the crux of the situation is in the proper establishment of the Pravda." She went on to say that otherwise there would follow material and political bankruptcy, and to reiterate Lenin's view that only a central organ could organize the movement.

Stalin returned to Russia and has never since left its borders. Malinovsky, the Okhrana agent, had attended the Krakow meeting. During the preceding months, the police, fearful of exposing their agent in the Duma, had refrained from arresting the Bolshevist leaders. They now demanded that Malinovsky help them seize Stalin and Sverdlov. As soon as Stalin arrived in the capital, he found himself pursued and shadowed at every turn.

"Why is there no news from Stalin?" wrote Mrs. Lenin to Podvoisky on March 8. "Is there anything the matter with him? We are worried." Two days later she urged upon the same correspondent the need for fullest cooperation with Stalin, and added:

"One must take good care of Stalin. It is clear that he is not very strong. He falls sick too often."

Stalin found shelter in the "sacred" home of the Duma deputy Badayev. Here he stayed in hiding for days and did not dare to show himself in the street. Outside, secret agents were snooping about and waiting impatiently for him to emerge. In the meantime Malinovsky had given a helpful tip to the secret service. A concert was scheduled to be held in a labor hall for the benefit of the Pravda. Such affairs were usually attended by large crowds. The unsuspecting Bolshevist leaders decided that it would afford them an opportunity, in the noise and confusion of the throngs, to meet and talk things over. Stalin decided to go to the concert. The police agents were scattered among the crowd. Stalin scented danger. He made for the stage exit, followed by his pursuers. Here a hasty attempt was made to throw a lady's cloak over him and have him spirited away. He was seized in the act.

Arrested early in April, 1913, Stalin did not regain his freedom until four years later, upon the overthrow of the monarchy.

IX

After spending several months in St. Petersburg prisons, Stalin was exiled to the Turukhansk district, in the province of Yeniseisk, on the Polar Circle. Stalin's seizure had been the signal for a series of raids in which Sverdlov, Spandaryan, and, later, Kamenev and the Bolshevist deputies in the Duma had been rounded up. In time, Turukhansk became a center for a colony of over three hundred political exiles, among whom the Bolsheviks were numerous. Stalin and Sverdlov were assigned to the remote hamlet of Kureika.

In September, 1913, a Bolshevist conference took place in Galicia, Austria, under Lenin's direction. It was decided to arrange for the escape of Stalin and Sverdlov. Malinovsky, who was present, immediately conveyed the information to the Okhrana. An order went out to the Siberian gendarmerie to take all measures to prevent their escape. Two special constables were attached to the exiles, to watch them. The following May, the police department, in a communication to the governor of Yeniseisk, warned of another attempt by Lenin to procure the freedom of his lieutenants. Stalin's record of escapes required exceptional watchfulness.

Lenin was in hot water at the time. The Mensheviks had filed a series of charges against the Bolshevist organization with the Socialist International, which was to hold its next world congress in August, 1914. It looked as if the Bolsheviks would be excluded from the International brotherhood, a most serious blow. Lenin planned to hold a conference of his own. The World War broke out and saved Bolshevism the disgrace of excommunication. At the same time, it overwhelmed the growing tide of revolutionary outbreaks and strikes in Russia.

What was Stalin's attitude during the World War? This is a crucial question which everybody Bolshevik must answer. Lenin at once assumed a position of violent hostility to the conflict, a position which became known in history as "defeatist." All the socialist parties of the world were split and demoralized. Most of the recognized leaders in the European countries supported their respective governments and voted for war credits. The Socialist International was virtually disrupted. In Russia, many of the revolutionary chiefs of hostile camps found themselves united on the issue of "defeatism." Lenin, Trotsky, Martov, and Chernov, the leader of the Socialist-Revolutionary Party, were now in accord. They had the support of Rosa Luxemburg and Karl Liebknecht in Germany and of similar minority socialists in other countries. In Switzerland, two conferences of "defeatists," took place, one in Zimmerwald and the other in Kiental, at which Lenin viciously attacked the patriotic socialists as traitors to the cause. To this day, Bolshevism regards these Swiss conferences as the birth of the Communist International.

Four thousand miles away, in the Turukhansk colony, the split was just as violent and sharp. The debates were passionate and vindictive. Stalin did not share in them. Trotsky has more than once asked Stalin to reveal his stand during the war. Having exposed to the world every scrap of writing showing the differences between Lenin and Trotsky prior to 1914, Trotsky has in turn demanded that Stalin produce his war record and publish his writings during the period. Stalin has failed to do so, which is indirect evidence that his position was certainly not so intransigent and orthodox as that of his chief. On the other hand, one of the Turukhansk exiles, the Bolshevik Shumyatsky, relates that Spandaryan was so violently opposed to the war that he was accused of being pro-German. "Then Stalin visited his friend, and the nagging of Spandaryan stopped. Stalin unhesitatingly took up a 'defeatist' position, and maintained it quietly to the end."

Stalin himself has preferred to remain silent on this period of his life. Only ten years later, speaking of Lenin, did he have something to say on the question, without however touching upon his own viewpoint at the time.

"The period of 1914–1917," declared Stalin, "the period of the imperialist war, when nearly all socialist parties fell victim to the general patriotic fumes, offering their services to the imperialism of their fatherlands, was the period when the Second International lowered its banners before capital, when the chauvinistic wave swamped even such men as Plekhanov, Kautsky, Guesde, and others. Lenin was then the only one or nearly the only one who commenced a decisive fight against the socialist chauvinists and the socialist pacifists, exposing the treason of the Guesdes and the Kautskys, branding the 'half-measures' of the small-minded 'revolutionists.' Lenin understood that he had with him only an inconsiderable minority, but that was of no decisive importance to him, for he knew that the only true policy, the one that had a future, was the policy of sequential internationalism, for he knew that politics guided by principle is the truest policy. It is well-known that Lenin emerged victorious from this battle for a new International."

Yet Stalin had apparently severed all his former connections during the war. He had drifted away from Lenin, although the underground means of communication reached even to the Polar Circle. Toward the end of 1915, Lenin tried hard to get in touch with his "wonderful Georgian." Stalin was in exile under his legal name of Djugashvili. Lenin could not recall the last name! In November of that year he wrote from Geneva to his friend Karpinsky:

"Great favor to ask of you: find out the last name of Koba (Joseph Dj——, we have forgotten). It is very important."

X

Stalin retired into his shell in exile. He became morose and irritable. He preferred isolation and evaded company. He abandoned politics and avoided doctrinaire arguments. He developed into a passionate nature-lover, and undoubtedly impressed his comrades as an unusual Bolshevik.

Turukhansk is a town with a population of two hundred, with a jail, a hospital, and a central police office. The exiles were settled either in the town or in the remote villages of the district. The native population is half Ostiak and half Russian. The land is swampy, the vegetation largely limited to brushwood. The local peasants are extremely poor. Bread is difficult to obtain. The river of Yenisei abounds in fish, and most of the local food is herring. The main industry is hunting, largely fox, ermine, and squirrels.

When Stalin arrived in June, 1913, "his coming was preceded by legendary reports of his ability to escape under any conditions," according to Shumyatsky. "He had a record of seven escapes. The party members, however, did not know that the 'fierce' Stalin was a member of the Central Committee."

Stalin and Sverdlov were both taken to the village of Kureika, consisting of three homesteads and situated on a river of the same name. Fifty miles away are lead mines, and in the summer freight steamers ply here. The two exiles shared a room in a peasant's cabin. They had no kerosene and were compelled to use candles during the long winter night. The children of the proprietor would make themselves at home in their room for hours at a stretch. In the evening, unwelcome visitors would drop in to talk to the learned men and waste their time with boring questions.

Stalin and Sverdlov took up hunting and skiing. They would go out into the tundra and cover fifteen miles a day on their joint expeditions. "The weather is marvelous, nature delightful, the air sweet. It is good to be on skis," wrote Sverdlov to a friend from Kureika.

The two friends began to quarrel. Sverdlov, who died in 1918, was the first president of the Soviet Republic and was one of the titanic figures in the revolution. His was a poetic soul and a lovable disposition. The letters from which we get this oblique sketch of Stalin were written long before the revolution, to a young woman, and were never intended for publication.

"There are two of us here," wrote Sverdlov, "the Georgian, Djugashvili, is with me, an old acquaintance whom I had met in exile before. He is a good fellow, but too much of an individualist in his everyday conduct. I, on the other hand, am a believer in a minimum of orderliness. On this point, I sometimes get nervous."

"I have a comrade with me?" Sverdlov wrote later to the same correspondent, in reply to her letter. "Yes. But we know each other too well. Moreover, and that is the saddest part of it all, in conditions of exile and prison, man bares himself and reveals himself in all his pettiness. It is a pity that he displays only the pettinesses of life. There is no room to show one's big side. We now live in separate quarters, and see each other but rarely."

Sverdlov secured a transfer to another village. His few lines indicate that then Stalin already exposed himself as lacking in sensitiveness and personal warmth, and as abounding in that rudeness for which Lenin later castigated him.

Stalin remained in isolation for nearly three years. Other revolutionists in similar circumstances developed melancholy, went insane, sometimes committed suicide, or frantically and repeatedly tried to escape or at least to change their place of banishment. Stalin, that son of the arid Caucasus, with his hot temper, acclimatized himself perfectly to the Polar Circle, the frightful blizzards, the monotonous landscape, the extreme cold and desolation.

On very rare occasions, Stalin visited his friends, Spandaryan and his wife, in the neighboring village of Monastyrskoye. Here, too, Stalin was uncommunicative. When Sverdlov and Spandaryan organized the colony, arranged meetings and debates, and applied to the government for permission to establish a consumers' cooperative store, it was without Stalin's participation. He maintained his aloofness.

Stalin became a fisherman, a hunter, and a trapper. In the winter he chased furred animals; in the summer he fished and hunted geese and ducks. "He surrounded himself," writes Shumyatsky, "with heaps of meshing, casting-nets, muzzles, shotguns, automatic traps, seines, blocks, baskets, etc." He became the marvel of the district. "He cast his nets under the ice, he disemboweled his catch himself, and even wove his own nets and made other equipment. He chopped wood, cooked his own food, and found time to work on his manuscripts. And all the while he was under the sharp watch of a special constable."

XI

If Stalin dreamed dreams, he did not give expression to them. If he seethed with ideas, he did not launch them in the world. By now the Turukhansk Bolsheviks, under Sverdlov, had established regular clandestine communication with their comrades in the capital and with Lenin in Switzerland. To inquiries from abroad as to what Stalin was doing, Sverdlov could only reply: "I do not know whether he has done any literary work during his stay in exile."

The world carnage had been going on for thirty months. The conservative Duma had turned anti-government. Rasputin had just been assassinated. Tsarist ministers were changing with kaleidoscopic rapidity.

In Zurich, Lenin was pacing the narrow alleys like a caged tiger.

Trotsky had been deported from France and Spain and, like a trapped lion, was now walking the deck of an old tub bound from Barcelona to New York.

Stalin, the bear, was hibernating in Arctic Siberia.

And then the war came to Stalin. There was not enough cannon fodder. A mobilization was declared in the Far North. "Twenty of our fellows have been called to military service," wrote Sverdlov early in 1917. "They were sent off today. Among those mobilized was Stalin, too, who has lived all the time in an obscure station far from the other comrades."

But Stalin's journey to the front ended on its first lap. Because of a well-concealed but real physical deformity, he was granted exemption and returned to his secluded abode. The hands that were to rule Russia were not able to wield a rifle. The army medical examiner found that—

Stalin's left hand is warped. It will not open.

Is it possible, in the light of modern psychology, that the iron claw of Bolshevism is not Stalin's mailed right fist at all but that impotent left hand dressed in a glove of steel?

CHAPTER SIX

A FELLOW CONSPIRATOR

I

REVOLUTION!

Ten thousand cannon and twenty-five million men under arms were hushed. Revolution in Russia! At last the war had found its Nemesis. At last a cannon had been forged that would silence all the howitzers on the battlefields. Fired by a hundred and seventy-five million people, its report let loose a tornado across scarified Europe, and ignited desperate blood with fantastic faith. If all the great navies had been sunk, if London had been destroyed by a fleet of Zeppelins, if the kaiser had been taken prisoner, it would have been an episode as compared with the effect of the arresting cry: Revolution in Russia.

At last, she was come. The Revolution of whom poets had sung for a century, for whom thousands had given their lives in ecstasy, to whom tens of thousands had looked forward from prison cells and exile, and of whom tens of millions had learned to speak in whispers, with deep fervor and fear. The sun had finally risen over that bleak continent. The miracle had been wrought, no one knew how. A dynasty that had just celebrated the three hundredth anniversary of its unlimited despotism melted away in an instant. The world echoed with the shout of the Russian Revolution. Nay, to the liberated Slavs it seemed that the world was too small to carry the word, that the universe itself had been startled out of its composure.

The smoke of the revolution cleared away, and the smoke of the war spread once more over the earth. A great revolution was born under an ominous star. No, it was born of it. Would the light of the revolution extinguish the light of all the artillery barrages? Or would the greatest of wars subdue and smother the greatest of human outbursts? The contest between the World War and the Russian Revolution developed with dizzying speed. Against the array of immense armies was arrayed a small group of visionaries with an idea. Against irrational destructiveness would be aligned destructiveness with a goal. Lenin and Trotsky and . . . Stalin would know how to harness the human lava, how to mold the shapeless mass into a new monster, more monstrous than the hugest of armies, more armor-plated than the mightiest of fleets. They would know how to transform the halo of the revolution into a hallowed flame, its inner fire into a fire-eating dragon, its unquenchable thirst into an all-devouring machine. They would know how to turn the fierce hatreds of the war into a new hatred, not of nations but of classes, a hatred so consuming, so enduring, that it would carry a whole civilization with its insane conflicts and spurious victories down, down, down.

And yet the downfall of the Romanovs was a thundering refutation of decades of insurrectionary theory. Here, indeed, was a classical revolution, an elemental blast from the depths. Where was Lenin's army of professional revolutionists? Scattered, crushed, dispirited, deteriorated, it had little to do with the popular avalanche that descended upon the capital in the middle of March. The autocracy tumbled down of itself, and it fell upon the existing skeleton of the Bolshevist conspirative organization with a force that exploded Lenin's pseudo-scientific theories as to the art of making revolution and caused concussion of the brain among his veteran disciples.

The conspirators emerged from under the débris dazed by the light. It was one thing to plot underground against the monarchy with the ultimate aim of social revolution. It was another thing to find one's way in the open to a new order of society. Lenin and Trotsky alone did not lose their heads. In spite of years of theoretical differences, they now found themselves in accord in the face of supreme action. From Switzerland, where Lenin was frantically trying to secure permission to get to Russia, fiery epistles went out urging the Bolsheviks back home to show no shadow of confidence in, or support of, the Provisional Government, and to remember that "the overthrow of every capitalistic government beginning with the Russian was the main point." Trotsky echoed this stand from New York and the Canadian concentration camp where he was detained on the way to his native land.

And Stalin? Softly, self-effacedly, he was making his way to the seat of the revolution from Siberia, across a turbulent sea of rebellion and victory. Stalin did not stop on the journey to deliver impassioned speeches. His soul was permeated with doubt. His gait was faltering. Shall the strife between the socialist factions now be buried? Shall unity prevail in the revolutionary camp? Shall the patriotic Soviets of workers and soldiers, represented in the new government by Kerensky, be supported? Did not the democracy of the liberals, Mensheviks, and Socialist-Revolutionaries deserve cooperation now?

The people were still celebrating the honeymoon of their freedom. Harmony was the watchword. The discordant Lenin and Trotsky had not yet arrived. Stalin responded to the environment. Together with Kamenev, Sverdlov, Zinoviev and others, he was able to forsake his doctrinaire heritage and let his pulse beat with the pulse of a reborn nation. But it was unheard-of heresy, from the viewpoint of orthodox Leninism. It is a weak spot in Stalin's dogmatic armor that he surrendered to the living force about him.

II

Stalin did not enter Petrograd like a hero or a liberated martyr. Nor did he return as a crusader. Unlike Lenin and Trotsky, whose appearance later was a signal for mass demonstrations, Stalin came back to his post the way he had come and gone for years. Without ado, he slipped into the offices of the Pravda, which had been reestablished a fortnight after the abdication of the tsar. Without ado, Stalin, Kamenev, and Muranov, all members of the Central Committee, perpetrated a coup in the administration of the paper and took it out of the hands of the junior Petrograd leaders. Stalin's first signed article appeared in the Pravda on March 27, three weeks before Lenin's triumphant and disturbing reentry of Russia. Stalin's opening salvo was mild, so mild that it tasted like syrup to the moderate elements, whose hearts were already then filled with fear of Lenin's wrecking crew. "The land to the peasants, protection of labor for workers, a democratic republic for all the citizens of Russia," such was the concluding climax of Stalin's manifesto upon his arrival.

The gulf between Stalin and Lenin at the time was as wide as that between Stalin and Trotsky today. Stalin took a position which was far less extreme than that of the "left" Mensheviks. But Lenin was coming back with an ax in one hand and a knout in the other. With the knout he would whip his flock together and shepherd his stray wards into his old lane. With the ax he would hack away at the coalition government of socialists, liberals, and capitalists, he would attack viciously the bourgeois system of democracy, he would have the World War turn into a civil conflict, and would marshal and drive the workers and peasants against the ruling class. Lenin would metamorphose Stalin's syrup into blood, and put a point on his pen which Stalin himself was not firm enough to give it.

Lenin would kill all sentimentality. The Provisional Government of free Russia was not sacred to him. He would demand its overthrow. Not so Stalin. He, too, was for ending the imperialist war, but by gentle pressure and not by onslaught. He was not for social revolution, but for social reforms.

"The day of the appearance of the first issue of the 'transformed' Pravda," writes Shliapnikov, the leader of the Petrograd Bolshevist organization, in his book, "was a day of jubilation in the camp of the war patriots." The Duma and the Menshevist leaders of the Soviet "were overflowing with the one news item: the victory of the moderate, judicious Bolsheviks over the extremists. In the Executive Committee of the Soviets we were met with venomous smiles. This was the first and only time when the Pravda won the approval of sworn war patriots. . . . When the issue reached the factories, it caused utter confusion among the members of our party and our sympathizers, and biting comments on the part of all our opponents."

There was enormous indignation in the workers' districts. "What was the matter? Why did our paper renounce its Bolshevist policy and take up that of national defense?" were the questions showered upon Shliapnikov and his associates. "But the Petrograd Committee, as well as the entire organization was caught unaware by the coup," he writes, "and when the proletarians learned that the Pravda had been seized by three of its former leaders who had arrived from Siberia, they demanded their exclusion from the party."

This document throws a penetrating light upon Stalin when contrasted with his conduct ten years later while in power. For Stalin eliminated one by one the chief figures of the Soviet Revolution on the ground of their past heresies. Yet Stalin was not alone in his waywardness. Most of the other Bolshevist chiefs were just as conciliatory, but they showed it in a more spectacular fashion. Stalin was more cautious. He was not violent in defending his views. His conspirative training stood him in good stead. He had long ago learned the value of silence. Perhaps it was his inability to shed the cloak of mystery he had worn all his life and which had become almost his second self.

Without ado, Stalin was elected a member of the Executive Committee of Soviets and joined the small Bolshevist delegation there. He made no flaming speeches. He did not share in the debates. Yet there was a curiosity about the man in revolutionary circles. His career had become a legend. He was expected to reveal his true stature now. Sukhanov, one of the most intimate recorders of the revolution, closely identified at the time with the Soviet and the Bolshevist activities, in his "Notes on the Revolution" describes Stalin as one of the few individuals holding the fate of the revolution in their hands, and continues:

"In any event, it was impossible not to be perplexed by the rôle of Stalin. While the corps of officers in the Bolshevist Party was of a low level, overwhelmingly casual and ignorant in composition, its generalship included a row of great figures and worthy leaders. On the other hand, Stalin, in the course of his modest activity in the Executive Committee, made—not only on me—the impression of a gray spot which flickered obscurely and left no trace."

Sukhanov, in his seven volumes, makes no further mention of Stalin, except to remark that "there is nothing more to add to the foregoing." Nevertheless, Stalin's share in the epochal year of 1917 was no casual one. It is inherent in the structure of Bolshevism, in Stalin's career, which epitomizes it so largely, it is part and parcel of a life of conspirative work, to escape attention.

In the limelight of 1917 were leading actors. Of them the observers wrote books and articles, for upon them the public gaze was centered. But backstage were the directors and the producers. Stalin was behind the scenes. He stayed there when the audience hissed and whistled. He also stayed there when the audience called for everybody to come to the curtain to receive its fickle homage.

III

In the palace of the *prima ballerina* Kseshinska, the elite of the once conspirative order met in solemn session. The home of the tsar's former favorite had been seized by the Bolsheviks and turned into party headquarters. Red flags were flying from the building. Inside, the expensive furnishings and precious vases had been replaced by plain tables and benches. Here a few score of underground professional revolutionists came together in secret conference. Stalin, Rykov, Kamenev, Krestinsky, Molotov, Shliapnikov and many others were present. It was April 12. Lenin was not yet back. There had never before been a Bolshevist conference without Lenin. Would they who had always derived their inspiration and guidance from their master know where to turn when left to their own resources?

To this day the stenographic records of this conference are suppressed in Russia. It seems that the ultra-Leninist Stalin played a most unenviable rôle then. He was a democrat, just another radical, a parlor-Bolshevik at best, but not the intrepid rebel of Tiflis. Freedom tasted well even to the Bolsheviks. The recognition that they were accorded in the Soviet and other official quarters tasted even better. Stalin was of course in the opposition, of the parliamentary variety, the kind that did not exclude handshaking with one's "class enemies." Indeed, what was Leninism coming to?

"Power has been divided between two organs," said Stalin at the secret conclave, according to the minutes, "of which neither possesses full authority. The two share it jointly: the Soviet is in reality the initiator of revolutionary reforms; the Soviet is the revolutionary leader of the arisen people, the organ which is building up the Provisional Government. And the Provisional Government is in reality playing the rôle of consolidator of the conquests of the revolutionary people. The Soviet mobilizes the forces. It controls. But the Provisional Government, in its obstinate and confused way, is fortifying the victories already won by the people. . . . In so far as the Provisional Government consolidates the advance of the revolution, it must be supported. But in so far as it is counter-revolutionary, it must be denied support."

Stalin spoke of the people and not of the proletariat. Stalin spoke of the Provisional Government headed by Prince Lvov, Miliukov and Gutchkov, all constitutional monarchists, as deserving support. He spoke of the Soviet then dominated by Kerensky, Tseretelli, Liber, and Dan, all patriotic socialists, as the revolutionary leader of the arisen country. This was sheer treason to Bolshevism, kotowing to the bourgeoisie, profanation of Leninism. Where was the dictatorship of the proletariat? Where was the social revolution? Where was the Chosen Party?

But Stalin did not reach the bottom of his fall

until the conference took up the proposal made by Tseretelli for a complete union with the Mensheviks. Said Stalin in the course of the discussion:

"We must go in for it. It is necessary to define our proposals as to the policy of such a union. It is possible to unite on the platform of Zimmerwald-Kiental."

And when the young Molotov expressed doubts as to the wisdom of such a fusion, Stalin replied:

"One should not run ahead and anticipate differences of opinion. Without such differences, there can be no party life. We will adjust small differences within the framework of the party."

This was the very same Stalin that eight years later, in the name of a "monolithic" party, condemned as treason any independent views on the part of all Bolshevist leaders, the man who expelled and exiled and imprisoned people like Trotsky, Rakovsky, Radek, Kamenev, Zinoviev, Rykov, Preobrajensky, and hundreds of veteran Leninists, for differences as to policy.

But the peace feast at the Kseshinska palace was coming to an inglorious finale. The last session of the conference was held on April 16, the day of Lenin's arrival. That irrepressible and fierce Swiss exile, met by vast crowds, was leaping from the railroad station across the city with a roar that struck terror not only into the hearts of the government but into those of his renegade disciples.

"What kind of revolution was it which permitted the capitalists to run the country?" bellowed Lenin at the official reception and at street corners on the way to the conference. "The piratical imperialistic war is the beginning of civil war in all Europe. . . . The dawn of the world socialist revolution is breaking." The listeners were dumfounded, the Bolshevist comrades escorting Lenin were dismayed.

In an hour, he was at the palace. Here two hundred of his party chieftains were assembled. Tea was served in a hurry. Then Lenin arose. He spoke for two hours. "It seemed as if all the elements had been let loose from their depths and the spirit of all-destruction knowing no obstacles, doubts, human difficulties and calculations, was sweeping through the hall of Kseshinska's mansion," writes Sukhanov. "I went out into the street and had the feeling of having been beaten on the head with chains all night."

The wrath of Lenin rendered all the Bolshevist captains speechless. No one argued or answered. "Was this freedom when all the printing presses are in the hands of the capitalists?" he asked. His indignation was boundless.

"Even our Bolsheviks display confidence in the government. One can explain it only by the fumes of the revolution. This is the destruction of socialism. You, comrades, regard the government with confidence. If that is so, our roads part. I would rather remain in the minority. One Liebknecht is worth more than one hundred and ten war patriots. . . . If you sympathize with Liebknecht but extend even one finger to the war patriots, you are committing treason to international socialism."

As to Stalin's demand in the Pravda that the Provisional Government renounce annexations, Lenin exclaimed:

"To demand of a capitalist government to renounce annexations is nonsense, it is a mockery that cries to heaven."

Lenin demanded the end of the war, no compromise with the Provisional Government, the Mensheviks, and the Socialist-Revolutionaries. He was for an immediate declaration of war against the capitalist order, for social revolution, for "all-power to the proletariat."

Stalin was crushed.

IV

To Lenin's old guard it seemed that their master had gone mad. His platform was so alien to the prevailing mood in the high party circles that the Pravda, publishing Lenin's famous April theses embodying his stand, attached to it a note expressing the editors'—of whom Stalin was one—disagreement with their chief. Yet it is this catechism that forms today the cornerstone of Stalin's doctrine of power.

Lenin went over the heads of his associates, and appealed directly to the masses. At the same time, he reached out for an alliance with the independent group led by Trotsky. He launched a campaign against "the old Bolsheviks who more than once played a sorry part in the history of our party by repeating a formula unintelligently learned, instead of studying the peculiar nature of the new and living reality."

"Kamenev and Rykov tried to resist," writes Trotsky. "Stalin silently stepped aside. Not one of his articles written about that period shows that

Stalin made any attempt to estimate his previous policy and win his way to Lenin's stand. He simply kept silent, because he had been too much compromised by his unfortunate leadership during the first month of the revolution. He preferred to withdraw into the background. He never made any public appearance to defend Lenin's views; he merely stood back and waited."

Stalin never denied his vacillations. The strength of his defense lies in the fact that he shared his views with many of the party leaders, and that he never pretended to be the originator of policies or the infallible leader that Trotsky would make himself. "It's no wonder that the Bolsheviks, having been scattered by tsarism in prison and exile, and only now able to come together from all the ends of Russia to work out a new platform, could not in one stroke find their way in the new situation. . . . I shared my mistaken viewpoint with the majority of the party, and surrendered it fully about the middle of April, adopting Lenin's April theses." Such was Stalin's apology years later.

In the first week of May, an all-Russian Bolshevist conference was held in Petrograd. Here Stalin came out in support of Lenin's resolution. From that moment on, he remained faithful to his master, a loyal fellow conspirator. Later in the summer the Bolshevist Party, after a lapse of ten years, once more elected a Central Committee. Stalin was one of its members. For the first time, the Central Committee formed the all-powerful Political Bureau. Stalin was on it. This bureau was fated to play a transcendental part in the evolution of the dictatorship and the career of Stalin in the next decade. The Central Committee was in charge of three secretaries. Stalin was one of them. The official organ of the party had an editorial council. Stalin remained one of the editors. He was one of the founders of Bolshevist publishing enterprises and presses. When the Soviet insurrection was in the process of being hatched, an organizational Committee of Seven and a political Committee of Five under Trotsky were appointed to consummate it. Stalin was a member of both.

There were many breaks and conflicts within the party during the following months. Sharp issues developed between Lenin and various groups of his followers. Stalin never shared in them. He either consciously abnegated all claim to independent thought, sincerely attaching himself to Lenin as a lieutenant in action, or he consciously chose to bide his time, to let others wrangle and fight and wear themselves out, so as to enable him to emerge at the proper moment with an unimpaired even if colorless political record.

V

From the moment of its birth the Russian Revolution suffered from a duality of power, as indicated by Stalin in his April speech. This duality runs like a red thread through the entire march of the history of Russia from the fall of the Romanovs to the triumphant rise of Stalin. Accompanying the two conflicting currents has been the duel of personalities in the revolution. Stalin's rôle since 1917 was determined by this fateful malady. With the overturn of the autocracy, two organs of power emerged simultaneously, the Duma representing the privileged classes and the Soviet chosen by the workers and peasants. So long as the latter followed the lead of the former, the Provisional Government was a united national power. The Duma stood for the state idea, the Soviet for the class idea. With the gradual atrophy of the Duma and the progressive influx of power into the Soviet, the balance was upset, and the Provisional Government step by step lost its hold on the masses. The Soviet became the representative of the state idea and the Bolshevist Party the carrier of the class concept. Long after the Bolshevist seizure of power, the revolution continued to swing between these two poles, until the Soviet became vitiated and the party concentrated in its upper sphere all authority, leading to an unlimited dictatorship.

How was Stalin able to capture so much power? This question is answered by the peculiar alignment of forces and leadership in the early stages of the Russian Revolution. Looking back thirteen years, it is now evident that this revolution produced three dominant personalities: Lenin, Trotsky, and Stalin. Trotsky dramatically impersonated the state idea of the great upheaval. That was not an accident. His natural gifts and past career made for the broadest outlook. His histrionic impulses made for popular acclaim. Stalin was the very opposite. He incorporated the party element. He had never sought the platform. He had always lived and worked in the shadows. He was an organizer and not a tribune, an engineer and not an architect. Lenin combined and coordinated the two phases. He was big enough to embody the Trotsky and Stalin currents, to conceive, plan, and build the revolution as the state of the future founded upon strict class rule.

If you would follow Stalin's path through the amazing year of 1917, go down into the depths of Lenin's political laboratory. The failure of the Provisional Government to make peace, the failure to give the land to the peasants, the failure to convoke the Constituent Assembly within a short time, the failure to heed the spontaneous clamors of the people, the dissemination of unpardonable canards as to Lenin's being an agent of the kaiser, the shady flirtations with monarchist generals and would-be saviors of the country—all these gave the Bolsheviks their increasing popularity, their expanding hold on the Soviet, at the same time driving them back as a party into the catacombs demolished by the first revolution.

Here Stalin found his opportunity. The Soviet seizure of the government was the handicraft of a highly organized subterranean conspiracy. It was here that Stalin left his marks. It was here that he flickered not like a "gray spot" but as an effective engine of insurrection. Trotsky's share in the Soviet revolt was immense by virtue of his stirring the imagination of the masses, mobilizing their emotions, and unfurling banners that gave the movement its color, pathos, hero-worship, and its world-wide sweep. Stalin's share was great, too, by virtue of his acting as chief of staff, organizing the cohorts, controlling the distribution of forces, executing the policies initiated by Lenin, and delivering to posterity that compact army which makes the Bolshevist Party such an astonishing phenomenon.

The revolution had its centrifugal and centripetal forces. Trotsky was with the first. Stalin with the second. While the revolutionary planet continued to shoot off meteors, to scatter stars and lights in its wake, Trotsky had his name blazoned forth and that of Stalin was wrapped in darkness. When all the fireworks of the revolution had been shot, all the rainbows cast, and the body that is Soviet Russia settled down to a prosaic, tenacious, hard process of integration, then it was found that in its center was . . . Stalin. But how had he made his way there? He had been there from the beginning! He had done his work on the quiet. And he was pragmatical enough to realize that the dictatorship of the proletariat, in addition to being a popular catchword, was after all a dictatorship that must eventually be wielded by one human being.

VI

Two men were sitting in the editorial office of the Pravda, Stalin and Demyan Biedny. It was the eve of the first grand demonstration organized by the Bolsheviks in protest against the Kerensky offensive at the front. The telephone rang. The Kronstadt sailors were asking for Stalin. Their inquiry was pointblank:

"Shall we or shall we not come out with our rifles?"

Biedny watched Stalin intently. "I was consumed by curiosity," he tells. "How would Stalin answer a question about arms over the telephone? Stalin humorously and slyly screwed up his face, stroking his mustache with one hand."

"What! Rifles, rifles? Why, comrades, you ought to know what to do," spoke Stalin. "We here are only scribblers and we always carry our arms, our pencils, with us. As to your arms, it is for you to decide."

Biedny was convulsed with laughter. "Stalin has always been a master at giving clear directions," he observes in his narrative.

It is a common fallacy to allot credit or discredit for momentous events in proportion to the contemporary reverberations rather than in accordance with actual performance. The world was set agog by the demonstration of the following day. The press was filled with fearful descriptions. Lenin and Trotsky were in the headlines in all the capitals of the globe. Yet it was the concealed Stalin that directed the march. His was not to speak to the multitudes through megaphones, but to put up the men with lusty lungs and to supply the audiences—armed. Four hundred thousand soldiers and workers poured out into the streets under the auspices of the Soviet. The demonstration became the first review of the Bolshevist forces. They marched with banners calling for peace and a Soviet government. Yet there were no observers to record that behind the banner of the Central Committee of the Bolshevist Party marched a tall and pleased Caucasian who was to stand out several years later as the one leader of the country.

The offensive at the front ended in disaster. The revolution ran away. The masses grew more radical than the Bolsheviks. Regiment after regiment demanded immediate action. On July 16, the populace poured out into the streets half a million strong. The soldiers and sailors clamored for the heads of the government. One of the Socialist-Revolutionary ministers, Chernov, was seized by the uncontrolled mob, and was saved by Trotsky. The government frantically appealed to the Soviet Executive Committee. The Bolsheviks had decided not to sponsor the demonstration, considering the moment unpropitious for an insurrection. But Lenin declared that the people were a hundred times to the Left of his party. To avoid anarchy, Lenin's Central Committee decided at the last moment, unable to stem the tide, to guide it into peaceful channels. Later, Lenin and his associates were saddled with responsibility for the wild outbreak.

"It was at three o'clock in the afternoon on July 16," relates Stalin. "In Kseshinska's mansion a city conference was being held to discuss municipal questions. Suddenly two delegates from the machine-gun regiment dashed in. 'Our regiment is on the point of being broken up. We are being mocked at. We cannot wait any longer. We have decided to rise, and sent out delegates to the factories and regiments.' The representative of the city conference, Volodarsky, declared that our party had decided not to demonstrate. The delegates left protesting.

"At four o'clock the Central Committee met. It decided against action. I was commissioned to carry this decision to the session of the Soviet Executive Committee. I conveyed all the facts. I proposed that they take the necessary measures.

"At five o'clock the city conference adopted a similar resolution. All the participants went to their districts and factories to restrain the masses from rising.

"At seven o'clock two regiments appeared in front of Kseshinska's mansion with banners reading: 'All Power to the Soviets.' Two of our comrades came out to persuade the soldiers to return to their barracks. They were met with cries: 'Down!' This never before had happened. At this time a procession of workers came up with the cry: 'All power to the Soviets.' It became clear to everybody that it was impossible to hold back the masses."

Late in the evening the Bolshevik leaders decided to reconsider their former decision and to organize the movement as a manifestation which would present the popular demands to the Soviet. The following day the Pravda appeared with a blank space; the earlier resolution had been taken out of type at the last minute. The city seethed for a couple of days. Then the government took the offensive. The military authorities demanded that the Bolsheviks remove the armored cars from Kseshinska's palace and that they send the armed sailors back to Kronstadt. This was done.

Stalin received an order from the military commander to clear the Bolshevist staff out of the palace and to have the rebel soldiers in the fortress of Peter and Paul vacate their position. At that time, the government's artillery, cavalry, and infantry were in readiness to attack. It was a critical moment. The Central Committee failed in its efforts to persuade the soldiers and sailors to yield without armed resistance. Stalin was dispatched to the fortress to break down the opposition of the Bolshevist hotheads by convincing them of the futility of a struggle. He succeeded, and the men agreed to return to their regiments and armories on condition that their arms be sent there too.

Martial law was declared. "We, fighting for the full power of the Soviets," said Stalin at the extraordinary conference held two weeks later, "found ourselves in the position of an armed opponent of the Soviet. It would have been madness for us to have accepted the challenge of battle."

"On July 19, there were no demonstrations," announced Stalin on a subsequent occasion. "Fresh troops from the front paraded the streets. The cadets had been mobilized. Secret agents were snooping about everywhere, verifying passports and arresting people helter-skelter. The previous night the Mensheviks and the Socialist-Revolutionaries had decided to declare a dictatorship and disarm the workers and soldiers. . . . We received an order to clear Kseshinska's palace at once. I went to the Soviet Executive Committee with the proposal to adjust matters without bloodshed. 'What do you want? To shoot us?' I asked. 'We are not rising against the Soviets.' Bogdanov answered me that they wanted to avoid bloodshed. We went to the military headquarters. The military met us in none too friendly a manner, and declared that the order had been issued. I got the impression that those gentlemen sought a bloodbath at all costs."

The decisive action was the publication of the forged documents purporting to show that Lenin and Trotsky were German spies. The attack on Lenin and his allies became in the nature of a hunt. This was one of the main factors in the ultimate success of Bolshevism. The offices of the Pravda were sacked, and the newspaper closed. Trotsky, Kamenev, and scores of others were put in jail. Lenin and Zinoviev, in accord with the decision of the Central Committee, resolved not to surrender. Once more the Bolshevist Party returned underground. Once more Stalin, the arch-conspirator, was called upon to execute delicate tasks. Stalin was back in his element.

VII

The hunt for Lenin was widespread. The whole city was talking of the sensational vanishing of Lenin and Zinoviev. Was it not proof of their guilt? Stalin was commissioned to find a hiding place for them. While the search was on, he had the two men transferred and concealed in the apartment of Alliluiev, his future father-in-law. Connections were established with a Bolshevik peasant in the country, and in the evening of Sunday, July 22, on one of the crowded boulevards of the city, one could have observed four men walking toward a certain point near a railroad station. Two of the men were Lenin and Zinoviev. The other two were Stalin and Alliluiev, who acted as guards. The two refugees were safely put on board a train, in charge of the peasant, who was to house them in a barn. Stalin went back to his work, but stepping more softly than ever, clinging to the shadows and leading the entire Bolshevist organization into a semi-legal channel.

During the weeks that followed, Stalin was the leader of the Bolshevist forces in the field. He, of course, represented Lenin, with whom he was in constant touch by secret channels. He was only the spokesman of Lenin, but even that was of special importance in a hierarchical organization such as the Bolshevist is. It was Stalin who represented the Central Committee at the extraordinary conference held after the July events. Again it was Stalin who delivered the keynote speech at the Sixth Congress of the party held in August. After the first session, the cautious Stalin had the whole body moved in the old conspirative manner to new quarters. He took no chances. Here were assembled the remaining captains of Bolshevism. Their arrest would be a catastrophe to the cause.

It was the first occasion that Lenin was not present at such a gathering. This congress it was that decided upon the policy of an armed insurrection against the Provisional Government. And it was at this congress that the formal alliance with Trotsky took place. "We must raise the new slogan of union with the left wing—the Internationalists—who have retained a dose of revolutionary honor, who are ready to fight against the counter-revolutionists," declared Stalin. And while Stalin was only the executor of the union, it is one of the many ironies of the revolution that under his guidance Trotsky was admitted into the Bolshevist sanctum, and elected for the first time a member of the new Central Committee, where he stayed until Stalin, in a different rôle, expelled him. Yet Trotsky's popularity was even then greater than Stalin's. Among the first four names announced as having received the highest number of votes—the others were kept secret for conspirative reasons—that of Stalin was not included. Those of Lenin and

Trotsky, both involuntarily absent, headed the list.

At this congress Stalin already formulated and expressed the view which he did not translate into action until ten years later. It was here, three months before the Soviet Revolution, that Stalin took up the bold position from which all his political and economic differences with Trotsky developed, in the future struggle for power—a struggle also complicated by personal animosities.

The fundamental difference between Stalin and Trotsky in that struggle was national socialism versus international socialism. Can social revolution be successful in one country or does its existence depend upon world revolution? Lenin at the time held that socialism in Russia cannot survive without the overthrow of capitalism in Western Europe. Trotsky stood and still stands on the same platform. But Stalin came out at this congress with what is probably the most significant utterance of the first forty years of his life.

When the resolution providing for the seizure of power came up for discussion, it stated that the purpose of taking over the government was "to guide it, in union with the revolutionary proletariat of the advanced countries, toward peace and the socialist reconstruction of society." One of the leading delegates, Preobrajensky, then proposed to change this clause as follows: "To guide it toward peace, and, in the event of the occurrence of a proletarian revolution in the West, toward socialism."

Stalin objected to the suggested change, and stated his reasons in this trenchant and original fashion:

"The possibility is not excluded that Russia particularly will be the country that will pave the way toward socialism. . . . The base of our revolution is broader than in Western Europe where the proletariat finds itself all alone face to face with the bourgeoisie. Our workers are supported by the poorest stratum of the peasantry. Finally, in Germany the machine of state functions incomparably better than the imperfect machine of our bourgeoisie, which in itself is a vassal of European capital.

"One must discard the antiquated idea that Europe only can show us the road. There is such a thing as dogmatic Marxism and creative Marxism. I stand on the latter ground."

The remarkable utterance of Stalin remained forgotten and of no consequence during the stormy years that followed. Moreover, Lenin certainly believed in the imminence of world revolution, and Stalin was not the man to press his doctrine. He wisely shelved it until other days. Stalin sensed that in an unbridled idealistic revolution one must conserve such a realistic idea.

Stalin knew how not to shoot his bolt prematurely.

VIII

The Provisional Government was now in the hands of Kerensky, who desperately clung to the fading colors of the republic—democracy and liberty. But he was sitting on a volcano. The gates of hell seemed to have broken loose in the depths. A dark and boundless sea of humanity blazed with the cry: "Peace and land!" From his shelter in the loft of the hay-barn Lenin poured oil into the gaping crater through the mouths of ten thousand frenzied agitators. The moderate socialists were losing out to the Bolsheviks, who by every election were gaining larger and larger power in the Soviets. Kerensky believed in the people, but the people no longer believed in Kerensky. On the one hand, the military were seeking to eliminate Kerensky and strangle the Soviets. On the other hand, the Left revolutionary groups were accusing him of dictatorial methods and an alliance with the monarchists and capitalists. Everything played into the hands of the Bolsheviks. The Allies' efforts to drive revolutionary Russia into an offensive against Germany produced the opposite results. The front was demoralized.

The Bolshevist efforts were centered upon organizing the coming insurrection. The adventurous attempt of General Kornilov to march upon Petrograd and "restore order," brought all the revolutionary factions together. Trotsky was set free. As president of the Petrograd Soviet, he headed the Revolutionary Military Committee which actually made possible the establishment of the Soviet government. Stalin was active within the party. Stalin never lost sight of the fact that the next revolution must be under Bolshevist control, that it must not be permitted to run away. To Trotsky, the main objective was to sweep onward. To Stalin, the main objective was to have the sweep properly harnessed. Trotsky believed that a Soviet revolution would mean the power of all the workers' and peasants' parties represented in the Soviets. To Stalin, the slogan "All Power to the Soviets" had but one meaning: All power to the Bolshevist Party.

Stalin had advocated a coalition with Trotsky at Lenin's behest, but not for the purpose of enthroning Trotsky. Always a party man, steeped in the Leninist tradition, Stalin was glad to welcome new converts into the fold, but kept in mind that they were converts. The Bolshevist Party being a hierarchy, it was not to be expected that strangers with an irregular record, however brilliant, would ever be permitted to rise to the pinnacle. Stalin always remained distrustful of fresh recruits. He ever remembered that he was among the first to embrace the faith and that Trotsky came upon the scene rather late. He would be useful, to be sure. And Stalin collaborated. When Kerensky convoked the national Democratic Conference in an eleventh-hour attempt to stave off disaster, Trotsky came out for the Bolshevist boycott of this so-called "pre-parliament." Kamenev and Rykov were against the boycott. But Stalin supported Trotsky. The following day, the latter received a jubilant note from Lenin.

"In the days of the Kornilov affair," writes one of Stalin's assistants, Pestkovsky, "I used to run into Stalin frequently in the Smolny Institute [where the Bolshevist headquarters were now established]. Here I observed that the main work of preparation for the October revolt was conducted by three members of the Central Committee, Stalin, Sverdlov, and Djerjinsky. The Petrograd Committee and the military organization worked under their guidance. It was Stalin who had exclusive charge of the political direction of the preparations. He was also the director of the party organ.

"The labor masses of Petrograd knew Stalin but

little at that time. He did not seek popularity. Lacking oratorical talent, he avoided appearing at mass meetings. But not a single party conference, not a serious organizational meeting of any consequence, was held without Stalin's addressing it. The active party members knew him well on account of that."

"In the first days of the revolution," wrote Stalin in October, "the slogan of 'All Power to the Soviets!' was a novelty. In April, it was first raised against the Provisional Government. In June, it was demonstratively recognized by a vast majority of workers and soldiers. In July, the slogan was the center of a battle between the revolutionary majority of the capital and the government of Lvov-Kerensky. At the end of August, the Kornilov rising caused the revolution to mobilize its forces. The Soviets suddenly came to life and took over power in Siberia and in the Caucasus, in Finland and in the Urals, in Kharkov and in Odessa. Without this seizure of power, the revolution would have been crushed. And so the slogan 'All Power to the Soviets!'—announced in April by a tiny group of Bolsheviks in Petrograd—became at the end of August the almost universal clamor of the revolutionary classes in Russia.

"The moment has come when this revolutionary slogan must at last be realized."

There is an unauthenticated story that Stalin met a former comrade about this time.

"Come with us," Stalin said, "now, before it is too late. If you don't, tomorrow you will be one of my bodyguards."

But if Stalin did not think of bodyguards, he certainly did think of power.

IX

The stage was now set for the world-shaking climax.

From his hiding place Lenin sounded the call to immediate action. He was furious. He was impatient with his lieutenants. The Petrograd Soviet now had a Bolshevist majority. Then why wait? But his aides in the field favored delay until the approaching meeting of the All-Russian Congress of Soviets. Lenin vehemently insisted on seizing power at once.

"Procrastination would be absolutely a crime," he wrote to his staffs. "The Bolsheviks have no right . . . to wait." He sent vitriolic messages that were actually destroyed without trace by his disciples, so offensive were they in content. Once more was Lenin ahead of his flock. He could not stand his isolation any longer. He returned to Petrograd. He was tired of preparations. He wanted a coup d'état without further postponement.

In the night of October 23, in Sukhanov's apartment, Lenin gathered his general staff. He came wearing a wig, to avoid recognition. Here in a ten-hour session, the conspiracy was hatched. It was decided to act, but, upon Trotsky's representations, also to wait for the Soviet Congress which was meeting at the beginning of November, in order to secure its approval of the Petrograd coup as a fait accompli. Only Kamenev and Zinoviev opposed the seizure of the government as an adventure, and favored delay until the Constituent Assembly met. Stalin sided with Lenin.

"What did it mean," discoursed Stalin in 1924,

speaking of Lenin, "to start a revolt at such a moment? . . . It meant to stake everything on one card. But Lenin was not afraid to risk, for he knew, he perceived with his far-sighted eye, that a revolt was inevitable, that it would be victorious, that a revolt in Russia would pave the way for the end of the imperialist war, that it would stir the tortured masses of the West, that a revolt in Russia would turn the imperialist war into a civil war, that it would produce the Soviet Republic, which would serve as a rampart for the revolutionary movement of the entire world."

But Stalin forgot to mention that on the very eve of this revolt he slipped badly and committed an almost fatal sin against Lenin. At that grave moment Kamenev and Zinoviev still continued to fight in the open the insurrectionary policy of the party. Lenin attacked them in print as "immeasurable villains." They published a statement in the Pravda explaining their stand. Stalin came out in the paper, without the knowledge of the Central Committee, with an editorial note, which said:

"We express the hope that the declarations by Zinoviev and Kamenev settle the matter. The sharp tone of Lenin's article does not alter the fact that fundamentally we are all in agreement."

Stalin was subjected to cross-fire at the next session of the Central Committee. The indignation expressed was so great that the minutes of that sitting were deleted when already in type from the 1917 records recently published by the Bolshevist Party, and remain unavailable in Russia. The minutes read:

"Comrade Stalin declared that he was resigning

from the editorship." That was four days before the Soviet revolt. In order not to aggravate matters at a critical time, Stalin's resignation was not accepted by the Central Committee.

One cannot help feeling that Stalin's rebuke of Lenin was amply justified. Yet how different Stalin became when put in the saddle!

The Soviet revolt was carried out under the leadership of Trotsky by the Military Revolutionary Committee of the Petrograd Soviet, which was formed under the disguise of defending the revolution. "Our purpose was to accomplish the revolt by means of a conspiracy," wrote Trotsky. The subterfuge was necessary to make it appear that it was the Petrograd Soviet which had seized the power, and to retain the support of the Left Socialist-Revolutionary Party, whose votes were needed to make a majority in the Congress of Soviets. When the executives of that party inquired what the aim of the Military Revolutionary Committee was, an insurrection or the maintenance of order, threatening to withdraw their deputies in the case of the former, Stalin replied: "Order, defense."

"The entire work of the practical organization of the uprising," wrote Stalin a year later, "was carried on under the immediate direction of the chairman of the Petrograd Soviet, Trotsky. One may state without hesitation that the party was indebted first and foremost to Comrade Trotsky for the garrison's prompt going over to the Soviet and for the able organization of the work of the Military Revolutionary Committee."

At two o'clock in the afternoon, on October 24,

while the government was already crumbling, Stalin reported to the Bolshevist caucus of the Soviet Congress the latest information in possession of the Central Committee. "They are advancing from the front against us," announced Stalin. "A Lettish regiment coming to our aid has been detained. The Provisional Government is vacillating. They sent men today to negotiate with us."

But the Bolsheviks had no intention to effect a compromise.

X

Revolt!

November Seventh—the reddest of all the red-letter days in the calendar of human history.

Thirty weeks before, two million people deluged the thoroughfares of the city and in a transport of creative joy threw off the chains of thirty decades, and proclaimed in one chorus the utopian reign of democracy, liberty, and justice.

That was Revolution, majestic, awesome, thrilling.

Now it is insurrection. The streets of Petrograd are deserted. The people are cowering in their homes behind shutters and locked gates. The city is chilled with fear. It is a funeral and not a birth. A nation steeped in suffering is burying its short-lived golden hopes.

Armed detachments move about on mysterious errands. They are occupying without resistance the central telegraph exchange, the railroad stations, the important state buildings. Several ministers of the government are already under arrest. Trotsky has announced that power has passed into the hands of the Soviet. "There was tense silence for a few seconds," he writes. And when the applause came, it was "rather thoughtful . . . a disturbed thoughtfulness. A sure historical instinct revealed itself here." Thus was the Soviet coup received in its own household.

The Winter Palace is surrounded but not yet captured. Kerensky's loyal cadets are still picketing and controlling the important streets. In the Smolny, Trotsky, Stalin, Podvoisky, and others are issuing orders and leading the insurrection. Lenin is still safely in hiding in the workers' quarters of the capital. His bodyguard, the Finnish communist Rakhya, has just brought him the news that Kerensky is about to raise all the bridges over the numerous canals of the city. Lenin paces the floor. Military tactics are foreign to him.

Suddenly he declares that Stalin must be found as soon as possible. He has to see Stalin at once. Rakhya argues. All means of communication are paralyzed. There is no way of reaching Stalin. Lenin insists: "We must go to the Smolny then."

In the evening Lenin and Rakhya slowly make their way to the Smolny. Lenin's face is bandaged with a kerchief to look as if he were suffering from a toothache, and he wears a cap and large eyeglasses. After many adventures, passing through the cordons of Kerensky's pickets unrecognized, they arrive at their destination.

Here bayonets are fixed, machine guns are trained. Lenin is challenged by the wakeful Bolshevist guards. With great difficulty does he pass through the lines. Discipline here is no longer the discipline of democracy. Dictatorship is posted at the doors, although its declaration has not yet been promulgated. In a few hours the Soviet government will be established, and the dictatorship of the proletariat proclaimed. A new and startling cabinet of ministers will be set up. Power of a novel kind, immense power, will be distributed among the handful of people in a littered smoke-filled room. And Stalin will get his share.

CHAPTER SEVEN

POWER COMES TO STALIN

I

"COMRADE STALIN, are you the people's commissar for nationality affairs?"

"Yes."

"Have you a commissariat?"

"No."

"Well, I will get one up for you."

"All right. What do you need?"

"Nothing but credentials so that I may get help."

"Very well."

The conversation took place in the Smolny several days after the Soviet revolt. The applicant, Pestkovsky, a Polish Bolshevik interested in the question of minority races, had decided to join Stalin's department. The interview having proceeded that far, "Stalin, who does not like to waste words," tells Pestkovsky, "went into the office of the council of commissars. In a few minutes he emerged with a mandate. I took it." Stalin's new aide started off to find quarters in the Smolny. He established himself in a large room half of which was occupied by some commission. He drafted into the service an old friend whom he accidentally met, and the two found a table and put up an improvised sign on the wall reading "People's Commissariat for Nationality Affairs." He then returned to Lenin's office where Stalin had his desk.

"Comrade Stalin, would you like to have a look at your commissariat?" Pestkovsky asked. "The imperturbable Stalin," he writes, "was not surprised by my speed and followed me to his new commissariat. Here I introduced to him my friend, Seniuta, the chief of the chancery. Stalin was agreeable. He looked over the place and emitted a sound which was either one of approval or of displeasure. He returned to Lenin's study. I ordered stationery and a seal, spending all the money we had. Once more I applied to Stalin."

"Comrade Stalin, we haven't got a penny."

"How much do you need?"

"A thousand rubles to begin with."

"Come back in an hour."

When Pestkovsky returned, Stalin asked him to apply to Trotsky for a loan of three thousand rubles.

"He has money," remarked Stalin. "He found it in the former ministry for foreign affairs."

Pestkovsky located Trotsky, got the funds, and gave him a formal receipt. "As far as I know," he tells, "Stalin never returned that loan to Trotsky."

A couple of days later Pestkovsky ran into Stalin in the lobby of the Smolny.

"Have you a typist in the commissariat?" asked Stalin, who had a paper in his hand.

"No, we have no need for one. We use the typist of the council of factory committees."

"If that is the case," declared Stalin, "find a reliable typist and have this paper copied. We need twelve copies. It is strictly confidential."

The paper was the historic ultimatum of the majority of the Central Committee to the group led by

Kamenev, Zinoviev, Rykov, and Lunacharsky, who were still trying to effect a coalition with other revolutionary parties. It practically said: "Submit or get out!" Pestkovsky was tremendously interested, but could learn nothing from the uncommunicative Stalin. He went to Muranov to inquire as to the differences. Muranov, waving his hand, replied:

"Our misfortune is not that we have too many Marxists. It is that we have too many Marxes."

II

Stalin's cabinet post in the early period of the Soviet régime was but a matter of an official title. Unofficially, Stalin became more than ever Lenin's right-hand man.

The revolution presented a scene of remarkable chaos. Within a series of overlapping and inchoate waves there was but one fixed point—Lenin. Kerensky was advancing upon Petrograd. The entire bureaucracy was on strike. The supreme army command was sabotaging the new government. The front was melting away. The Germans were threatening an advance. The Ukraine and half a dozen other territories declared their independence. Here and there tsarist generals were already organizing armies to wage war against the Soviet power. The socialists in the All-Russian Soviet were fighting Lenin. The National Railwaymen's Union, under Menshevist control, paralyzed traffic and demanded a coalition government.

Within the high councils of the Bolshevist Party, pandemonium reigned. Lenin's idea of a party dictatorship and his suppression of the non-socialist press led to one crisis after another. He was attacked viciously by his own disciples as an adventurer, an opportunist. His resignation was demanded. Half a dozen members of his cabinet, led by Rykov, Ryazanov, and Nogin, resigned. "We take the view that it is necessary to form a socialist government of all the Soviet parties," they wrote in their declaration. "We think that there is only one other way, the preservation of a purely Bolshevist government by means of political terror, upon which the council of commissars has entered. We cannot and will not enter upon it. We see that it leads to the estrangement of the proletarian masses from the political leaders and to the establishment of an irresponsible régime and the wrecking of the country and the revolution." Kamenev, Zinoviev, Rykov, Miliutin, and Nogin resigned from the Central Committee.

Lenin's steamroller crushed these lily-livered rebels, stamped out their spirit, and turned them into servile office-holders. Stalin was at the wheel of the steamroller. Lenin was at the height of his glory, at the true pinnacle of his career, in this maze of pitfalls and dangers. With this suite of stalwarts, he executed one attack after another, always on the offensive. His shadow was Stalin. Lenin had the impulses, Stalin conveyed them. Lenin had the will, Stalin put it into effect. Stalin was the carrier of Lenin's armor.

"The period of 1917-18," writes Stalin, "was crucial for our party and our state. The party then first became the ruling power. For the first time in the history of humanity a new power arose, that of the Soviets of workers and peasants. To transfer our party, which had hitherto existed illegally, onto new rails, to create the organizational foundations of the new proletarian state, to find the forms for the relations between the party and the Soviets, to insure the leadership of the party and the normal development of the Soviets—all of these constituted the most complex organizational problem facing our party."

In the process of consolidating the embryonic dictatorship of the proletariat into a party dictatorship; in the fateful transformation of the social revolution into a Leninist revolution; in the all-important preservation of the party control and premiership of power against the encroachments of the new state machine that was threatening to wrest authority from the hands of the Bolshevist circle, Stalin performed a colossal amount of labor. Yet his rôle was singularly lacking in color, in initiative. It would seem as if he had said to himself: "I erred once. I shall follow Lenin blindly from now on." And he absorbed the personality of his chief at this stage perhaps more than anybody else or than at any other time in his career.

Stalin at this time laid the foundations of his subsequent power. Possibly it would be more just to say that Stalin, even as Lenin himself, was a tool in the hands of a force that was less obvious but more potent than the organized Bolshevist machine. The breakdown of all boundaries was so complete, the overflow of the revolution so immeasurable, the disintegration of all cells in the national organism so thorough, that at the very climax of the dissolution, and in proportion to its vastness and momentum, was the force of integration. It was the chaos that in the end produced the dictatorship. From this disunion came union, from decentralization—centralism; from diffusion—solidification.

While Trotsky was publishing the secret treaties of the tsar to a gaping world, while he was preparing to occupy the grand stage at Brest-Litovsk against the kaiser's equally theatrical personages, Stalin was clinging close to the heart of the revolution, to its center of gravity. He was the child of destiny.

III

The first act of the new government was to issue the decree, drafted by Lenin in pencil, giving all the land to the peasants. The next day, armed with this great popular victory, Lenin turned his attention to the defense of Petrograd. The Red Guards were poorly organized, and a division of troops could have marched into the capital and overturned the new régime. Podvoisky, in charge of the military organization, describes the moment as follows:

"On November 8, we began to form and send Red Guard regiments to the front. Comrade Lenin apparently grasped in the most realistic manner the critical position. Unexpectedly for us, he appeared at the staff headquarters with Stalin and Trotsky." The result was the mobilization of the Kronstadt forces which saved the situation.

The next step was to secure peace. In the night of November 9, Lenin and Stalin, accompanied by War Commissar Krilenko, went to communicate directly over the ticker-telegraph with the commander-in-chief at Moghilev, General Dukhonin. This historic conversation lasted from two to half past four in the morning. The general refused to recognize the authority of the new government, and to honor its demand for the immediate initiation of armistice negotiations with the enemy.

After a brief conference on the spot, the following was dispatched over the wire:

"In the name of the government of the Russian Republic, at the command of the council of people's commissars, we dismiss you from the post you hold for disobeying the orders of the government and for conduct which is causing unheard-of suffering to the laboring masses of all the countries and especially to the armies. We order you under the threat of martial law, to continue in command until the new commander-in-chief, or the person empowered by him, arrives at headquarters to take over your office. Lieutenant Krilenko is appointed supreme commander-in-chief. Lenin, Stalin, Krilenko."

"It was in the first days after the October Revolution," Stalin himself describes the episode, "when the council of people's commissars endeavored to compel the rebel general, Commander-in-Chief Dukhonin, to stop military activities and to open negotiations with the Germans for an armistice. I recall how Lenin, Krilenko, and I went to the staff headquarters in Petrograd to conduct over the direct wire conversations with Dukhonin.

"It was an anxious moment. Dukhonin and the army headquarters categorically refused to carry out the order of the council of commissars. The high officers of the army were entirely in the hands of the headquarters. As regards the soldiers, it was unknown what would be said by the twelve million men under the control of the so-called army committees, which were in a mood of opposition to the Soviet authority. In Petrograd itself there was being prepared an uprising of the cadets. Besides, Kerensky was advancing on Petrograd to make war. I recall how after a short pause at the wire, Lenin's face became lit up with an unusual light. It was clear that he had made his decision. 'Let us go to the radio station,' said Lenin. 'It will render us a service; we will issue a special order removing General Dukhonin and appoint in his place as commander-in-chief, Comrade Krilenko, and we will appeal to the soldiers direct, over the heads of the officers, to surround the generals, to suspend military operations, to establish contact with the Austro-German soldiers, and to take the business of peace into their own hands.'

"This was a jump in the dark. But Lenin was not afraid of this jump. On the contrary, he was eager for it, for he knew that the army wanted peace, that it will fight for peace, sweeping away any and all obstacles on the road to peace; for he knew that such a method of establishing peace will not be a lesson in vain to the Austro-German soldiers, that it will let loose the longing for peace on all fronts, without exception."

Upon Krilenko's arrival at the front, Dukhonin was arrested. In spite of all attempts to save him, the deposed commander-in-chief was attacked and lynched by a mob of infuriated soldiers.

In the meantime traffic in the country was still paralyzed, Kamenev's negotiations with the Menshevist railwaymen were at a standstill, and Stalin was dispatched by Lenin to carry the fort. After many endless night conferences, he broke down the resistance of the democratic brotherhood.

In his capacity as commissar of nationality affairs, Stalin turned his attention to the East, to carry out Lenin's program of undermining the colonial empires of the great powers. On December 7, a proclamation was issued by the Soviet government, bearing the signatures of Lenin and Stalin, and addressed to the "Laboring Moslems of Russia and the East." This was a strange document for Marxists to issue. It was an appeal to the faithful to rise against their oppressors and put an end to foreign rule in Asia. But at the same time, the manifesto canceled the traditional tsarist policies in the Orient.

"Constantinople must remain in the hands of the Mohammedans. . . . We announce that the agreement as to the partition of Persia between Great Britain and the tsar's empire is torn up and annulled. . . . We announce that the agreement as to the partition of Turkey and the seizure of Armenia is torn up and annulled."

This declaration was effective and far-reaching propaganda. But Lenin's strategy also included the immediate extension of the social revolution to the neighboring countries. Close to Petrograd was Finland, and it was highly desirable to have it Sovietized. Stalin was charged with the mission. He engineered the communist revolt in Finland. It is true, the Red régime in that country did not last more than six months. But then Finland is a European nation. And Bolshevism has never been able to maintain a foothold in the West.

IV

With bated breath the world watched the Soviet government enter into separate peace negotiations at Brest-Litovsk with the Central Powers. Upon the outcome, it seemed for a while, the issue of the World War depended. A finer piece of international showmanship Bolshevism has never staged. The Teutonic governments sought a speedy conclusion of peace, to enable them to strike decisively at the Allies before the Americans were ready to take the field in force. The Bolsheviks parried for time, in the hope of a revolution in Germany.

There is preserved in the Lenin Institute in Moscow a curious document in the handwriting of Lenin and Stalin, drafted at the session of the council of commissars of December 10, 1917. It bears the title of "Outline of Program for Peace Negotiations with Germany." Lenin attempted in this paper to draft for the Soviet Peace Delegation, then led by Joffe, the concrete terms of peace on the basis of the principle of no annexations and no indemnities. But somehow Lenin stopped in the middle. Lenin was never strong on concrete application of ideas. He could lay down policies and expound theories, but he could not clearly define the mechanics of their execution, he could not translate them into practical steps. He could prescribe a formula and let Stalin prepare the corresponding prescription.

The half-finished script of Lenin's remains an amazingly incoherent and inept document. Lenin, however, knew his weakness, and turned the paper over at the session to Stalin, who knew how to apply ideas, and who proceeded to set down point by point the basis for the negotiations. And Stalin's draft it was that later became the Soviet program of peace, as presented to the Germans on December 22, and broadcast throughout the world.

This document illustrates clearly the relation between Lenin and Stalin. The part that Stalin had in the Brest-Litovsk drama was not one of heroism but of technical performance, not of policy but of politics. While the Soviet envoys, first Joffe and then Trotsky, were in the spotlight, defying the Germans who were bent upon dictating an oppressive peace, the Bolshevist Party was in the throes of unprecedented dissension. Lenin stood for peace, to save the hearth of world revolution. He was in the minority. A powerful Left faction under Bukharin cried for a holy, revolutionary war against the Central Alliance. So violent was this opposition that at one time a plot had been perfected to kidnap Lenin. The negotiations were procrastinated to the limit. The peace delegates went back and forth. At the seat of power, the Central Committee, confusion was supreme. Trotsky came out with his famous conciliatory formula of "No peace and no war." This Lenin characterized as futile phraseology.

At the session of the Bolshevist general staff of January 19, 1918, Stalin declared: "The way out of the grave situation has been shown us by the middle course—the position of Trotsky." By a vote of nine against seven this policy was approved. Lenin fought it with devastating ferocity. The Left elements simply could not understand how a proletarian government could sign a humiliating treaty with the imperialist kaiser without defeating the very aims of Bolshevism. The Germans then began their advance, moving into Russian territory by leaps and bounds. Lenin submitted his resignation. In the end, it was Trotsky's realization of his error and his single vote that gave Lenin the necessary majority to carry the final round and have the onerous peace approved.

During the inconceivable turmoil of clashing forces and ideas, what was Stalin's stand? The records of the many sessions with their fluctuating votes and ever-changing formulas tell the story of Stalin's consistency. He had no original policy. He gave birth to no winged phrases. Whenever Lenin voted "Yes," Stalin did likewise. When he ventured a suggestion, it was not happily received. Thus at the critical session of February 23, Stalin proposed that the German terms should not be signed and that another attempt be made to recommence negotiations. Uritsky answered him by explaining that it was too late, that the Germans had already taken Dvinsk and were rushing forward at great speed. Lenin declared:

"Stalin is wrong when he says that one need not sign now. These terms have to be signed. If you do not sign them, you will be signing the death sentence of the Soviet government in three weeks."

Stalin bowed. Trotsky maintains that Stalin had not taken any independent position. He writes:

"He was simply waiting and calculating. 'The old man is still hoping for peace,' he would nod to me, referring to Lenin. 'He won't get any.' Afterward he would go to Lenin and probably make the same sort of observation about me. . . . My principal object—to make our conduct in the question of peace understood by the world proletariat in the best possible light—was no doubt a matter of secondary importance to Stalin. He was interested in 'peace in one country,' as he later was in 'socialism in one country.' "

But Stalin's "confused and helpless position" was not quite as confused as Trotsky would have us believe. When Trotsky wired Lenin from Brest-Litovsk on February 15, asking for further instructions, Lenin replied:

"I should like to consult first with Stalin before replying to your questions." Three days later, at the critical hour, Trotsky conversed with Lenin over the long-distance telegraph ticker. Once more an important decision had to be made. Lenin replied:

"Stalin has just arrived. We will confer with him, and immediately give you our joint answer."

And as to Trotsky's principal object of arousing from Brest-Litovsk the world proletariat, well, it proved secondary not only to Stalin but to Lenin. The Brest-Litovsk peace was the first compromise on the part of the international revolution, a surrender of Bolshevist principles from which the cause of world communism has never recovered. It was a struggle between pure revolutionary doctrine and the realities of the state. Bolshevism made peace with imperialism against its own principles, justifying the compromise on the theory of preserving the source of social revolution in power. The subsequent overthrow of the monarchies in Germany and Austria proved but a slight compensation to communism.

Yet it was a compromise that the pragmatical Stalin could well understand. Power is not won to be surrendered to theory. Theories are shaped to fit power.

V

This was brought home to Stalin more than ever in his position as commissar for nationality affairs. Under his direct control, the international revolution made its second vital compromise, in a field that was less spectacular but not less effective. And in the process, Stalin discovered the first of the three magic keys to the treasure-chest of power.

The son of a suppressed minority race, Stalin as commissar for nationality affairs turned his attention to the subjected and backward peoples that formed half of the population of the great country. He had in the past specialized in the study of the national question and was recognized as one of the leading Bolshevist authorities on the subject. But, once in power, he discarded his earlier Marxist theories as to absolute political independence of all subjected peoples and carried out a policy that eventually caused bitter friction between him and Lenin.

Stalin more than other leaders of his party, is responsible for the cementing of the federation known as the Soviet Union. It was a problem of the first magnitude. Within the confines of former Russia, live ten score different races, from the highly advanced Armenians and Georgians to the backward

Yakuts and Bashkirs. Many of these peoples occupy solid blocks of territory, and have traditions that go back for thousands of years. Many of them had been robbed of their independence by tsarism in recent times, and developed vigorous revolutionary movements for national liberation. Some of the minor nationalities boast cultural heritages equal if not superior to that of the dominant race, the Great Russians. Others, like Bokhara and Turkestan, were mere colonies of imperialist Russia, having the same relation to Moscow as Haiti to the United States or Mesopotamia to Great Britain.

The policy of the Soviet government has been to satisfy in full the demands for cultural autonomy of all the minority races, without granting them an ounce of real political power. Within the framework of a highly centralized dictatorship, the so-called independent republics forming the Soviet Union enjoy unlimited freedom in education and the arts but no economic or state sovereignty. Moscow has in effect said to them: "You may have your own national schools, but no statehood."

When Stalin was in Vienna in 1913, he formulated the original Bolshevist doctrine on the national question. He opposed federalism as oppressive, as an instrument of imperialism, and favored separatism in the future social revolution for all the nationalities seeking independence. That year Lenin came out with a virulent declaration advocating the absolute right of secession for all the subjected races in Russia.

When Stalin returned from exile after the overthrow of tsarism, he wrote an article in the Pravda in which he analyzed the suggestion that Russia be built into a federal union like the United States. After an able exposition of the origins and development of the American federal system from 1776 to our own times, he drew a parallel between the American colonies and modern Russia, and found that their economic conditions were distinctly dissimilar. He also pointed out that the American federation consisted of states along geographic lines whereas in Russia the various territories presented separate ethnic units.

"It is clear," he wrote, "that federalism in Russia does not and cannot decide the national question and . . . can only turn back the wheel of history." His conclusion was that the Bolshevist solution of the question must be radical and final: "The right to secession for such nationalities which cannot and do not wish to remain within the general framework of the state."

Seven months later, a week after seizing the government, Lenin and Stalin, in their joint Declaration of the Rights of the Peoples of Russia, issued on November 15, 1917, proclaimed to the world "the right of the peoples of Russia to free self-determination, including separation and the organization of an independent state."

Two months later, Bolshevism executed its first face-about on the national question. In January, 1918, Lenin announced in a declaration approved by the Central Committee: "The Soviet Russian Republic is constituted on the basis of a free union of free nations, as a federation of Soviet national republics." Forgotten was the old Bolshevist theory that federalism was coercive and imperialist, and that "a free union" was incompatible with the principle of federation.

That year Stalin attempted in an essay to explain and justify the new policy. It was a well-written piece, but carried little conviction. He propounded the view that the internationalist character of the Soviet Revolution lifted the nationality question from a domestic status to a world level. The Soviet Republic, he asserted, was a bridge in the world-wide revolutionary front for the liberation of the colonies and dependencies from the imperialism of the West. Hence, the justification for the forcible inclusion of the subjected peoples and countries in the Soviet federation. Was it not to the ultimate interest of Bokhara or Afghanistan to be under Soviet rather than under British control?

Life was rapidly overtaking theory. The following year, Stalin was able to incorporate in the new program of the Communist Party the proposition of a "federative union of states." When the Soviet Constitution was drafted soon afterward, there developed a bitter feud between the "Great Russian" Lenin and the Georgian Stalin. It was the latter who was accused of imperialist tendencies! Lenin insisted, however, upon recognition of the right to secession on the part of the members of the federation. This provision was carried against Stalin's opposition, but it remains, of course, a dead letter.

Reviewing after Lenin's death the road "traversed by the party from the denial of the principle of federation to its recognition," Stalin acknowledged that the structure of the Soviet Union was a complete negation of previous Bolshevist theory.

Such is the effect of power upon doctrine. Traveling from conspirative haunts to the Kremlin, Bolshevism and Stalin shed their internationalist feathers for the garb of nationalism. Nothing illustrates more strikingly this transformation than the march from separatism to federalism, from the principle of secession to that of a centralized dictatorship which extends over domains and races that have no proletariat and no immediate or genuine interest of their own in socialist revolution.

Under tsarism, the numerous oppressed peoples were held together by the iron rule of a military-bureaucratic machine—imposed from above. Under Bolshevism, they are bound by the iron rule of the ramified party machine—imposed from within.

Stalin, as commissar for nationality affairs, had opportunities for creating living, personal relations with every section of the proletarian empire such as no other member of the government had. The delegates and representatives of a hundred races came to know Stalin. For the framing of the network that enabled him later to become the "boss" of the entire Soviet Union, Stalin's first office was invaluable.

In building the national political machine which was to bring him to the pinnacle of the dictatorial pyramid, Stalin learned that unlimited power is impossible in a decentralized, separatist state.

First it was necessary to frame the hundred-odd national staves into one body, one vessel.

The second step was to forge that spiral hoop of steel which is the modern Communist Party.

The third stage would be to bind the vessel with the hoop, and power such as the world has never seen would be secured.

Stalin attained the first goal. But before the second task could be undertaken, the great prize would be in jeopardy, the revolution would be in real peril, and Stalin would fight the initial round of his great battle with Trotsky—for power.

VI

What kind of man was this coming "boss" of the Soviet Union in his immediate environment? How did he exercise his power while presiding over the commissariat for nationality affairs? In his own department, Stalin was neither imperious nor hard. He was not a thunderer. His close collaborator in this work, Pestkovsky, described Stalin's relations with the collegium or council governing his commissariat.

"There were Lettish, Polish, Lithuanian, Esthonian, and other elements," writes Pestkovsky. "They were afflicted with the ideas of Left Bolshevism. I myself belonged to that faction. . . . Stalin faced the difficult task of fighting within his own organization. I am almost certain that Trotsky, who accuses Stalin of 'dictating,' would in three days have dispersed the oppositional council and surrounded himself with his own followers. But Stalin acted differently. He decided to educate us by slow and persistent efforts, and displayed much discipline and self-control. He had his conflicts with individual members of the council, but was loyal to the body as a whole, submitted to its decisions even when he disagreed, with the exception of such cases where there was a violation of party discipline. Then he would appeal to the Central Committee and, of course, carry his point."

Sometimes Stalin would grow weary at the conferences with his department chiefs, but he would never lose his temper. When his reserve of patience became exhausted as a result of interminable discussions, he would suddenly disappear. His usual trick was to excuse himself with the remark: "I'm stepping out for a minute." He would then vanish and hide in some corner in the Smolny, while the government was in Petrograd, and in the Kremlin, when it was transferred to Moscow.

"It was almost impossible to find him," tells Pestkovsky. "At first we would wait for him. Later we learned to break up and go home. I would occasionally locate him in the most unexpected places. A couple of times I ran into him in the home of the sailor Vorontzov, in the kitchen, where Stalin, lying on a couch and smoking a pipe, would be sunk in thought.

"Lenin could not get along without Stalin for a single day. It was probably because of that that our office in the Smolny was next to that of Lenin. In the course of the day, Lenin would telephone Stalin innumerable times, or he would drop in and take Stalin with him. Stalin spent most of the time with Lenin. What he did there I do not know, but once, entering Lenin's office, I observed an interesting scene. On the wall was a large map of Russia. Two chairs were in front of it. On the chairs stood Lenin and Stalin and with their fingers traced the northern boundary, I think, in the neighborhood of Finland.

"At night when the confusion in the Smolny

would subside somewhat, Stalin would go to the main telegraph office where there was a direct line to the front, and stay there for hours. He conducted lengthy conversations, now with our army commanders, and now with our enemies; for example, with the war minister of the Ukraine with whom our government carried on negotiations."

In the scramble for office space upon the arrival of the government bureaucracy in Moscow, Stalin's commissariat did not fare well. At first, two private houses were placed at its disposal.

"Watch out that these are not taken away from you," Stalin warned his aide. A dozen Lettish guards were then hired and posted by Pestkovsky outside the buildings. In a short time, two more dwellings were required to house the bureaus. Stalin was dissatisfied.

"Now it will be impossible to keep track of the organization. It would be better if we had one large building," he said.

"I secured the Grand Siberian Hotel," announced Stalin several days later, "but the supreme economic council has seized it without authority. However, we must not let them get away with it. Tell the Alliluiev girl to type out on the machine several signs reading: 'This Building Belongs to the Commissariat for Nationality Affairs.' Don't forget to take some tacks along with you."

But the revolution was still young then. Occupation meant possession. Formalistic authority was not yet enforced. The building remained in the hands of the tenants that seized it. It was one of those few cases where Stalin suffered defeat and did not exact retribution.

Chapter Eight

THE DISOBEDIENT WARRIOR

I

THE revolution sought peace and found war. It would not fight the Central Powers, but it was eager to fight its enemies at home. It had no backbone against the imperialists and militarists of the German and Austro-Hungarian monarchies, but it discovered a backbone against the monarchists, landlords, and capitalists within its own frontiers. One army of millions had been dissolved. But hardly had it melted over the surface of the land before it began to crystallize into a new army. In 1917 there were twelve million soldiers at the front. Early in 1918 there was none. Two years later the new Red Army numbered six million men.

Revealing are the forces of revolution. The deserters of yesterday become the heroes of today, and the heroes of yesterday the cowards of today. The Red Army, improvised as it was in a brief span of time, was both a spontaneous and a cultivated shoot from the tree of renascence. The spontaneity sprang from the storm and stress of the period of destruction, from the will to revolution, from the party that incarnated that will; the cultivation came from the state mold which the revolution assumed, from the necessity to maintain a position in the new balance of power in the world.

These two elements, the elements of individualism and collectivism, of partizanship and statecraft, of guerrilla warfare and machine militarism, clashed within the Red Army in the persons of Stalin and Trotsky.

It is one of the ironies of Stalin's career that he who was the embodiment of the idea of discipline, of obedience, of party unity and control, should have represented at the front the individualist trend. While Trotsky, the supreme commander, always an individualist in the past, always outside the party machine, a typical guerrilla revolutionist, should have incorporated at the front the idea of the state as the supreme institution of the revolution.

The story of this first round in the Trotsky-Stalin bout remained hidden in the Kremlin archives for years, and did not become known until after the death of Lenin. Yet the rift between the two men commenced in the first year of the revolution, when it was less of a struggle for power and more of a conflict as to policy. But even then the personal elements already entered into the fight.

Stalin was jealous for the heritage of his party and distrustful of "aliens'" gathering too much authority into their hands. Trotsky was above politics, but he was imperious, flushed with an exaggerated sense of his importance, and flaunted his ego in a manner that made people think of Napoleons in embryo.

The Red Army, according to Bolshevist theory, was not to be built up on hero-worship. It was to reflect the dominant class, under the leadership of the proletariat and not personalities. There is no question that Trotsky violated this principle. The statutes of the Red Army contained a biographical section dealing with Trotsky. It concluded with the glamorous words: "Comrade Trotsky is the leader and organizer of the Red Army. Standing at the head of the Red Army, Comrade Trotsky is leading it to victory over all the enemies of the Soviet Republic."

This spirit Trotsky displayed from the beginning of his great military career. It was dictated by sound considerations of mass psychology, but it bred envy and fear in the hearts of the Leninist old guard. Stalin, with his natural suspiciousness, his reticence, his self-control, his gentle touch but tenacious grip, was an admirable executioner of any potential or incipient Bonaparte. He remembered the lessons of the French Revolution perhaps a little too well. And he would be more zealous, more watchful than his master, Lenin. For is not that the historical rôle of all disciples of prophets?

Trotsky's surpassing contribution to the victory of the Soviet forces over all their powerful enemies in the field was the placing of the technical control of the Red Army's strategy and operations in the hands of experts. With magnificent courage and vision, Trotsky drafted tens of thousands of tsarist officers, many of them brilliant military scientists who never had had an opportunity under the corrupt old régime, and placed them under the supervision of revolutionary commissars. It was an anomalous situation—the sight of tsarist officers in the Red Army. But then perhaps one reason for the failure of all past revolutionary attempts was their lack of professional generalship.

Stalin distrusted this method of organizing the

army. He distrusted Trotsky's "specialists." Stalin by his training could not comprehend such a policy on the part of a revolutionary government and could not help undermining it in the interests of the revolution he had helped bring into the world. Moreover, did not Lenin himself have his misgivings and anxieties on the subject?

II

Gruesome and majestic is civil war. It is primitive, but, unlike the modern warfare of attrition, its nature is one of sweeping movement.

All of Russia was now ablaze. In every direction of the compass, looking from Moscow, fronts were rising. In the Ukraine, an "independent" government was in control with the aid of German troops. The Cossack generals in the northern Caucasus and the Don territory were whipping one army after another into shape. The Czecho-Slovak Legion was advancing from Siberia upon Ekaterinburg where the Romanov family was imprisoned. The Socialist-Revolutionaries attempted insurrections against the Soviet government in Moscow and in Yaroslavl.

During 1918-1920, Russia became an arena for the greatest civil war in history. The revolution spread and recoiled. The Bolshevist power was beleaguered. A solid circle of steel enveloped the heart of the country. In the east, Kolchak swept on from the Pacific to the Volga. In the south, the line ran from General Dutov in Asiatic Russia to the Roumanian borders. General Denikin, later followed by Wrangel, moved from the Black Sea to the center of Muscovy. In the west, the Poles, Letts, Esthonians were on the offensive. In the north, Finland, the Archangel Expedition, and, above all, the forces of General Yudenitch hammered at the besieged fortress. The British, the French, the Japanese, and the Americans were present to tighten the stranglehold. The blockade was in force.

The revolution called. Stalin was one of the first to go to the front. He had never been a soldier. He brought to the battle-line, however, an organizing skill, a stubbornness, a resoluteness, and an authority which made him one of the most feared war commissars. He also brought with him a distrust of Trotsky's policies and a disdain of military science.

Early in June, 1918, Stalin was dispatched to the lower Volga, to Tsaritsyn—now Stalingrad—the outlet for the rich grain-producing districts of the northern Caucasus. His position there was one of controller of food supplies. Upon his arrival, he found that the Red forces were highly disorganized. The Cossacks were getting close to the city, and the Bolshevist rule was feeble in the region. Stalin immediately applied himself to the job of stamping out all disorganization and introducing a state of martial law. He at once came into conflict with the army commanders who were under the orders of the revolutionary war council of which Trotsky was the chief. The first decisive conflict with Trotsky developed here.

Stalin was in constant touch with Lenin. "I am driving and bullying all who require it," wrote Stalin to Lenin, July 7. "Hope soon to restore the position! You can rest assured that we shall spare nobody, ourselves or others, and the grain will be obtained. If only our military 'specialists' (what cobblers!) would not sleep and idle, the line would not have been broken; and if we restore the line it will not be thanks to the officers, but in spite of them."

When Lenin expressed his anxiety about the possibility of a rebellion in Tsaritsyn on the part of the Left Socialist-Revolutionists, Stalin replied:

"As for the hysterical ones, rest assured, our hand will not falter, we shall deal as enemies with our enemies."

Stalin's relations with the commanding officers were strained from the beginning. On July 11, he telegraphed to Lenin:

"Everything is complicated by the fact that the headquarters staff of the North Caucasus Command has proved to be absolutely incapable of fighting against the counter-revolutionists. It is not only that our 'specialists' are psychologically incapable of striking the decisive blow against the counter-revolution, but also that they, as 'staff' workers, are capable only of 'drafting plans' and elaborating schemes of reorganization, and are entirely indifferent to military operations . . . and, generally speaking, behave as if they were outsiders, guests. . . .

"I intend altering this and many other local shortcomings. I shall take measures, even to the dismissal of those officials and commanders who are ruining the cause, despite the formal difficulties which, where necessary, I shall break through. Of course, I shall take full responsibility before all higher institutions."

This was nothing short of disrupting the military organization that Trotsky was attempting to build. It was a breach of army discipline for which court-martial is the established code. But Stalin at this time still had the full support of Lenin in Moscow. On the spot, he had the backing of a group of old Bolsheviks, of whom Voroshilov and Minin were the leaders, Voroshilov is now the commissar of war of the Soviet government, in the office that Trotsky held then. Stalin and Voroshilov worked hand in hand. The latter was in command of several detachments of irregular troops, largely free-lancers, and he fought for their independence and against subordination to the regular army system.

Trotsky soon learned that Stalin's ruling group was sabotaging the high command. His efforts to establish discipline and normal military order were nullified at Tsaritsyn by Stalin. Once Trotsky sent a telegraphic message urging the need of leaving the army staff and the war commissariats alone, so as to permit them to function properly. On this message, Stalin made the following inscription:

"To be ignored!"

Trotsky did not know at the time it occurred of Stalin's countermanding his order. But it was the talk of Tsaritsyn, and led to the further destruction of the morale of the military officers and staff workers. Lenin was apprised of the situation.

"Every day I would receive from the high command," writes Trotsky, "or the front command such complaints against Tsaritsyn as: it is impossible to get executions of an order, it is impossible to find out what is going on there, it is even impossible to get an answer to an inquiry. Lenin watched the conflict develop with alarm. He knew Stalin better than I did, and obviously suspected that the stubbornness of Tsaritsyn was being secretly staged by Stalin. The situation became intolerable; I decided to enforce order in Tsaritsyn."

III

What was Stalin doing in Tsaritsyn? First of all, he proceeded to clean up the town. There were too many white-collared people in the streets. There were military bands playing in the public gardens. The bourgeois aspects had to be eradicated. Stalin was bent upon turning the city into a proletarian war camp. He set up a special division of the Cheka (Extraordinary Commission) which went about its task of stamping out counter-revolution ruthlessly.

An officer who was in Tsaritsyn at the time, Colonel Nosovitch, who later deserted from the Red Army and joined General Krasnov, described in a White newspaper Stalin's activities. Expecting to draw from the northern Caucasus the food supplies needed in central Russia, Stalin found shortly after his arrival this source cut off by the enemy's advance.

"But it was obviously," wrote Nosovitch, "not in the nature of such a person as Stalin to leave unfinished work once begun. We must be fair to him, and admit that any of the old administrators have good cause to envy his energy; and it would be well for many others to learn from his capacity to adapt himself to his work, and the local circumstances.

Gradually, as his work grew less or, rather, as his direct tasks became smaller, Stalin began to examine the work of all the administrative departments of the town, and the task of organizing the defense of Tsaritsyn in particular, and the whole of the Caucasian, so-called revolutionary, front in general.

"By this time, the atmosphere had become heavy at Tsaritsyn. The Cheka was working at full speed. Not a day passed without plots being discovered in what had seemed to be the most reliable and secret places. All the prisons of the town were full. . . .

"The fighting at the front had reached its culminating point. . . .

"After July 20, the chief moving spirit and executor was Stalin. A simple conversation on the direct line with the center, concerning the difficulties and unsuitability for work of the existing form of administration, brought a command along the main wire from Moscow, that Stalin was to take charge of the whole of the military . . . and civil administration. . . .

"By now the local counter-revolutionary organizations had become considerably strengthened and, having obtained money from Moscow, were preparing an insurrection to help the Don Cossacks to free Tsaritsyn.

"Unfortunately, the leaders of this organization who had arrived from Moscow, the engineer Alexeyev and his two sons, were not well acquainted with the existing state of affairs and, as a result of a badly arranged plan . . . the organization of this plot was discovered. . . .

"Stalin's resolution was short:

" 'To be shot!'

"Engineer Alexeyev, his two sons, and a considerable number of officers with them, some of whom had been members of the organization while others were suspected of participation in it, were seized by the Cheka and shot without trial."

"I was commissioned to secure food for Baku," one of the partizan chiefs told Jerome Davis several years later. "At that time Baku had a population of two hundred thousand, with seventy-five thousand workers. Grain was collected at the mouth of the river Volga to be distributed all over Russia. I carried my own armed force. After months of desperate work we had three hundred thousand poods of wheat. Then I had to get boats to ship it to Baku. All was arranged, and I was happy, when officers of Stalin's appeared and confiscated it. In vain I showed my order from the communists. Stalin's men said, 'It makes no difference what orders you have. If we do not get grain and go back to Stalin with empty hands we shall be shot.' These men had a larger fighting force, and I realized that it would either mean a terrible fight or else surrender. Baku was starving. I decided to appeal personally to Stalin.

"At that time Stalin was virtually a dictator in the matter of securing grain. He almost never received anyone in his room except his lieutenants. He was like a lion in his cage, always pacing up and down. In spite of everything, I managed to get to him and plead for Baku. Stalin brushed the plea aside with the statement, 'What nonsense you are talking. If we lose Baku, it is nothing. We will take it again inside of a few months or a year at the most. If we lose Moscow, we lose everything. Then the revolution is ended.' The grain went to Stalin and Moscow."

But Stalin also set an example at the fighting line. After the repressive measures in the rear had been put into effect and "revolutionary order" restored, he set out for the front, which then stretched over three hundred and fifty miles.

"I remember, as if it were today, the beginning of August, 1918," writes Voroshilov in his reminiscences. "The Krasnov Cossacks were attacking Tsaritsyn, trying with one concentrated drive to throw back the Red Army units to the Volga. For many days the Red troops, headed by the Communist division composed entirely of workers from the Donetz Basin, withstood the extremely powerful attacks of the excellently organized Cossack units. These were days of great trial. You should have seen Comrade Stalin at that time. Calm as usual, deep in thought, he literally had no sleep for days on end, dividing his intensive work between the fighting positions and the army headquarters. The position at the front became almost catastrophic. The enemy front, formed into a horseshoe, with its flanks resting on the Volga, pressed closer each day. We had no way out.

"But Stalin cared nothing for this. He was inspired with one single thought—victory! To smash up the enemy whatever happened! And this indomitable will of Stalin was passed on to his closest colleagues, and despite the almost hopeless position nobody doubted in our ultimate victory."

IV

When Stalin countermanded Trotsky's order, he usurped authority. When he defied the high command, he acted as a partizan chieftain and not as an army officer of rank. But he displayed his independence behind Trotsky's back. He did not inform his chief of his act or his reasons for it. He did not bother to notify general headquarters of the measures he was taking or canceling.

This is characteristic of Stalin, but even more so was the manner in which he took his punishment. His bravado turned into diffidence.

The issue was now: Trotsky or Stalin. Trotsky proceeded to Tsaritsyn determined to get Stalin out of the way. . . . Trotsky won.

"I insist categorically on Stalin's recall," he wired Lenin on October 4. "The Tsaritsyn front is in a bad way, despite the abundance of troops. Voroshilov can command a regiment but not an army of fifty thousand soldiers. Nevertheless I leave him in command of the Tenth Tsaritsyn Army on condition that he submit to the commander of the southern front, Sytin. Until now the men in Tsaritsyn have not even sent reports of operations to Kozlov [general headquarters]. I made them undertake to send in reports of operations and reconnoitering twice a day. If this is not done by tomorrow, I will commit Voroshilov and Minin to trial and announce it in an order to the army. So long as Stalin and Minin remain in Tsaritsyn, they are endowed, in accord with the constitution of the revolutionary war council, only with the rights of members of the war council of the Tenth Army. There is only a short time left for an offensive before the roads become impassable for infantry or cavalry. Without coordinating operations with Tsaritsyn no serious action is possible. There is no time for diplomatic negotiations. 'Tsaritsyn' must either submit or get out of the way. We have a colossal superiority of forces but complete anarchy at the top. With this one can cope in twenty-four hours on condition that you lend your firm and decisive support. In any event, this is the only way out that I can see."

The following day Trotsky transmitted to Lenin without comment an order of the commander-in-chief nullifying an order of Stalin's, and stating that "the activities of Stalin are wrecking all my plans."

Lenin agreed to Stalin's recall from Tsaritsyn.

Anxious for peace, aware of Trotsky's method of dealing summarily with recalcitrants, and having acceded to Trotsky's demand for Stalin's recall, Lenin wanted to avoid a demoralizing row. He dispatched Sverdlov, the president of the republic, to the scene, to take Stalin to Moscow and smooth over things upon Trotsky's arrival. Sverdlov came to Tsaritsyn by special train. He suggested to Trotsky that he have a talk with Stalin. Here is how Trotsky describes this meeting:

" 'Do you really wish to dismiss them all?' Stalin asked me, in a tone of exaggerated humility. 'They are fine boys!'

" 'Those fine boys will ruin the revolution, which can't wait for them to grow out of their adolescence,' I answered him. 'All I want is to draw Tsaritsyn into Soviet Russia.' "

Stalin returned to Moscow with Sverdlov, his erstwhile roommate in exile. Trotsky confined himself to stern warnings. He had a conference with Voroshilov, who also became very meek and who confessed that the Tsaritsyn Stalinists had executed only such orders from general headquarters as they had deemed proper. Trotsky warned his eventual successor that in case of further disobedience, he would have him arrested and sent to Moscow for trial before a revolutionary tribunal.

A year later, after Trotsky's successful campaign to save Petrograd from General Yudenitch, the Political Bureau met to award to him the Order of the Red Banner, the highest decoration granted by the Soviet government. Kamenev then proposed that a similar award be made to Stalin.

"For what?" asked Kalinin. "I can't understand why it should be given to Stalin." But the decoration was approved. When the meeting adjourned, Bukharin rushed at Kalinin:

"Can't you understand?" Bukharin argued. "This is Lenin's idea. Stalin can't live unless he has what someone else has. He will never forgive it."

Trotsky, in describing the episode, tells of the solemn session of the Soviets at the Moscow Grand Opera House at which the decorations were ceremoniously presented.

"Stalin himself was wisely absent," writes Trotsky. It was the kind of wisdom which Trotsky never understood. Stalin did not crave ovations. He craved power.

Six years later, Tsaritsyn—the Russian for the "city of the tsars"—was renamed Stalingrad.

V

Stalin did not yield. Upon his return to the Kremlin, he swayed Lenin and secured a considerable measure of support from him. He cultivated and led the widening opposition to Trotsky's policy of employing military specialists and to the rigorous discipline introduced in the Red Army. Trotsky ignored party traditions, and high-handedly punished alike old Bolsheviks and new revolutionists when they failed to perform their duty. This was a dangerous course which alienated proletarian support. Stalin took advantage of this. He also sowed distrust in Lenin's heart of Trotsky's rapid ascent to power.

"Today Stalin returned bringing with him news of three big victories by our troops before Tsaritsyn," Lenin wrote to Trotsky. "Stalin persuaded Voroshilov and Minin, whom he considers very valuable and quite irreplaceable workers, not to leave, and to obey in full the orders of the center. . . . Stalin is anxious to work on the southern front. He hopes that in actual work he will be able to demonstrate the correctness of his view. . . . In informing you of all these statements of Stalin's, I request that you consider them and reply, first, as to your willingness to talk the matter over with Stalin personally—for this he agrees to visit you—and second, if you think it possible to remove the friction by certain concrete terms and to arrange for the joint work which Stalin so much desires. As for me, I think it necessary to make every effort to arrange to work in conjunction with Stalin."

Lenin played Stalin against Trotsky. He sincerely sought a truce, but he also thought it safe to checkmate the two powerful men. Trotsky agreed to a compromise. Stalin was appointed a member of the war council on the Ukrainian front. The patched-up peace, however, did not last. Voroshilov, who had been transferred to the Ukraine, and Mezhlauk, the collaborators of Stalin, continued here the Tsaritsyn policy. Trotsky complained that "the line pursued by Stalin, Voroshilov and company means the ruin of the entire enterprise."

Lenin again endeavored to achieve a compromise. "A compromise is of course necessary," replied Trotsky, "but not one that is rotten. In point of actual fact, all the Tsaritsyn men are now gathered at Kharkov [the capital of the Ukraine]. . . . I consider Stalin's patronage of the Tsaritsyn policy a most dangerous ulcer, worse than any treason or betrayal by military 'specialists.' "

In the meantime, the northeastern front was in bad shape. The Red forces surrendered the city of Perm. The supply department collapsed. The Third Soviet Army lost eighteen thousand men and large quantities of equipment. The enemy advanced rapidly. The situation was grave. Lenin decided to send somebody to that sector to inquire into the causes of the disaster and to restore the front.

Voroshilov, in his official sketch of Stalin's military career, quotes the following telegram from Lenin to the president of the Revolutionary War Council of the Republic—without identifying that gentleman as Mr. Trotsky:

"There are several party dispatches from Perm

concerning the catastrophic condition of the army and drunkenness. I thought of sending Stalin—am afraid Smilga would not be firm enough in his attitude toward . . . who also, it is said, drinks and cannot restore order."

This telegram has been published and broadcast in Russia in recent years as evidence of Stalin's high authority under Lenin. Yet it is indicative of the manner in which history is being written in the Soviet Union, that the commissar of war deemed it necessary to delete certain vital parts from Lenin's message without pointing out the omissions which are italicized in the following complete text:

"To Trotsky, the President of the Revolutionary War Council, at Kozlov or wherever he may be. Moscow, December 31, 1918. There are several party dispatches from Perm concerning the catastrophic condition of the army and drunkenness. *I am sending them on to you. You are asked to go there.* I thought of sending Stalin—am afraid Smilga would not be firm enough in his attitude toward . . . who also, it is said, drinks and cannot restore order. *Telegraph your opinion."*

Trotsky replied the following day, his message concluding with the phrase: "I agree to Stalin's journey with the powers of the party and the revolutionary war council."

The suppression of the full correspondence between Lenin and Trotsky concerning Stalin's appointment is considered necessary for the prestige of Stalin. Upon receipt of Trotsky's consent, Stalin and Djerjinsky were designated "to investigate minutely the causes of the surrender of Perm. . . . And to take all needed measures for the speedy restoration both of the party and Soviet work in the whole region of the Third and Second armies."

In the Ukraine, the tug of war between Trotsky and the Stalin faction continued for months. Finally, Trotsky succeeded in forcing the issue. The Political Bureau took up the matter. Lenin sent word to the insubordinate chiefs that he was in full harmony with Trotsky, and demanded that Voroshilov and Mezhlauk obey the supreme command, "otherwise Trotsky will call you to his headquarters the day after tomorrow and will issue detailed orders."

Once more Stalin went down to defeat, and he remembered it.

VI

Stalin developed prodigious energy on his mission, and together with Djerjinsky performed valuable service in reorganizing the shattered northeastern front. The two commissioners sent out a call for reenforcements, and they were able to stem the advance of the enemy and to consolidate the line. At the same time, they reported to Moscow, "a serious cleansing of the Soviet and party institutions is taking place in the rear." Revolutionary committees were organized in the various localities. The proletarian forces were mobilized, the military intelligence department combed and purged. "The provincial Cheka has also been cleansed and reenforced by new party workers."

But Stalin also did not neglect any opportunities to deliver thrusts at Trotsky. He severely criticized the conduct of the revolutionary war council of which Trotsky was president. In their report to

Lenin on the causes of the Perm catastrophe, Stalin, and Djerjinsky dwelt upon "the outrageous and criminal methods employed by the Revolutionary War Council of the Republic [read: Trotsky] which actually paralyzed the front with its contradictory instructions and which deprived it of every possibility of coming to the speedy assistance of the Third Army."

Stalin did not surrender his conviction as to the damaging policy pursued by Trotsky. He blamed him for "the unreliability of reenforcements from the rear, which is explained by old methods of formation." He and his associate reported to the council of defense, of which Lenin was the head, that "the army cannot work as an air-tight, entirely autonomous unit," that it lacked proper means of contact with the adjacent fronts, that the orders of the high command were wrong.

Stalin now carried the battle into Trotsky's own field, that of army organization. "A régime of strictly centralized action on the part of individual armies," wrote Stalin and Djerjinsky, "must be instituted on all fronts, and primarily on the eastern front, for the carrying out of definite, seriously thought-out strategic instructions. Arbitrary action and thoughtlessness in the defining of instructions, without a careful consideration of all data, and the rapid change in instructions necessitated thereby, and also the indefiniteness of instructions themselves, as the Revolutionary War Council of the Republic often lets pass—all this makes it impossible to lead the armies, causes waste of time and energy, and disorganizes the front."

Stalin's labors enabled the Soviet forces to assume the offensive in the east, but all his achievements were wiped out by the huge advance of the Kolchak army a few months later. A critical situation now arose at Petrograd where General Yudenitch advanced in the spring of 1919, with the aid of the British. Groups of military "specialists" and officers at the Kronstadt naval base betrayed the Red Army, and several regiments went over to the enemy. Two forts, the "Red Hill" and the "Gray Horse," rebelled. Stalin was sent to stop the demoralization. The city was put in a state of martial law. Stern measures were taken to organize the inner defense of the capital. But Stalin did not limit himself to the rear. He telegraphed to Lenin:

"On the heels of 'Red Hill' we have liquidated 'Gray Horse'; their big guns are in complete working order. . . . The naval specialists assured us that the capture of 'Red Hill' from the sea would overthrow all naval science. There is nothing left for me but mourn the loss of this so-called science. The speedy capture of the 'Hill' was the result of the most brutal interference on my part, and that of civilians generally, in the operations, including the canceling of orders on land and sea, and giving our own instructions.

"I consider it my duty to declare that I shall continue to act in this way, despite all my reverence for science."

This contemptuous attitude toward military science was the expression of the psychological difference between Stalin and Trotsky. At Petrograd, Stalin was able to turn the tide by a counter-attack which he organized when Yudenitch was within thirty miles of the city. Voroshilov, dealing with this period, relates that Stalin "liquidated the most perilous situation before Red Petrograd," leaving the impression that it refers to the main Yudenitch thrust. In reality, the success was far from decisive. Three months later, Yudenitch resumed the offensive and got as far as the gates of the city. That was in October, 1919, when the announcement was made in Paris that Petrograd had been captured. On that occasion, it was Trotsky who saved the situation and destroyed the enemy. After all, there is such a thing as science in warfare.

VII

Stalin's star was rising in the military firmament. That of Trotsky suffered a temporary eclipse. Stalin returned from Petrograd with the halo of a conqueror. Trotsky at this time made the gravest blunder of his war career.

The clash between the two leaders approached a climax. Trotsky had overreached himself on the eastern front by ordering the court-martial of a number of leading Bolshevist commissars, without due investigation of their responsibility. This gained for him fresh and powerful opposition and for Stalin new allies. Furthermore, Trotsky removed the commander of the eastern front with disastrous results.

But it was on a question of strategy that the crisis developed. Kolchak had been thrown back from the Volga to the Ural Mountains. This was a great victory for Trotsky. But Denikin was moving forward at an alarming rate and threatening central

Russia. The question arose: Shall the campaign against Kolchak be prosecuted to the bitter end or shall the main forces be diverted to stop Denikin's advance? Trotsky stood for the latter solution. If his plan had carried the day, Kolchak would have been left in possession of Siberia and given a respite to enable him to reorganize and to assume the offensive. The plan adopted, however, by the council of defense, resulted in the complete annihilation of Kolchak's forces. While it permitted Denikin to get close to Moscow, it also accelerated his rate of advance and made his front correspondingly vulnerable. On the other hand, it enabled the Red Army to bring later from the east a victorious force which successfully smashed the center of Denikin's line and sent it reeling back to the Black Sea.

Five years later, speaking of the Trotsky legends in relation to the conduct of the war, Stalin said:

"Among these widely circulated legends is the story that Comrade Trotsky is the 'only' or 'main organizer' of our victories in the civil war. I must declare in the interests of truth that this story does not at all conform to the facts. I am far from denying the important part played by Comrade Trotsky in the civil war. But I must insist with all resoluteness that the high honor of bringing about our victories belongs not to individuals, but to the great collective of the advanced workers of our country—the Russian Communist Party." Stalin then recited Trotsky's failure to perceive the right strategy in the crucial campaigns against Kolchak and Denikin, and concluded with the challenge: "Let them try to deny these facts!"

Stalin now took the offensive, and urged upon Lenin the dangers of Trotsky's military direction. He sought the removal of his opponent. On June 4, 1919, he wrote to Lenin:

"The whole question now is whether the Central Committee can find enough courage to draw the proper conclusions. Has the Central Committee sufficient character and firmness?"

Trotsky submitted his resignation as commissar of war, as president of the revolutionary war council, and as member of the Political Bureau of the Central Committee.

This was a bombshell. It caused a serious crisis in the government. If Trotsky harbored Napoleonic designs, according to his accusers, they were not sustained by his unqualified resignation from power. The highest Bolshevist organs, the Political and Organizational Bureaus, met in joint session to consider Trotsky's act. And it was here that Stalin proved signally lacking in "sufficient character and firmness." He did not push his viewpoint at the meeting. Was it due to Lenin's influence? Or was it because of Stalin's realization that the time was inopportune to strike? In any event, on July 5, one month after privately urging Lenin to remove Trotsky, Stalin was one of the seven to affix his signature to the unanimous declaration which was transmitted to Trotsky, and in which his resignation was declined as "absolutely impossible" and of the "greatest detriment to the republic."

This document was worded in a fashion sufficient to please even the vanity of a Trotsky. It granted him the widest power. Yet it must be said that Trotsky proved himself big enough later to acknowledge his own mistake on the strategic issue and to confess that the plan approved by the Central Committee was the right one.

Despite Stalin's joining in the declination of Trotsky's offer to resign, he balked at orders to proceed to the Denikin front at the moment of grave danger. He retaliated by insisting upon three conditions before accepting the appointment. They were:

1. That Trotsky should not interfere in the affairs of the southern front, and should not cross its boundary line.
2. That a number of workers whom Comrade Stalin considered unsuitable for the work of restoring the position among the troops were to be immediately withdrawn, and—
3. That new workers, to be chosen by Comrade Stalin, should be immediately dispatched to the southern front, who would be capable of fulfilling the task.

Trotsky was not eliminated from the southern front. But Stalin's conditions were accepted! Such was Lenin's magic touch. He knew how to deal with his disciples. When Stalin arrived at the front, he displayed considerable perspicacity. He quickly analyzed the situation and urged the adoption of a new plan.

"Circumstances and conditions," he wrote to Lenin, "are not only ready for this, but urgently demand a change. . . . Without this, my work on the southern front is simply futile, criminal, useless; which gives me the right, or rather forces me to go anywhere, to the devil even, rather than remain on the southern front."

But Stalin found his path crossed by Trotsky and all his measures thwarted. He submitted his resignation.

The Political Bureau informed Stalin that "it considers it absolutely inadmissible to support one's business demands with ultimatums and declarations of resignation."

It was a painful blow to Stalin's pride.

VIII

Stalin's health was breaking down. His temper became irritable. He was being employed to stop dangerous gaps, but he never received proper credit for his work. He did the inside jobs. Trotsky garnered the glory.

Stalin complained to the Central Committee that he "was being transformed into a 'specialist' for cleaning out the stables of the war department."

When a breach developed on the western front, Stalin was rushed there. At a meeting of commissars in Minsk, he turned to the Polish communists present with the remark: "Your Pilsudski is an old woman. If he had any brains, he could march into Russia with two divisions and take Smolensk."

When Denikin's cavalry raids made it imperative for the Soviet forces to organize cavalry units of their own, Trotsky came out with the winged cry: "Proletarian—to horse!" Several detachments were formed under Trotsky's direction. But it was Stalin who conceived the plan, a bold step not in accord with professional military opinion, of creating a cavalry army. He overcame all opposition, and on November 11 organized under Budienny the famous First Cavalry Army.

When in January, 1920, a crisis arose on the Caucasian front, Stalin was requested by the Central Committee to go there to institute "genuine unity among the commanders" and to utilize "as widely as possible local forces and resources." He was informed that "the Political Bureau has resolved that it is absolutely necessary that you enter the revolutionary war council of the Caucasus front. . . . Inform us when you leave for Rostov."

Stalin was sick. He was tired of being shifted from one front to the other. He wired Lenin that this going back and forth would make the local leaders incline to "accuse me of frivolously jumping from one sphere of army activity to another, in view of the fact that they are not informed of the decisions of the Central Committee."

Three days later, Lenin telegraphed him: "I have not yet lost hope that . . . everything will come right without your being transferred."

But shortly afterward he was again urged to go to the Caucasus. On February 20, he telegraphed Lenin:

"It is not clear to me why the care for the Caucasus front should be put first upon me. In the order of things, the care of consolidating the Caucasus front lies wholly on the Revolutionary War Council of the Republic, the members of which, according to my information, are in full health, and not on Stalin who, as it is, is overburdened with work."

Lenin's reply is characteristic of the treatment

which that master had always accorded his lieutenants:

"The task of expediting the arrival of reenforcements from the southern front to the Caucasus front is entrusted to you. One should generally be helpful in every way, and not become a stickler for departmental spheres of authority."

When in the early summer of 1920, the Russo-Polish War broke out on a large scale, Stalin was the commissar in charge of the southwest front. During the historic advance of the Red Army to the gates of Warsaw, Stalin was largely responsible for the great thousand-mile march of Budienny's First Cavalry Army, its rout of the Polish forces, and its rapid advance into Galicia. In the catastrophe which the Red Army suffered at Warsaw, Trotsky would saddle Stalin with the blame for the rapid advance because of an anxiety to capture Lemberg, the capital of Galicia, first. But it is a fact that the right flank, under Smilga, also composed of cavalry, rushed at such headlong speed that it was saved only by seeking internment in Prussia, whereas Stalin saved his army.

When General Wrangel reorganized the remnants of Denikin's force in the Crimea and resumed the offensive, the Central Committee once more called upon Stalin. The resolution called for him to organize a war council and to concentrate on the Wrangel front. Lenin wrote to Stalin: "The Political Bureau has just finished dividing up the fronts, so that you are engaged exclusively with Wrangel."

During the entire period of civil war, Stalin was in the midst of battle. But not for a moment did he relinquish his campaign against Trotsky. He continued to ignore and slight him. He did not bother to send copies of his dispatches to the high command. Lenin usually forwarded the important Stalin messages to Trotsky. Once he instructed the latter to send to Stalin a message under his, Lenin's, signature, as follows:

"Address all military communications also to Trotsky, otherwise there may be a dangerous gap."

There *was* a dangerous gap. But it was not of a military nature. Rather was it political and personal in character, and for that reason fraught with even graver peril.

IX

Stalin was wilful, Trotsky was overbearing. Stalin was wily, Trotsky was unambiguous. Yet Stalin's line of conduct was consistently for the good of the revolution. This Lenin fully realized.

Stalin's ear was always to the ground. After all, a political party even in war time remains a political party, with its jealousies and ambitions, with minor functionaries climbing to the top and higher functionaries receiving homage and information from the lower ranks. Stalin gathered and gave expression to all the discontent, just and unjust, to all the criticism, fair and unfair, that inevitably accompanies the conduct of a great war.

But Stalin was more than that. He was the master-mind of the "inner defense" of the revolution, even as Trotsky was of the "outer defense." His chief concern was the rear, whereas that of Trotsky was the front. Stalin was thinking in terms of the

STALIN IN THE BACKGROUND.
This is the Second Congress of the Communist International the summer of 1920. Lenin in the center, Kamenev to the right and Zinoviev to the left. At the right of Stalin, Bukharin, to his left Sokolnikov.

victory of Bolshevism, while Trotsky was thinking of the victory of the army. "The weak spot in our armies is the instability of the rear," reported Stalin to Lenin, "chiefly due to neglect of party activity, incapacity of the Soviet departments to put into operation the instructions of the center, and the exclusive, almost isolated, position of the local Cheka institutions."

Stalin solidified revolutionary sentiment. Wherever he went, he introduced that reign of terror which both the Reds and the Whites considered indispensable for the conduct of civil war in Russia. Stalin fathered the course that to make the workers fight and win it was first necessary to wage in the rear a campaign of exterminating and terrorizing the non-proletarian elements. At the same time, he stood up more than once for Bolshevist commanders who were in trouble for insubordination. Thus when Parkhomenko, who later distinguished himself at the head of a cavalry division, was sentenced to be shot, Stalin, hearing of it, demanded and secured his immediate release.

Stalin's opposition to the employment of tsarist military experts grew out of his fear for the safety of the revolution. He was anxious lest these officers gain the upper hand over the political commissars and eventually seize control of the army. Lenin supported him in this, and shared the same fears. He even once suggested to Trotsky to dismiss all the military "specialists" and to appoint a veteran Bolshevik as commander-in-chief. When Trotsky informed him that there were thirty thousand such officers in the Red Army, Lenin at once realized the impossibility of his request and became enthusiastic over the magnitude of Trotsky's performance in impressing such a great body of enemies into the service of the revolution.

Stalin's apprehensions, however, were not allayed. He conducted an elaborate intrigue, and insinuated to Lenin that Trotsky was grouping hostile men against him. When Menjinsky carried the news to Trotsky, the latter was bewildered and declared: "I don't even want to talk about it." He confronted Lenin with the story, and Lenin's excitement confirmed its truth.

Stalin's intrigue was in keeping with his character. Suspicion runs in his blood. It was his sincere way of serving the revolution. Trotsky contributed to it by his aloofness, his self-sufficiency, his inability to form intimate, confidential friendships. To place in the hands of such a person a powerful army was enough to breed alarm in any conspirator's soul.

The gap between Stalin and Trotsky was bridged by Lenin in the realm of military affairs. In the political sphere, it widened and deepened as soon as Lenin passed away. He was able to tame Trotsky and squelch Stalin, but he was not able to cure the festering sore in the headquarters of Bolshevism.

X

War and love. Revolution and romance. Stalin and . . . marriage.

Such is the sequel extraordinary to this chapter of an heroic military career.

The clock of history struck 1919.

The desperate and decisive year of the revolution; the year of hunger, terror, cholera, of swift victories and defeats; the year of supreme tension, when the curtain of fire enclosing the besieged fortress of Bolshevism was at its summit, when every ligament in the Soviet body was ready to snap, when the very atmosphere vibrated with the convulsions of an agonized land.

Imagine Lenin or Trotsky in connection with an adventure in love at any time during the titanic struggle.

But Stalin was not a Lenin, not a Trotsky.

Stalin did not give himself entirely and undividedly to politics and war. Between his conflicts with Trotsky and his frequent missions to the various fronts, he prosaically consummated the great love affair of his life.

Stenka Razin, the tradition runs, flung his mistress into the Volga at the critical hour of his rebellion.

Napoleon Bonaparte took a new mistress, Countess Walewska, at Warsaw on his march to Moscow.

Stalin was neither a Razin nor a Bonaparte.

He obtained a divorce and then married again.

He had been separated from his first wife for years. One day in 1919, a special messenger from the Kremlin went to the bureau of marriage and divorce. He carried with him the necessary application blanks filled out by Stalin. The divorce was granted by proxy. The marriage license was issued in the same manner.

Stalin was almost forty.

Nadya Alliluieva was barely seventeen.

He had known Nadya's parents before her birth, he had known her in her cradle, he had known her when she was a schoolgirl. And like a true son of the Caucasus, he married her as soon as she reached her full adolescence.

Such is the stark outline of the romance of the inscrutable Stalin.

CHAPTER NINE

DISOWNED BY LENIN

I

THE curtain was now rising upon the second act of the great revolutionary drama.

The play of social forces was inevitably turning into a melodramatic piece in which a handful of characters shared the principal rôles.

In the forefront of the stage were half a dozen actors. There was Zinoviev, wily and lustful, a coward and a despot, a hypocrite and an oracle, a demagogue with a double chin.

There was Kamenev, weak, deceitful, urbane, an ambitious yet humane intellectual, with a dark stain on his record—resembling a minor orchestra conductor more than a proletarian warrior.

Standing apart was Rykov, honest but vacillating, addicted to drink, an amateur economist, with an illuminated countenance, who looked as if he had stepped out of the novels of Dostoyevsky and Turgenev and could not quite adjust himself to this topsyturvy dreamland.

Hovering in his vicinity was Tomsky, making a study in Slavic contrasts. Stultified in his physical growth, wiry, compact, this former metal-worker, sad in appearance but tense in motion, was endowed with keen native intelligence. What he lacked in education, he made up in will-power.

Pacing back and forth was Bukharin, youthful,

erudite, sometimes brilliant, almost always hysterical, a subjective thinker with no will-power—all brains and all nerves.

To the right, was Kalinin, the "little father" of the new régime, naive in appearance but crafty at heart, holding an olive branch to the peasantry, at first regarded as an "extra," who showed, however, that he could act a leading rôle.

In the center was Stalin, repressed, silent, brusk, collected and often phlegmatic in his manner. There was irony in his eyes. Inflexible in his circumscribed but upright purpose, he was wilful, unscrupulous in the selection of his means.

In a corner, aside from the rest of the troupe, was Trotsky, overbearing, disdainful, conscious of his superiority, unselfish, unafraid, waiting for the acclaim of the populace, expecting to be crowned at the proper moment.

Lenin was directing the company when the curtain rose. But as the play progressed, he would be stricken. He would be fearful. As he appeared from time to time, his speech would be that of a paralyzed god. He would realize that a scramble for power was unavoidable. Now and then he would call to Trotsky for aid. Pathetically he would threaten to smite his conspiring disciples. But his threats would carry no more weight, his tongue no more fire. His withered hand would fling no more thunderbolts. He had created a monster, and the monster would hasten his collapse.

The heroic period of the revolution at the front was also the period of the fateful adolescence of this monster. It is known in history as "military communism." At the very beginning of the civil war, Lenin gave it its first impetuous start, and he was never able to stop it. "Dictatorship is a great word," he hurled at the party congress in 1918, "and great words should not be thrown to the wind. Dictatorship is iron power, bold and swift in revolution, implacable in the suppression of exploiters as well as hoodlums. And our power is altogether too soft, it resembles jelly much more than iron."

In the furnace of military communism the great word became red-hot iron, as Lenin willed it. But at the same time the knights of the Bolshevist order forged their pens into swords, their pamphleteering and oratorical pasts into political machines.

When the blaze subsided, it was found that the revolution had congealed into molds. Zinoviev was the "boss" of a party steamroller of his own in "Red" Petrograd. Kamenev became the ruler of the Greater Moscow political organization. Trotsky was the misunderstood but envied possessor of a mighty military structure.

And Stalin, the shrewdest of them all, what would be his share in this new scheme of things?

Rykov, as the head of the Supreme Economic Council, was in charge of the nationalized industries and commerce. Tomsky, as the chief of the national trade-union movement, was marshaling labor into the government service. Bukharin, the editor of the Pravda, was the spokesman of the Kremlin.

But Stalin? Was he destined to remain Lenin's Man Friday, a confidant of his master, a mere messenger, at best a glorified private secretary? Lenin's tutelage was becoming irksome. Stalin was too much of a realist not to see the distribution of power going on about him. He had his eye upon the center of gravity—the party. He would make his own place there, and automatically the most coveted of all prizes would be his.

II

Throughout his entire career in power, Stalin has held cabinet posts but twice. In both instances, the commissariats of which he was the head, later went out of existence. In both cases, Stalin used his office as a stepping-stone to greater authority. Where Stalin gravitated, there his departments went. He invariably and completely identified his government agencies and their functions with those of the party. Under him the political machine swallowed the state apparatus.

Stalin became the inspector-general of the republic. In 1919, Lenin conceived the idea of forming a state department of control and inspection, which became known as "Rabkrin," to combat the boundless spread of corruption and bureaucracy. He called upon Stalin to take charge of it. At the session of the council of commissars at which the organization of the new department was discussed, Lenin handed Stalin a note in which he stressed the need of making it an organ of the masses. He wanted a popular campaign against red tape, arbitrary rule, criminal inefficiency or dishonesty in office.

Stalin's reply, as written upon Lenin's memorandum, was characteristic, inasmuch as it said that Lenin's suggestions were merely questions of policy within the new commissariat. Stalin's departmental mind could not be imbued with the spirit of the creator of the Rabkrin.

The antagonism between Lenin and Stalin developed first in this sphere. Lenin kept worrying Stalin. Lenin attributed the greatest significance to his work. He wanted the Rabkrin to become an instrument of democracy under a dictatorship! He grew irritated. Early in 1920, in a letter to Stalin, he reminded him that the object of his original plan was "to lead the entire mass of workers, men, and women especially, to participate in the Rabkrin."

It was obviously an impossible wish. The dictatorship excluded free activity on the part of the masses. Stalin made the Rabkrin an inquisitorial body, the only logical step in the prevailing system of government. Yet Lenin did not perceive the logic of the situation. He did not blame the centralized dictatorship as the source of the evil, he did not admit that the suppression of democracy within the party and the masses inevitably led to stoppage of all creative impulses and processes. He blamed Stalin, who was only carrying out his prescription, for curing bureaucracy with more bureaucracy.

Lenin's jabs and thrusts at Stalin continued. But the bureaucratic disease kept on growing, until it clogged every artery in the life of the nation. The government harbored hundreds of thousands of shady careerists. The party became the shelter for hundreds of thousands of mere adventurers. The Central Committee created a Control Commission of its own, which carried out the first general housecleaning with the result that two hundred thousand members were expelled from the Bolshevist ranks.

Stalin failed as inspector-general. But he succeeded in the first requisite of building a political machine, namely, putting his own people in controlling positions. He brought the Rabkrin and the Control Commission close together. Instead of having the bureaucracy checked from the bottom, as Lenin had hoped, it was supervised by a corps of functionaries from the top. And these functionaries were, of course, high party officials.

After three years in this office, Stalin was forced by Lenin to have the Rabkrin reorganized. New blood was introduced into the commissariat. But no improvement occurred. In a note to the new board, written in August, 1922, Lenin expressed this view and incidentally his criticism of Stalin's performance. "From my questioning of Stalin, I could not see any improvement. You may now have a staff of eight thousand instead of nine thousand," wrote Lenin. "But you should cut it to two thousand, and pay the salaries of six thousand, and thus increase the efficiency threefold."

But Stalin had achieved his object. If Zinoviev had his political machine in Petrograd, if Kamenev had his in Moscow, Stalin would have his in the entire country. The Rabkrin had given him the necessary foothold in every branch of the administrative system.

At the Eleventh Congress, held in March, 1922, Zinoviev proposed that Stalin be elected secretary-general of the Central Committee. Up to that time, the position was one not of power so much as of a technical nature. But in the hands of Stalin it would mean the development of the one and only seat of power in the country. Stalin seized the opportunity to build a national political machine, of which he was to become the first "boss" on the European scene.

In order to attain his destiny, Stalin needed but one more stroke.

Lenin was stricken.

III

For twenty months Lenin lay ill, staging astonishing recoveries and suffering the inescapable relapses. In the medieval Kremlin, a conspiracy was woven, with the Asiatic Stalin in the center, which had all the elements of a dark plot of ancient Muscovy.

Trotsky would have us believe that even before Lenin's first stroke, Stalin had been maneuvering to isolate and replace the grand master of Bolshevism. It is a fascinating theory, but there is not a shred of evidence to support it. At the time Lenin was stricken, there was animus between him and Stalin, but of a transitory character. There was, however, enmity between Trotsky and Stalin. But Stalin was comparatively unknown and Trotsky was at the apogee of his glory and had the fullest cooperation and confidence of Lenin.

Then how did it come to pass that the satellite Stalin should emerge as a rival of the Olympian Trotsky? How was it possible for that obscure mechanic to get the controls and shut off the chief engineer from the current of power?

It was possible because Lenin and Trotsky had

themselves cultivated the soil of Stalin's future rise.

Before proceeding with the action of the drama, it is necessary to turn back for a rapid survey of what military communism had done to the Soviet government and how it had paved the way for one-man rule.

Lenin suffered the first attack from arteriosclerosis in May, 1922. But the revolution had been afflicted with the hardening of the arteries for over three years. In 1917, power had been seized by Lenin under the slogan of the dictatorship of the proletariat. Step by step, during the following four years, it was transformed into a one-party dictatorship. In the ruling Bolshevist organization, these steps were marked by the following guideposts:

First.—The Seventh Congress of the party, in 1918, which ratified the dishonorable peace with the Central Powers, also declared that the primary and fundamental task was the taking of the most energetic, relentless, decisive, and Draconic measures for the raising of party discipline, the creation of iron cohorts of proletarians, and universal military training of the entire adult population irrespective of sex.

Second.—That congress elected a commission of seven, which comprised Lenin, Trotsky, and Stalin, to frame a new constitution for the party which was then renamed from Bolshevik to Communist. This ironclad constitution is still in force.

Third.—The power conferred upon party members made hundreds of thousands of non-revolutionists join its ranks in order to become officials, and bred during the period of military communism bureaucratic wantonness and misrule.

Fourth.—The suppression of all opposition within the party, particularly the first workers' groups that fought for freedom of opinion and democratic control of the political machines, established the precedent that all criticism was counter-revolutionary. Unity became an aim and not a means.

Fifth.—The Central Committee was enlarged to include two score party leaders. Its executive power was transferred to the small Political Bureau. The once supreme highest organ became in reality a Sanhedrin of a consultative nature.

Sixth.—The instrument of terror, the Cheka, created to combat counter-revolution against the state was turned into a party weapon for the cruel and unscrupulous destruction of all non-Bolshevist groups and for the rooting out of heresy within the Bolshevist household.

The effects upon the state structure of the policies pursued during the civil war were just as profound in the life of the revolution. They were as follows:

First.—The Soviet government had a coalition with the Left Socialist-Revolutionists during the first year of its existence. This is not generally realized. It was not until 1919 that the non-Bolshevist commissars were forced out from Lenin's cabinet. The council of people's commissars then became a training school for statesmanship under Lenin's guidance. Its power was transferred to the Political Bureau.

Second.—The Soviets of workers and peasants, which were in the beginning representative bodies although elected without secret and universal suffrage, were gradually transformed into bureaucratic civil-service departments, adjuncts of the party dictatorship. But it was not until the climax of military communism that the minority socialist deputies in the Soviets were silenced, dispersed, exiled, imprisoned, and finally eliminated completely.

Third.—The capitalist press was not destroyed until 1918. The socialist newspapers and magazines languished until the spring of 1919. It was at the end of that year that freedom of assembly for non-Bolshevist revolutionaries was abolished.

Fourth.—The trade unions retained their independence, with a certain measure of internal freedom and democracy, until the height of military communism. It was then that Trotsky proposed the militarization of labor. Lenin and Stalin opposed for tactical reasons this "state-ization" policy, but the labor unions became in fact if not in name obedient state organs.

Fifth.—The taxation of the peasant assumed a form of forcible requisition of his produce, frequently by means of armed detachments. The fight against the *kulak,* with the aid of the poorer peasants, grew out of economic necessity. It was justified by the theory of promoting the hegemony of the proletariat, but it alienated the great majority of the agricultural toilers of the country.

Such were some of the developments of the period of military communism in the organism of the dictatorship. Without these, Stalin would never have had his opportunity.

Military communism exploded with a force that rocked the Soviet régime to its foundations in the spring of 1921, when Kronstadt, which had cradled Bolshevism, rose in rebellion. It was not a White conspiracy. Thirty per cent of the Kronstadt Bolsheviks took up arms. Forty per cent more supported them. Together with other revolutionary elements, the rebellion fought against the party dictatorship, for free elections to the Soviets, for freedom of press and assembly, for democratic rule of all the toilers.

It was a spontaneous renascence of the revolution of 1917. At the same time a wave of peasant revolts swept the country. While Lenin dispatched Trotsky to crush Kronstadt with an iron hand, he hastily and resolutely shifted his entire course.

Lenin proclaimed the NEP—the New Economic Policy. Bolshevism beat a retreat on the economic front, but it could not relax its grip on political power. The party congress which formally adopted the NEP, also approved a policy of the resuscitation of democracy within the party. But it was too late. This policy remained inoperative. The process of the hardening of the arteries in the body of the dictatorship had gone too far. Moreover, political power has a tendency to increase in proportion to economic decentralization—under an absolute government. The monster had been loosed. It was a question as to who would ride it. Stalin had his dreams.

IV

Lenin had his forebodings. He had his definite fears as to the direction which the monster would take. He had his deep suspicions as to Stalin's designs upon it. "This cook will serve peppery dishes," he said of Stalin.

Six weeks before Lenin was paralyzed, at the congress which elected Stalin to the post of secretary-general, Lenin declared:

"The machine isn't going where we guide it, but where some illegal, or lawless, or God-knows-whence-derived speculators or private-capitalistic business-men, either the one or the other, are guiding it. A machine doesn't always travel just exactly the way, and it often travels just exactly not the way, that the man who sits at the wheel imagines."

Several days before the first stroke, Lenin wrote to Stalin:

"It is beyond doubt that we are living in a sea of lawlessness, and that the local influence is one of the greatest, if not the greatest, enemy of the establishment of lawful and civilized conditions. There is hardly a person who does not know that the cleansing of the party has revealed, as a predominating fact in the majority of the local commissions, the settling of personal and local accounts under the disguise of purifying the membership of the organization."

Lenin's message had no effect. Stalin was too engrossed in the absorbing labor of gathering all the threads of power into his hands. He devoted himself to the building up of the organizational bureau, the nerve-center of the national political machine. He distributed patronage, he penetrated through thousands of office-holders of his selection into every department, he made the dictatorship into a living reality in the form of a closely knit hierarchy of functionaries. In a word, Stalin was the "boss" and it was he who pulled all the inside strings of authority.

But Stalin's prestige was insignificant as compared with that of Trotsky. While Lenin was convalescing, the popularity of Trotsky was rising. Zinoviev, Stalin, and Kamenev lived in the shadow of Trotsky's light. The three were bound by a community of interests. They were all machine politicians. They were all veteran Bolsheviks who had expected to inherit Lenin's mantle. They were all envious of Trotsky. Zinoviev was by far the most ambitious and unscrupulous of the three. Kamenev was the most gullible. Stalin was satisfied to say little and to think deep.

In the supreme Political Bureau, the partnership of these three began to loom as a triumvirate. Of the remaining four members, only Trotsky stood out. But he towered so high above his opponents that they were driven to more intimate union because of him. The conspirators had not yet reached a secret agreement, but the understanding was already complete among them.

While Lenin was in a state of isolation, a battle took place in far-away Georgia, the homeland of Stalin, where two factions were struggling for control. It was an episode of the revolution, but it turned into a test of power between Lenin and Stalin. One of the factions was headed by Mdivani, an old Bolshevik, who interpreted the Soviet Constitution too literally and stood for a large measure of independence for Soviet Georgia. The other faction was led by Ordjonikidze, a henchman of Stalin's. It ended in a physical attack. The man who had formerly been a cellmate of his present boss, and who had been beaten up in the Baku prison by comrades for his roughness, now attempted to carry out Stalin's policy with his fists.

Mdivani had the support of Lenin. But Lenin was shut off from outside contacts. Although he was recovering rapidly, Stalin kept the facts of the situation in Georgia away from him. Stalin displayed a high-handed attitude. He won over to his policy Djerjinsky, the head of the Cheka, and these two sons of oppressed races—for Djerjinsky was a Pole—proceeded to act like Great Russian imperialists! Lenin had always suspected that tendency among his non-Russian disciples. And there was nothing that would enrage him to a higher pitch.

Without conferring with his associates on the Political Bureau, Stalin took the initiative and responsibility, simply in his administrative capacity, for staging a coup d'état in Georgia, sweeping out the people in power and substituting his own faction at the head of the Transcaucasian government. Mdivani betook himself to Moscow. He was bent upon getting redress. Lenin was rapidly regaining his faculties. Mdivani laid all the facts before the chief. Stalin was compromised. But he did not surrender. Lenin made a great issue of the Georgian affair. To him it was a question of national policy. Incidentally, at this writing, Mdivani is in a Soviet prison.

Lenin called for Stalin at the end of September, 1922, to discuss the matter with him. He then addressed a letter to the members of the Political Bureau in which he wrote: "In my opinion the question is supremely important. Stalin has a slight tendency toward hurry. . . . Stalin has already agreed to one concession. . . . Stalin agreed to postpone introducing the resolution in the Political Bureau until my arrival. . . . Here is my preliminary project. On the basis of a conversation with Mdivani and other comrades, I will fight for it and change it."

Stalin replied to Lenin the same day, attaching his comments on the project. After rejecting the proposal for the organization of the federal government into a "lower house" and an "upper house" as one which "will give us nothing but conflict and debate," Stalin added:

"In my opinion, Comrade Lenin himself 'hurried' a little. . . . There is hardly a doubt that this 'hurriedness' will 'supply fuel to the advocates of independence,' to the detriment of the national liberalism of Lenin."

The coarseness of Stalin's tone in his dealings with the sick Lenin is typical of the man. His accusation of national liberalism leveled at Lenin is amusing. But not so amusing was Stalin's continued insubordination and sabotage of Lenin's policy. Lenin was forced to carry the fight against the political machine into the open. But first he made an attempt to break Stalin's power with the aid of Trotsky.

Lenin summoned Trotsky to his room. The conversation turned on ways and means of combating the paralyzing growth of bureaucracy in the Soviet system. Trotsky clearly saw the mainspring of the disease, and pointed out to Lenin that it was the party political machine with its cliques and spoils in the shape of office that was at the core of the trouble. Both Lenin and Trotsky were thinking of Stalin.

"I propose a struggle with Soviet bureaucratism, and you want to add to that the bureaucratism of the organizational bureau of the party?" Lenin said.

"I suppose that's it," Trotsky replied with a laugh.

"Well, all right, I propose a bloc," declared Lenin.

"I am always ready to form a bloc with a good man," answered Trotsky.

This potential alliance of Lenin and Trotsky against Stalin at the end of 1922, shows that Lenin did not underestimate Stalin's ability. But Stalin got wind of the plan, perhaps largely by intuition. If a healthy Lenin in union with Trotsky could have easily smashed Stalin's power, Stalin would prove himself capable of overcoming Trotsky supported by a sick Lenin.

V

Lenin's health began to give way again. As his condition grew worse, the insolence of Stalin increased. The entente between Lenin and Trotsky on a number of political questions threatened the positions of Zinoviev, Kamenev, and Stalin. The triumvirate was being framed while the father of the revolution was suffering one relapse after another.

Here was a truly oriental setting. The world knew nothing, the country knew nothing, and the proletariat knew nothing, of what was transpiring behind the thick and high walls erected by Ivan the Terrible around his apartments. An emaciated little man, whose will-power had turned a world upside down, was lying in a bed under the care of the foremost German specialists. Every now and then that mysterious and inexhaustible fountain of energy with which nature had endowed him, would break out in a blast. Then the soft-treading figures in the background would scurry to cover. When his voice died down, they would emerge again and reach for the bounty that was his. The great flame of the revolution was flickering in the silent chamber. The dying man with the burning eyes read the handwriting on the wall. But he could do little more than that.

Sometimes he would turn to Trotsky for help. But he knew that Trotsky was not fit for the rôle of political manipulator. Trotsky could make revolutions, but not coups d'état. Trotsky could lead the masses, but not cope with palace conspiracies. Trotsky did not even understand Lenin's utter loneliness. He did not see how studiously and methodically the master had been isolated from all the sources of information, kept in the dark and often misled as to what was going on. It was too late to educate Trotsky in practical politics.

The conspirators grew bolder. They now reached the point of suppressing the writings of the man in whose name the cult of Leninism would be established under their nimble hands. Lenin wrote an article on the national question, a direct attack on Stalin's policies. "This question worried him extremely," wrote his secretary, "and he was preparing to speak on it at the party conference." He had taken care to send a copy to Trotsky. The latter, unsuspecting, asked if he could show it to Kamenev.

"Under no circumstances," replied the secretary.

"Why?" asked Trotsky.

"Vladimir Ilyitch [Lenin] says: 'Kamenev will immediately show everything to Stalin, and Stalin will make a rotten compromise and then deceive us.'"

Trotsky was taken aback. Was it possible that Lenin did not trust Stalin to carry out an honest compromise?

"Yes," replied Lenin's political secretary, "he does not trust Stalin, and wants to come out against him openly, before the entire party. He is preparing a bomb."

With a herculean effort, Lenin gathered all his remaining strength. For a few weeks, early in 1923, he displayed fabulous vigor and clarity of vision. His bomb was loaded with dynamite. What happened to it when it was detonated was another story.

In the meantime, he launched one blow after another at Stalin. He denounced "the hastiness and administrative impulsiveness of Stalin" as fatal, and "his spite" as equally damaging, adding: "Spitefulness in general plays the worst possible rôle in politics." The following day he wrote Trotsky that "it is of course necessary to hold Stalin and Djerjinsky responsible for all this Great Russian jingoistic campaign." In a strictly secret and personal note, he requested Trotsky to represent him against Stalin and company in the Georgian affair.

At the same time Lenin decided to strike at the vitals of Stalin's edifice. He attacked him at the most vulnerable point, the Rabkrin—the seat of the bureaucratic cancer. He wrote an article in which he unequivocally declared that the Rabkrin "does not enjoy at the present time a shadow of authority. Everybody knows that a worse organized institution than this one does not exist, and that under the present conditions you can expect nothing whatever of this institution."

Lenin watched for the article to appear in the Pravda. It did not appear. Daily he grew more indignant and excited. His wife telephoned Trotsky and asked him to intervene on Lenin's behalf. Lenin's condition was grave. Trotsky immediately called a meeting of the Political Bureau. All the members insisted that Lenin's plan of reorganizing the department was wrong. They also opposed the publication of the article. One of the Stalin lieutenants, Kuibishev, proposed that a special number of the Pravda be set up and printed with Lenin's article, so as to appease the sick man, but to conceal the piece from the party and the country.

Trotsky finally carried the field. It was too dangerous a weapon for the conspirators to leave in his hands. The article was published. It became in time one of the gospels of Stalin's Leninism. And Kuibishev was later appointed head of the reorganized Rabkrin!

VI

Lenin was now on the eve of his second stroke, from which he would never fully recover. Before the collapse, he waged his battle with uncommon vigor. In a note to Mdivani, he wrote: "I am working in your behalf with all my heart. I am outraged at the rudeness of Ordjonikidze and the connivance of

Stalin and Djerjinsky. I am preparing for you notes and a speech."

The notes and the speech and the article on the national question were all the ingredients of the bomb Lenin had been preparing to launch at Stalin at the forthcoming Twelfth Congress of the party. Fearful of another attack, he forwarded all the material to Trotsky, together with a copy of the note to Mdivani. Another copy went to Kamenev. It struck the three conspirators like a bolt from the blue.

Stalin in the meanwhile had endeavored to encircle Lenin completely and remove him from all unfriendly sources of information and influences. But Lenin's wife, Krupskaya, was in the way. A clash developed between her and Stalin. After all, to whom did Lenin belong, to his wife or to the party? For Stalin there could be but one answer. Moreover, the party meant the Central Committee, of which Stalin was secretary-general, and not Trotsky the arrogant novitiate.

Stalin had treated Krupskaya in his customary roughshod manner. Lenin became extremely agitated. He called for his stenographer and dictated a letter to Stalin in which he broke off all personal relations with his lifelong aide.

Krupskaya called Kamenev. She was in a state of high excitement. She told him of Lenin's latest move. It was an unprecedented act, indeed. She added:

"But you know Vladimir. He would never have decided to break off comradely relations if he had not thought it necessary to crush Stalin politically."

This was the last letter ever written by Lenin. The prophet had excommunicated his high priest.

Events crowded swiftly that night. Trotsky sent for Kamenev. At last the lion was ready to leap upon the cowering conspirators.

If Trotsky had then been in possession of a mysterious sealed envelope left by Lenin and marked, "To be opened and read at the party congress after my death," Stalin's destiny and that of the revolution might have been decisively changed.

The frightened Kamenev answered the summons. Trotsky snorted fire. But instead of declaring war he confined himself to a drastic ultimatum. He did not seek to remove Stalin and his flunkeys. He demanded a reversal of Stalin's policy on the national question in general and in Georgia in particular; a cessation of the arbitrary persecution by Stalin's party machine; the stoppage of all intrigue and restoration of honest collaboration in the high circles; and an immediate apology to Krupskaya on the part of Stalin and a change in his future conduct.

How characteristic of Trotsky was this straightforward challenge and magnanimity before going into battle. He had spent his life studying social theories and forces. He had had his opportunities in France and the United States to study the workings of a political machine, but he had never availed himself of them. Marx had not provided for party division within the proletariat. Trotsky had never learned the American saying: "All is fair in love and politics." The ultimatum as a weapon was never devised for use in practical politics.

Kamenev at once proceeded to see Stalin, who

was in the country. Stalin beat a quick retreat. He bowed to Trotsky's demands. In a few minutes, his letter of apology was on the way to Lenin's home, Krupskaya read it with relief, but it came too late to provide comfort and strength for Lenin.

The second stroke had come. Lenin's last act was irrevocable. He had disowned Stalin.

VII

Dawn was breaking upon snow-blanketed Moscow. But the suns of all the universes could not penetrate the man-made secrecy of the Kremlin. Born of deep darkness, the Bolshevist comet was now back at its conspirative source. Around Lenin's bed of agony stalked the ghosts of the fear that he had cultivated, the plotting that he had cradled, the amorality he had professed and preached—all in the name of an impersonal, objective social ideal and system which mocked at human nature.

But human nature now leered at the helpless Lenin in the persons of Stalin, Trotsky, Kamenev, Zinoviev, who went about fighting for the masses in the depths of conspiracy, who shrouded the revolution in silence, who were afraid to take even the "chosen class" — the proletariat — into their confidence, who shut off all but a mere handful of the party leadership from the scene of action.

The catacombs of the revolution had been lifted from the bottom and installed at the top. But the occupants of the august secret chamber were themselves unaware of the existence of that mysterious envelope in which the innermost of all secrets had been sealed under Lenin's direction.

It was Lenin's political testament, the most extraordinary of all documents ever penned by a communist or Marxist. He had written it two months before his breakdown, to insure the stability of the dictatorship.

"I have in mind stability as a guarantee against a split in the near future," wrote Lenin on December 25, 1922. "And I intend to examine here a series of considerations of a purely personal character.

"I think that the fundamental factor in the matter of stability—from this point of view—is such members of the Central Committee as Stalin and Trotsky. The relation between them constitutes, in my opinion, a big half of the danger of that split, which might be avoided, and the avoidance of which might be promoted, in my opinion, by raising the number of members of the Central Committee to fifty or one hundred.

"Comrade Stalin, having become secretary-general, has concentrated an enormous power in his hands; and I am not sure that he always knows how to use that power with sufficient caution. On the other hand, Comrade Trotsky, as was proved by his struggle against the Central Committee in connection with the question of the people's commissariat of ways of communication, is distinguished not only by his exceptional abilities—personally, he is, to be sure, the most able man in the present Central Committee—but also by his too far-reaching self-confidence and a disposition to be too much attracted by the purely administrative side of affairs.

"These two qualities of the two most able leaders of the present Central Committee might, quite innocently, lead to a split; if our party does not take measures to prevent it, a split might arise unexpectedly."

Lenin then proceeded to characterize several other high members of the party. Ten days later, on January 4, 1923, he added a postscript to his testament, as follows:

"Stalin is too rude, and this fault, entirely supportable in relations among us communists, becomes insupportable in the office of secretary-general. Therefore, I propose to the comrades to find a way to remove Stalin from that position and appoint to it another man who in all respects differs from Stalin only in superiority—namely, more patient, more loyal, more polite, and more attentive to comrades, less capricious, etc.

"This circumstance may seem an insignificant trifle, but I think that from the point of view of preventing a split and from the point of view of the relation between Stalin and Trotsky which I discussed above, it is not a trifle, or it is such a trifle as may acquire a decisive significance."

Lenin could foresee his death and seek to provide for such a contingency, but he could not foresee that he would linger on for a year in a completely paralyzed and idiotized state, his petrified hand resting on the helm of the ship he had launched.

CHAPTER TEN

THE SQUABBLE FOR THE SCEPTER

I

IF Lenin had completely recovered, the feud between Trotsky and Stalin would have gone down into Soviet history as another episode. Trotsky once more emerged victorious. Stalin was forced to retreat another time. As to the intrigue and conspiracy, they were not radically different from the methods pursued during the first struggle between the two men at the front.

The personal elements in the latest conflict were, it is true, more bitter than ever before. They overshadowed the issues. But the issues were there nevertheless. Stalin resorted to foul means, but his convictions were genuine. He honestly although violently disagreed with Lenin on the national question as well as on that of the control of the bureaucracy. And there is a great deal to be said for Stalin's viewpoint, given the premises of a dictatorship. Stalin regarded Lenin's insistence upon "independence" for the minor races as a fiction—a logical and legitimate conclusion. Stalin considered Lenin's aim to have the people control the government machinery under a non-democratic system as an aberration, a contradiction—again a natural and pragmatical attitude.

Stalin the politician was nearer to the realities than either Lenin or Trotsky. The revolution had moved away from its creators. The machine was going God knows where. The Bolshevist Party was no longer the party of pre-revolutionary days. It gravitated into channels alien to Lenin and Trotsky. With power, came stupefaction of intellectual life. With fulfilment, came an end to searchings. It was replaced by a smugness, a longing for domesticity, for enjoyment, which carried the seeds of deterioration of the old idealism. In a word, Bolshevism was completing the cycle of all human fruition.

Stalin realized that Lenin and Trotsky sought the impossible. They were trying to recapture the dreams of yesteryear. The tide ran with Stalin, and Stalin preferred to run with the tide. The New Economic Policy had shattered many a theory and formed many a crack in the rock of Bolshevism. Private commerce was reestablished. The middle peasant was declared an ally of the proletariat. And even the *kulak* was pronounced by certain Bolshevik leaders to be the legitimate rebuilder of the country's economy. Foreign capital was courted. Concessions were invited. One capitalist state after another extended recognition to the Soviet government. Everything seemed to support Stalin's favorite theory of socialism in one country. So long as the Soviet state retained the political dictatorship and the nationalized basic resources of the land, Stalin was satisfied.

Trotsky could never be satisfied. Trotsky, like Lenin, had a demoniacal and unquenchable thirst for revolution. The joy of living for Trotsky is to stem an avalanche single-handed. From 1923 to 1928, this man alone deflected the natural tide of the revolution and drove Stalin's vessel from the right to the left and from the left to the right, arresting a flow which in the end, as he later realized, nothing could stop. Whenever the ship deviated from its internationalist course, Trotsky's arm shoved it back. Stalin was at the rudder, but he turned in accordance with the Trotsky menace.

In the light of this gigantic process, and only in that light, can the five-year combat between Trotsky and Stalin be understood. It ended by Trotsky's landing on an island in Turkey, but it was for Stalin a trial which few men could have withstood and which involuntarily raised him from the rank of a politician to that of a statesman.

II

If Lenin had died immediately from the second stroke, Trotsky would have succeeded him in power. Lenin's testament was a sharp spear that would have felled Stalin at the time when his other conflicts with Lenin were still fresh and when his machine was not yet consolidated and that of Trotsky was unimpaired. But Lenin's last will could not be revealed until after his actual death. During the eleven months of his virtual death, Stalin had ample time to prepare for the emergency.

No sooner had Lenin relapsed into a coma than Stalin and Kamenev and Zinoviev proceeded to break the pledges of the understanding with Trotsky arrived at as a result of his ultimatum. Kamenev left for Georgia to carry out the reversal of policy there as desired by Lenin and demanded by Trotsky. On the way he received a telegram from Stalin informing him of Lenin's collapse. The agreement was immediately forgotten, and Stalin's policy put into effect in spite of the "bomb" which Lenin had manufactured for the coming congress.

Yet Stalin at this congress displayed a disposition to cooperate with Trotsky. When the question of the selection of the keynote speaker came up before the Political Bureau, Stalin suggested that Trotsky was the logical man for the occasion. Neither Stalin nor Trotsky insisted on the additional honor. But Zinoviev did and intrigued for it. He was given the privilege, but Trotsky undertook to deliver the report on industrialization.

The Twelfth Congress met in April, 1923, six weeks after Lenin's debacle. With the help of the Petrograd and Moscow delegates, controlled by Zinoviev and Kamenev, Stalin was able to consolidate his national machine. The decisions adopted were compromises with Trotsky, but their execution was a different matter. It was not a question of intrinsic accord between Stalin and his two allies. Rather was it the envy and fear of Trotsky that made Kamenev and Zinoviev rush to Stalin's support and to help him distort the enactment of the policies approved.

Before his collapse Lenin had suggested to Trotsky the reorganization of the party court, the Control Commission, into an organ for combating the bureaucracy. Lenin and Trotsky were to be identified with it, and achieve the objects that the Rabkrin under Stalin had failed to accomplish. Trotsky now raised the problem of freeing the state apparatus from the control of the party machine. This was a chimera under a monopolistic government. It was, of course, intended as a means of wresting power from Stalin. The congress resolved to create such a party tribunal, and fuse it with the Rabkrin, but without Trotsky in it. The sword that Lenin had forged turned against him and Trotsky. At the head of the new body was put Kuibishev, one of Stalin's trusted men.

Thus came into being the Central Control Commission, the Bolshevist "senate," or more correctly, the Inquisition, which has been functioning ever since alongside of the Central Committee, the Bolshevist "parliament" or consistory. Both remained under the firm hand of the secretary-general, Stalin.

As to Lenin's "bomb" on the national question. Stalin and his allies were able quietly to extinguish the fuse and avert an explosion. This was Stalin's strong point. He delivered a trenchant report in which he made it clear that Lenin had not been fully acquainted with the character of the opposition in Georgia. But all the material which Lenin had prepared in rebuttal was shelved in committee, and was not read before the entire assembly. Once more Stalin triumphed. And because of his conciliatory attitude, Trotsky voted for his resolution.

Three years later, when torrents of water had run under the bridge, Stalin "forgot" the facts of his bitter conflict with Lenin and accused Trotsky of "gossip." Having suppressed the documents in the case, he blandly faced the executive of the Communist International and indulged in the following reminiscences:

"I never had any differences on the national

question with the party or with Lenin. Trotsky probably referred to an insignificant incident when Lenin, before the Twelfth Congress, reproached me with having conducted an overly severe organizational policy with regard to the Georgian half-nationalists, half-communists of the type of Comrade Mdivani, who was recently our commercial envoy in France, saying that I had 'persecuted' them. However, subsequent facts proved that the so-called deviators of the type of Mdivani had really deserved more rigorous treatment than I had applied in my capacity as one of the secretaries of the Central Committee. . . .

"Lenin did not know and could not know these facts, as he was sick; he was in bed, and he had no opportunity to follow developments. But what bearing could this insignificant incident have on the principled position taken by Stalin? Trotsky, apparently in a gossipy way, has hinted of certain 'differences' between me and the party. But is it not a fact that the entire Central Committee, including Trotsky, unanimously voted for the theses of Stalin on the national question?"

The congress adjourned, after reelecting Stalin as secretary-general. Trotsky had made no effort to have him ousted. Absorbed in the economic problems, desirous of devoting himself to the task of leading the peasant country into an industrialized lane, as the only way to socialism, Trotsky treated the political aspects with little consideration.

Lenin's testament remained buried and unknown. Trotsky underestimated the Stalin opposition and was persuaded to follow a course of harmony. When he awoke to the manner in which the political machine was conducting itself, it was too late. Stalin had secured an opportunity to entrench himself in a position from which nothing could dislodge him.

III

Stalin was strong with the machine, Trotsky was strong with the masses. Stalin had with him a band of hardened and rough politicians. Trotsky was followed by a group of brilliant intellectuals. Stalin staked everything on the status quo. Trotsky sought to upset the apple-cart.

Trotsky wanted the helm of power. He wanted it to end the planless drifting of the revolution, to steer a course upon intensive industrialization, to break the political misrule and return to workers' democracy. But what he really wanted was to replace Stalin at the wheel.

Stalin sought peace with Trotsky, and was willing to let him have any post in the service of the state so long as the party control remained unchanged. As great as the dissatisfaction was with the Stalin methods in the upper circles, there was an even greater fear of letting Trotsky become the industrial and political "dictator" of the country.

In spite of the befogging issues, a group of Bolsheviks attempted to make peace not on these grounds, but on purely personal bases. Trotsky had retired during the summer of 1923 to Kislovodsk, the mineral resort in the Caucasus. Here a scheme was devised which had nothing to do with the great questions of policy but with a modus of satisfying the respective ambitions of the leading characters in the squabble for the scepter.

The Political Bureau was to be deprived of its former power and the secretariat-general of the party made the chief instrument of the dictatorship. It was proposed, mainly by friends of Trotsky, that a triumvirate be created consisting of Trotsky, Stalin, and Zinoviev. This was, of course, a conspiracy against the professed traditions of the party.

Stalin would have nothing to do with the "intrigue" of those who had entered the "Cave of Adullam at Kislovodsk."

"In the year 1923," he declared two years later, "after the Twelfth Party Congress, those who have now entered the 'cave,' elaborated a platform in accordance with which the Political Bureau was to be abolished and the secretariat was to become the leading political and organizational body. It was to consist of Zinoviev, Trotsky, and Stalin. What was the meaning of this platform? It meant that the party was to be led without Rykov, without Kalinin, without Tomsky, without Molotov, without Bukharin. The platform came to nothing, not only because it did not represent any principles, but also because the party cannot be led without the aid of the comrades I have just named. When a written question was addressed to me from the depths of Kislovodsk, I refused to have anything to do with the scheme, and said that, if the comrades should wish it, I was ready to give up my own position—quite quietly, without either open or hidden discussion, and without formulating demands for the protection of the 'rights of minorities.' "

This offer of resignation on the part of Stalin may or may not have been sincere. But Trotsky has never chosen to reply or refer to the incident. On the other hand, Stalin's statement that the party cannot be led without Rykov, Tomsky, Bukharin, does not stand up well in view of their eventual fate.

Conditions in the country favored Trotsky at the time. An economic crisis developed, accompanied by strikes, unemployment, and widespread distress in the cities. The agricultural recovery had been far greater than that of the Soviet industries. The communist economic engine was being towed by the peasant cart, and the bumps were violent. Dissatisfaction in the party took the form of several clandestine groups opposing the official machine. Trotsky's popularity was augmented by the circulation of the suppressed facts as to the differences between Stalin and Lenin. Trotsky's industrialization program was a striking and bold document, and his attack on the chaotic drifting, on the absence of a unified plan, won him wider support than ever. The stupor inhibited by military communism was evaporating under the NEP, and within the Bolshevist Party, which incidentally was losing members, there grew a potent current of opinion that was irrepressible. The masses looked to Trotsky to lead them out of the morass and into the promised land of socialist reconstruction.

Stalin was politician enough to sense the surcharged atmosphere and not force issues. Trotsky was not enough of a politician to take advantage of his opportunity and to force the issue on personal grounds.

IV

Trotsky took the offensive. Stalin took the defensive. Trotsky's attack was directed along one front. Stalin's defense was being organized at another front. Trotsky came out for workers' democracy. This meant, in view of his popularity, that he would be elevated to the highest position by the will of the masses. Stalin knew this meaning of the battle-cry of democracy. He quickly applied himself to the strengthening of his inner line, the political machine. He extended his patronage wider than ever, and selected and appointed his henchmen at every strategic position in the fortress of the dictatorship.

Early in October, Trotsky addressed a letter to the Central Committee in which he assaulted the use of the Cheka, now renamed G. P. U., in suppressing party differences. Stalin had together with Djerjinsky enunciated the new policy of espionage within the party, making it obligatory for members to become informers and deliver to the authorities any of their friends who formed groups in opposition to the official policies. Trotsky then dwelt on the "extraordinary deterioration of the situation within the party" during the preceding six months.

"In the fiercest moments of military communism," he declared, "the system of appointment within the party did not have one-tenth of the extent that it has now. Appointment of the secretaries of provincial committees is now the rule. That creates for the secretary a position essentially independent of the local organization. . . . The bureaucratization of the party machine has developed to unheard-of proportion by means of the method of secretarial selection. . . . There has been created a very broad stratum of party workers, entering into the administrative apparatus of the party, who completely renounce their own party opinion, at least the open expression of it, as if assuming that the secretarial hierarchy is the apparatus which creates party opinion and party decisions. Beneath this stratum, abstaining from opinion, there lies the broad mass of the party, before whom every decision stands in the form of a summons or a command."

The reply of the Political Bureau, led by Stalin, Kamenev, and Zinoviev, was that Trotsky could have had, as a member of the government, and in the capacity of vice-premier which Lenin had offered him, every opportunity "if he wished to, to demonstrate in action that the party might trust him with those practically unlimited powers in the sphere of industry and military affairs toward which he strives. But Trotsky preferred another method of action. . . . He never attended a meeting of the council of people's commissars, either under Lenin or after his withdrawal. He never attended a meeting of the council of labor and defense, either before or after its reorganization. . . .

"Trotsky categorically declined the position of substitute for Lenin. That evidently he considers beneath his dignity. He conducts himself according to the formula: 'All or nothing.' "

Of course, the position of premier which Lenin held was now nominal. Trotsky did not want nominal honors. The power that Lenin had exercised was of

Lenin. Trotsky would not be permitted to inherit that. Yet Stalin and his associates had to beat a retreat and get their revenge in other directions. Several days after Trotsky's broadside, a group of forty-six veteran and popular Bolsheviks addressed themselves to the Central Committee with a message in which an insistent and powerful demand was made for the introduction of democracy in the party and a change in the methods of the political machine.

A compromise was arrived at. After many heated sessions, the Political Bureau and Trotsky worked out a resolution which was signed unanimously and which was to become known as the manifesto announcing the New Course. A decisive change was to be inaugurated, so as to permit the popular will of the organized proletariat to assert itself. It looked for a while as if the conflict had been liquidated.

But Stalin and Kamenev and Zinoviev had no illusions as to the effect of genuine democracy upon their ultimate fates. The system of appointing secretaries—local political bosses—from the center was continued. On the other hand, the ranks of the three anti-Trotsky leaders closed tighter than ever. Trotsky was a member of the Political Bureau, but in fact another Political Bureau functioned in secrecy without Trotsky's knowledge. His place there had been taken by Kuibishev. Bound by conspirative vows, this august body descended to secret codes, to creating anti-Trotsky groups within the provincial centers. While officially factions and groupings were banned, this applied only to Trotsky followers. The dictatorial clique made use of this method in weeding out officials and leaders who were suspected of leanings toward Trotsky. Instead of carrying out the New Course, the old course was driven deeper underground, and the entire machine, in so far as possible, was being made "orthodox" from the standpoint of the ruling triumvirate.

Fear was the dominant feature of this amazing campaign. It was amazing because here was a great party, controlling a great country, priding itself upon its iron discipline and cohesion, terror-stricken by the apparition of one man. Whether the fear was justified or not, whether it was selfish or selfless, the digging under Trotsky assumed ratlike characteristics. His name upon the traditional lists of honorary chairmanships at official functions was shifted from the head to the bottom. Sometimes it would be omitted altogether. Since all elections had been manipulated for years, and all such lists prepared in advance in the Central Committee, and then sent to the various assemblies where they would be "voted," it was a system of juggling and "education" which was obvious to everybody, but which no one had any courage to question or challenge.

"We have no democracy because we are afraid of you," Bukharin confessed later to Trotsky.

While Trotsky was advancing along the front of democracy, Stalin struck at his hearth—the war department. Trotsky's right-hand man was removed. One of the heads of the Cheka, Unschlicht, was transferred to the general headquarters of the Red Army to "cleanse" that institution. The pretext was Trotsky's neglect of the office. The purpose was to weed out anti-Stalinists and replace them by obedient tools of the machine.

V

The massive gates of the Kremlin were thrown open. An auto-sled sped out and fairly flew across the snow-bedded city to the country. In it were Stalin, Zinoviev, Kamenev, Kalinin, Bukharin, and Tomsky.

It was a few minutes past six in the evening of January 21. The private wire in the Kremlin had just carried the message:

"Lenin is dying."

Out in the open, where the birch trees were more silvery than ever and the air more rigid than even the dictatorship could make it, in a villa at Gorky, after an hour of last agony, crowning three years of fierce resistance to paralysis, Lenin had at last dropped the scepter and closed his eyes upon the progressive paralysis which was overtaking his only child—the party.

Rykov was lying ill in bed. Trotsky had suffered an attack and had been ordered to the Caucasus by the physicians. The six old conspirators were flying to make a conspiracy with death.

Moscow knew nothing of Lenin's end. All night a handful of trustees were in conference over the body. It must be said that their eyes were red and their faces heavy. The only one who did not weep was Stalin. The party that Lenin had raised was kept in ignorance of the news. The newspaper presses continued to print the dialectical articles and the stereotyped denunciations of the bourgeoisie. In the morning, the papers did not have a word of Lenin's death. People were arrested in the streets for spreading the rumor. The censorship was clamped down tight. The "old guard" had to have its breathing spell. Fourteen hours after Lenin's death, the obliging censor telephoned the information to all the newspaper correspondents. They would not be permitted to send it out for another four hours.

Lenin's death came somewhat as a surprise. For several months the patient had been showing signs of improvement. He had learned to walk. He had learned to utter sounds and speak a few words. There was hope of eventual recovery. This condition had its effect upon the struggle within the party. It acted as a deterrent to Stalin and Zinoviev. Their hands were now untied. Fortune helped them by keeping Trotsky away.

At the railroad station in Tiflis, on the way to the Black Sea resort of Sukhum, Trotsky received a wire from Stalin announcing Lenin's death. In spite of his high temperature, Trotsky went to talk to the Kremlin on the direct wire. He wanted to know whether he could get back in time for the funeral. He was informed by Stalin that it would be held on Saturday, which did not permit him enough time to reach Moscow.

The funeral was held on Sunday. Trotsky could easily have got there to attend it. But Stalin did not want him there.

By the time Lenin died, the peace between Trotsky and his enemies had been shattered. The New Course was announced early in December; the floodgates of discussion had been opened wide. The party and the press were filled with exchanges of opinions. All that had been dammed in for over four years had now come to the surface. Lively meetings were taking place all over the country, and the views of the various groups were being aired without restraint.

Trotsky was unable in person to avail himself of the numerous invitations to address the meetings. He stated his point of view in an article on the New Course which was read in his name at a gathering in his district and which was published in the Pravda with Stalin's knowledge and approval. If Trotsky had not written that essay on democracy under proletarian dictatorship, he would have fared much better. It provided a number of loopholes for his enemies. Zinoviev and then Stalin interpreted certain passages in it as a masked attack against their leadership. It would appear that at first there was no unanimity among the members of the triumvirate. Before its publication, the article had rested in the hands of the secretary-general for four days. There was ample opportunity to ask Trotsky for a correction of certain parts. When Trotsky asked Stalin as to the reason for the delay in its publication, Stalin laughingly assured him that it would appear soon.

It took several weeks before the Trotsky article was turned into a battering-ram against its author. It was denounced by the machine politicians and writers from a thousand angles. The brunt of the attack was against Trotsky's alleged incitement of the youth as opposed to the deteriorating old guard. Zinoviev took the lead in the campaign. "It was a rupture of the achieved agreement," he thundered. "Comrade Trotsky has gone to war on the Central Committee, notwithstanding the fact that every concession that he demanded has been made to him in order to achieve unanimity."

Stalin followed suit. And then Kamenev joined in. These experts in the art of politics, these sons of a perverse culture which had taught them in their youth to read between the lines and to write for those who can read only in such a manner, these cabalists of Marxism to whom footnotes meant more than text, to whom construction was the soul of theory, now were at their finest.

Lenin died in the midst of the din of sharpened quills and dialectical wits. His death did not end the strange crucifixion by means of the spoken and printed word. It provided a splendid new opportunity. On that night Trotsky died too. Trotskyism was born.

It was inhumanly hard to eliminate Trotsky. But it would be far simpler to attack Trotskyism. For Lenin was dead. That would enable the guardians of his heritage to set up Leninism. What one could not do with the aid of a sick Lenin, one could accomplish with the help of a dead one.

The whole attack could be summed up in Stalin's words that Trotsky did not "have in mind the interests of the party, but had designs for undermining the authority of the majority of the Central Committee, the guiding nucleus of the Bolshevik old guard."

VI

Down with Trotskyism! Long live Leninism! Today Leninism is such an accepted concept that it seems strange to read Bolshevist historians and philosophers who shortly after Lenin's death hesitated to employ the word and most of all to define it. There had been communism, socialism, Marxism. But Leninism, what was that if Bolshevism was strict Marxism?

Stalin was never good at creating cults. He excelled in dynamics and not in messianic inspirations. He could use them once they hardened into ponderable forces. Zinoviev excelled in cult-making. He might have been a false Messiah in more remote times. It was he who conceived the fantastic idea of mummifying Lenin. It was perhaps indispensable to the launching of Leninism. There was a slight contradiction between scientific socialism and Pharaonic ritual. There was the further obstacle of overcoming the disgust and pain of Lenin's wife, sisters, and brother. But Leninism was needed to defeat Trotskyism, so that Stalin and Kamenev and Zinoviev would be secure in their seats of might.

Bolshevism had returned to its mother's womb. Darkest Eurasia was again enthroned where Tatar khans once feasted seated on the bodies of Russian princes. From now on the battle of intellect would be a losing one. Once more Russia could have her ikons. Instead of gilt images, red-draped pictures of Lenin would be installed in a million corners.

But there was one trifle still in the way—Lenin's testament. It expressly urged the removal of Stalin from his post. It made reference to Kamenev and Zinoviev, to their inglorious past in the revolution of 1917, when Lenin had characterized them as strikebreakers and deserters, and now pleaded for consideration for them. It was to be read before the plenary session of the next national congress of the party.

The Thirteenth Congress met in May, 1924, to the accompaniment of exciting rumors as to Lenin's mysterious last message. It was a hand-picked conclave. By this time, the great majority of the independent party leaders had been assigned to various scattered posts. Many of them were abroad in the Soviet diplomatic and commercial agencies. The delegates were properly coached. The majority had been welded in advance. In spite of Krupskaya's pathetic attempts and her demonstrative friendship with Trotsky, the steamroller was in no romantic mood. Stalin once more, or twice even, permitted himself a few rude gestures at the expense of Lenin's widow. The testament was not read before the whole body but in committee. Stalin nonchalantly offered to resign his post in conformity with the testament. But the machine had been properly oiled by Zinoviev, Kamenev, and Molotov. After all, was Lenin in full possession of his faculties at the time he had drawn up his will? The congress reelected Stalin as secretary-general. The testament was never published in Soviet Russia. Its existence was denied for years afterward. Its dissemination made one liable to severe punishment. Such was Leninism in practice.

Trotsky was reelected to the Central Committee and the Political Bureau. But no time was lost in completing the job of shearing his remaining power. Several thousand commissars and officers in the Red Army were dismissed or shifted to other fields. Prior to the Thirteenth Congress, a commission had been dispatched by Stalin to Sukhum to "coordinate" with Trotsky the contemplated reorganization of the commissariat of war. "This was sheer farce," writes Trotsky. "The renewal of the personnel in the war department had for some time been going on at full speed behind my back, and now it was simply a matter of observing the proprieties."

Although Trotsky valiantly fought the intimidation and intrigue used in "reorganizing" his own stronghold, there was some justification for the process. He had turned to other and more vital matters. The war had long since ended. The burning questions were now of finance, industry, the relation to the peasant, and international communism. Zinoviev as the head of the Communist International had missed an opportunity in the German communist uprising the previous year. There were tendencies on the part of Stalin's aides to arrive at a compromise with the Right, moderate elements in the West as well as in the East. At home, the same Right policies were followed in connection with the peasantry and the development of the industries along the lines of state capitalism. All this fitted in with Stalin's theory. It also provided Trotsky with fresh and powerful ammunition.

Lenin's death had been the signal for another outburst of terror and a tightening of the dictatorship. In spite of the general attack upon Trotsky from the top, it did not diminish but increased his popularity at the bottom. It is fairly certain that Trotsky could have seized power in the fall of 1924, the high-water mark of his prestige. There was an organized opposition to the governing triumvirate, which was influential and which drew its nourishment from the economic difficulties. The harvest that year was almost of famine paucity. But in order to take over the reins, a coup d'état was necessary. Trotsky refused to countenance such a plan. He even refused to sponsor the opposition officially. And yet he made himself liable to another thrust that well-nigh finished him.

VII

In November, 1924, upon the occasion of the seventh anniversary of the Soviet régime, Trotsky published a book on the events of 1917 with an introduction entitled "Lessons of October." Undoubtedly it was in part aimed at the unenviable rôle played by Kamenev and Zinoviev during the critical days of the conspiracy for the insurrection. It fell like a spark upon an exposed powder magazine. Ten thousand speakers, thousands of newspaper columns, and hundreds of books and pamphlets poured venom and slander upon the author. There perhaps has never been since the invention of the printing press a case where one article of several thousand words evoked such a deluge of comment, interpretation, rebuttal, criticism.

Trotsky's introduction and his book unquestionably showed a bias as to the history of the Bolshevist seizure of power. Moreover, it suffered from the fact that it was a vivid and imaginative piece of writing, displaying a flair which is Trotskyist, but which was perilous in the circumstances.

After the first edition of the book had been rapidly exhausted, several weeks elapsed before the next was permitted to appear. In the meantime, the

Niagara of slander became boundless. Thousands of meetings were held at which Trotsky's book was denounced by people who had never read it. "Unanimous" resolutions were passed by party organizations all over the land, under the tutelage of the official bosses, which arraigned Trotsky's infidelity and treachery to Bolshevism. All the time Trotsky and his followers were forced to remain silent. It was something resembling a national panic. The vituperation, the falsification became stereotyped in the mouths of the standpatters.

"A firm supporter of Trotsky," tells Eastman, who was in Russia at the time, "who attended one of these meetings was asked why he did not raise at least one voice against the resolution." He replied:

"In that fanaticized crowd, if I had not applauded the resolution, I should have been beaten up."

Leninism had indeed come to life with a vengeance. All the ethics of expediency, all the calumny that Lenin had for years showered upon the non-Bolshevist socialists of the world, all the skill he had employed in interpreting certain notes of Marx to justify a communist experiment in a backward peasant country, a party dictatorship under the disguise of a proletarian commonwealth, all that and more was the Leninism which now stalked across the front pages of the Pravda and choked the state printing presses of the Soviet union. (And there are no other presses.)

Trotskyism became a favorite sporting preserve. In it everybody hunted. They who had vainly sought for years to make careers now found it easy by the simple method of digging up an old pre-revolutionary Trotsky article or letter in which he had differed with Lenin. Trotsky's pictures disappeared from the offices. In private homes they had to be removed even by sympathizers in order to escape the arm of the G. P. U. His books were eliminated from display windows. Invitations extended to him to speak were mysteriously canceled. The director of the state firm which published his book was dismissed. His achievements in the Red Army were belittled. His past conflicts with Lenin were magnified beyond human credence. The Trotskyist heresy became the worst of all heresies, and, as customary in history, it was used as a shield by unscrupulous careerists to cover up all their own sins.

In the van of this concentrated publicity campaign were Zinoviev and Kamenev, who had been directly affected by Trotsky's account of the 1917 revolt. Stalin lent his aid, but could afford to remain more detached. He let loose his two Cerberi and watched their inquisitorial blood-hunt with a sardonic sneer. He even then knew that their day of reckoning was coming. He would know how to use the ammunition that Trotsky had emptied against his two associates better and more effectively when the moment for their slaughter was ripe. He did not intend to dampen this particular powder. It was too good.

"How did our differences begin?" asked Stalin two years later, when he was out to kill Kamenev and Zinoviev politically, and replied:

"They began with the question: 'What are we to

do with Comrade Trotsky?' That was toward the end of 1924. To begin with, the Leningrad group wanted to expel Comrade Trotsky from the party. The Leningrad provincial committee passed a resolution demanding the expulsion of Comrade Trotsky.

"We, that is to say, the majority of the Central Committee, were not in favor of such a step. After a struggle, we were able to persuade the Leningrad comrades to delete the sentence about expulsion from their resolution.

"A little later, when the Central Committee met in plenary session, the Leningrad members, supported by Comrade Kamenev, proposed the immediate exclusion of Comrade Trotsky from the Political Bureau. We could not accept this proposal of the opposition either.

"We were in the majority on the Central Committee, and were content to remove Comrade Trotsky from his position as people's commissar for war. We did not agree with Comrades Zinoviev and Kamenev, for we knew that the policy of lopping-off might entail grave dangers for the party. The method of lopping-off, the method of blood-letting (it was blood-getting they wanted) is dangerous and infectious. Today, you lop off one limb; tomorrow another; the day after tomorrow a third—and what is left of the party?"

Thus spoke Stalin on the eve of his emergence as the finest surgeon of his kind, the most meticulous and thoroughgoing but bloodless "lopper-off" to be found in the records of any great revolution.

In January, 1925, Trotsky "resigned" as commissar of war.

Far from reaching for the scepter, his arm was sent groping back in search of lost opportunities, scattered armies, terrorized and persecuted Trotskyists. It clutched in its fall the hand that had knifed it, only to precipitate the now inevitable ignominy.

Chapter Eleven

THE UNHOLY ALLIANCE

I

NO sooner had the Trotsky cloud lifted from the Stalin horizons than a new menace arose. Zinoviev had not demanded Trotsky's blood for nothing. Zinoviev had a world reputation as the leader of the Communist International. Lord Curzon and Secretary of State Hughes had enhanced his prestige. He had long considered himself the rightful heir to Lenin, and had harbored the ambition of becoming the supreme guide of all the Soviet policies. He would let Stalin convert them into mechanical energy. But Stalin had his own thoughts on the subject.

The squabble for Lenin's scepter continued, but the circle of actors narrowed for the moment. Its character too was different. Trotsky had no political machine. Zinoviev had Leningrad "sewed up." Kamenev's hold on Moscow was not so tight, because of the presence of the Central Committee—the headquarters of Stalin's national organization.

A series of incidents occurred during 1925 which tended to show that Zinoviev's machine was attempting to wrest the power from the hands of Stalin. One of Zinoviev's henchmen, Sarkis, attacked Stalin's spokesman, Bukharin, in the press for expressing "syndicalist and un-Bolshevik views." This article had not been sent to the secretary-general for approval before publication. "It was a gross infringement of the elementary rules of comradely discussion," declared Stalin. "I need hardly say that this affair could not fail to make relationships within the Central Committee worse than they were before."

Then Zinoviev attempted to set up in Leningrad, without the knowledge of Moscow, a center of the Union of Young Communists. "Of course, we could not tolerate that, side by side with the Central Committee of the Union of Young Communists," observed Stalin, "there should come into existence another central body competing with the former and setting itself up against it. According to our Bolshevist principles, no double leadership of this sort can be permitted."

The new attempt was suppressed by means of the G.P.U. Some of Zinoviev's lieutenants were removed from office. But Zinoviev would not down. He proposed to establish in his stronghold a central press organ, to be called the Bolshevik. This was unheard-of impudence. "We could not agree to this proposal," said Stalin, "and declared that a newspaper of the sort, appearing side by side with the Moscow Bolshevik, would inevitably become the organ of a group, the organ of a faction; that such an opposition paper would endanger the unity of the party. In plain terms, we prohibited the publication of this periodical."

There was satanic irony in the situation. But a year before Trotsky had been denounced for his factionalism, and his thesis of proletarian democracy was arraigned by Zinoviev as Menshevist, renegade and what-not. Now Zinoviev clamored for democracy. Stalin's machine was at least impartial. The cry of Leningrad was dismissed with the very words that Zinoviev had coined in the past for such occasions.

Up to now, however, there were still certain traditions intact in the higher spheres. Articles could be suppressed, but articles by whom? Certainly no one would have thought that an article by Lenin's widow, a veteran of veterans, could be kept out of the public prints. But Krupskaya allied herself with Zinoviev. She wrote a piece which was aimed at Bukharin's heretical slogan: "Enrich yourselves!" That slogan was the reflection of Stalin's economic policies of the moment, which were based on an understanding with the peasants.

"Comrade Krupskaya wrote an article against Bukharin and demanded that it should be published," Stalin relates the incident. "Comrade Bukharin retaliated by writing an article against Comrade Krupskaya. The majority of the Central Committee decided neither of the articles should appear, that no discussion of the kind should be opened, but that Comrade Bukharin should be asked to admit publicly in the press that the slogan 'Enrich yourselves!' was an incorrect one. . . .

"Now Comrades Kamenev and Zinoviev think they can frighten us by talking about 'prohibitions,' and are as indignant as any liberal could be because we refuse to allow the publication of Comrade Krupskaya's article. They won't frighten anyone by this sort of talk. In the first place, we prohibited not only the appearance of Krupskaya's article, but also that of Bukharin. In the second place, I should like to ask why we should not have the right of prohibiting the publication of an article by Krupskaya if we think that this prohibition is in the party interest? What is the difference between Krupskaya's position and that of any other responsible comrade? Do you think that the interests of any individual comrade are to take precedence over the interests and the unity of the party? Surely the comrades of the opposition know that for us Bolsheviks formal democracy is a trifle, and that the real interests of the party are all-important!"

Stalin could not help identifying the party with his political machine, the Central Committee with his secretariat, so that the "we" inevitably meant "I." In spite of the fact that the Central Committee was composed largely of hand-picked Stalinists, the denial of the liberty of press to unquestionably responsible Bolsheviks was as much of Stalin's artificial making as it was a natural outgrowth of the system of Leninism.

Rebuffed by the strong arm of Stalin and thwarted in their ambition to seize the national reins, Zinoviev and Kamenev turned from organizational conflicts to criticism of Stalin's general guidance. Here they found ample ammunition. They borrowed a great ideal of Trotsky's powder, and opened fire along a wide front.

II

In 1925, the Stalin of the Five-Year Plan was not yet. In fact, he stood very far from it. His fundamental premise was the stabilization of world capitalism. His international policies were in accord with this doctrine. Internally, the Stalin who five years later was to lead the grand campaign against the elimination of the *kulaks* as a class, advanced the slogan of "an alliance with the great mass of the peasantry." As far as the communist movements in the West were concerned and the eastern, especially the Chinese, developments, Stalin stood for support of the moderate groups, even going to the extent of backing Chiang Kai-Shek, who later turned upon his Kremlin ally.

This was, in a sense, good Leninism. For the help given by Lenin to Kemal Pasha was repaid in the same manner as were Lenin's and Trotsky's flirtations with the adventurous nationalist, Enver Pasha. There were many other good precedents for the opportunist policy of Bolshevism to seek support in non-communist quarters so long as the adventures were directed against the imperialist enemies of Soviet Russia. In this, the nationalist character of the Bolshevist revolution asserted itself.

But it was a vulnerable and perilous line of conduct for Stalin. The Communist International had been organized as the most extreme wing of world revolution. The cry went up that Stalin was betraying the international cause, that his policy at home and abroad was opportunist, leading to a degeneration that would culminate in a Bonapartist era.

Zinoviev opened fire on the peasant problem, making Bukharin his target, in an article entitled "The Philosophy of an Epoch." It was sent to Stalin for revision before publication.

"When Comrade Molotov sent me this article—

I was traveling at the time," Stalin described the affair several months later, "I answered it somewhat acrimoniously."

"Yes, comrades, I am a plain-spoken and rather rough sort of fellow. I don't deny it. I criticized it rather savagely, for really it is a little more than I can put up with when Comrade Zinoviev, for a whole year, systematically suppresses and misrepresents the most important features of Leninism as far as the peasant problem is concerned, and is dumb about the present slogan of our party concerning the alliance with the great mass of the peasantry."

Stalin expressed the opinion in his letter to Molotov that the article must be radically reconstructed. This was a pretty pass indeed. That Stalin should edit an article by Zinoviev, the oracle of Marxism! Lenin might have treated a schoolboy that way. He would have, however, permitted its publication in the case of a comrade of Zinoviev's standing, and then replied to it in print. Stalin simply sent Zinoviev to kindergarten.

Zinoviev retaliated in Leningrad. He applied here with a vengeance the Stalin methods. He weeded out the Moscow appointees. He consolidated his machine and was coming to the next, the Fourteenth Congress of the party, with a solid block of delegates behind him. A conference was held in the former capital in which Stalin's rule was subjected to severe bombardment. Zinoviev was going to war against the Moscow clique. Certain members of the Central Committee who had been installed in the Leningrad organization by Stalin were not "elected" to the congress.

In the periodic economic crisis that the country was undergoing after two years of comparative recovery without any planning, the fragments of discontented groups flocked into Zinoviev's camp. Kamenev could not marshal the Moscow machine as blatantly as his ally in Leningrad was able to do. But he excelled in intrigue and in bringing to the front a number of scattered leaders. Sokolnikov, the commissar of finance, later Soviet ambassador to Great Britain, joined the new opposition with the cry that Stalin was guiding the revolution to state capitalism. Lashevitch, one of the Red Army leaders, the man that Lenin had once proposed for the post of commander-in-chief, a veteran Bolshevik, a personal friend of Trotsky's joined in the new alignment. The opposition appeared with a platform. It carried strings of quotations from Marx and Lenin, but the barrel of its heavy artillery was quite simple. It was aimed directly at Stalin's fort, the secretariat of the Central Committee.

Stalin, recalling that during the Trotsky fight these new opponents had sought to achieve a compromise by introducing Zinoviev and Trotsky into the secretariat, very aptly said:

"It would seem that what they want now is not that the secretariat should undertake the political guidance of the party, but that it should confine its attention to technical questions. What they want is no longer the abolition of the Political Bureau, but the omnipotence of the Political Bureau.

"Well, if the transformation of the secretariat into a single technical apparatus would really be to Comrade Kamenev's liking, perhaps we ought to see what can be done about it—but I am afraid that the party would never agree. . . .

"But why do they go on talking about the omnipotence of the Political Bureau? Is not a demand of this kind positively ludicrous? Does not the Political Bureau possess supreme authority?"

What Kamenev and Zinoviev wanted was to replace Stalin. Two days before the congress met, a compromise proposition was submitted by a group of leaders, including Bukharin, Rykov, Tomsky, Kalinin, and Stalin, "to avoid the danger of a possible estrangement of the Leningrad organization." A number of concessions of secondary character were made by the Stalin faction. The opposition refused to accept the compromise.

"It preferred open and savage war at the party congress," said Stalin. "We are opposed to the policy of lopping off. Of course, this does not mean that the leaders will be entitled, with impunity, to do anything that takes their fancy. Certainly the party will not prostrate itself before any individual leader. . . . We are opposed to the idea of a special press organ for discussion. . . . Discussion must not be driven too far. We must never forget that we are a *ruling* party. . . . We must not forget that any open expression of our differences may reduce our influence in the country—to say nothing of the effect it may have abroad.

"The unity of the party must be and will be maintained—provided that the party and party congress do not allow themselves to be intimidated. If any one of us should get a swelled head, he will be called to order. This is necessary, it is absolutely essential.

The only possible way of leading the party is by a collectivity of some sort. Now that Lenin is dead, it is absurd to think, or talk, or dream of anything else."

With this specter of fear, with his powerful club of patronage, with his song of collective leadership, Stalin rode over the opposition and came out at the beginning of 1926 more than ever the head of the dictatorial government.

Once more he offered his resignation, making it an issue between his direction and that of the opposition. The several hundred office-holders representing the local organizations would not hear of it.

III

Trotsky was writing books and studying modern economics. He was running the concessions committee and the scientific-technical board of industry. He had been appointed to these posts several months after his resignation from the war office, upon his return from the health resorts. He had watched the beginnings of the Stalin-Zinoviev struggle with justifiable satisfaction, but he did not participate actively in politics. At the congress, he was present but did not speak.

During this period Trotsky first advanced and elaborated a five-year plan for the industrialization of the country. It was entitled "The Report of the Special Conference for the Restoration of Basic Capital and State Industry." Stalin took it up publicly in 1930, to criticize its conservative chart as compared with the bold map of the plan he had put into operation. He spoke of the declining Trotskyist curve as against the ascending Bolshevik curve, when new opponents cropped up to challenge the tremendous pace that Stalin had set. But he never denied the existence of the plan of Trotsky, just as he never denied that the issue of industrialization had first been forced by Trotsky.

But the new activities of the former head of the Red Army gave no peace to the zealous Stalinites, who were afraid of his creating a new fighting front.

"The Stalin apparatus followed on my heels," writes Trotsky. "Every practical step that I took gave rise to a complicated intrigue behind the scenes; every theoretical conclusion fed the ignorant myth of Trotskyism. My practical work was performed under impossible conditions. It is no exaggeration to say that much of the creative activity of Stalin and his assistant Molotov was devoted to organizing direct sabotage around me. It became virtually impossible for the institutions under my direction to obtain the necessary wherewithal. People working there began to fear for their futures, or at least for their careers."

Armed with the renewed confidence of the congress, Stalin set out to employ the unlimited powers at his command to ferret out the new heretics. The familiar scene of persecution, of removing people from their posts, of imprisonment and exile, of misrepresentation, now unfolded in connection with the Kamenev-Zinoviev following. But it proved a far harder task than in the anti-Trotsky campaign. The leaders of the new opposition were old craftsmen, and controlled quite an impressive sector of the governing apparatus.

In the spring of 1926, Lashevitch, a member of the Central Committee and acting commissar of war, organized in the woods an illegal meeting—it was impossible to hold a legal political gathering—at which the plan of a united opposition to Stalin was outlined. The main purpose was to force the machine to permit a wide-open discussion within the party of all the issues. To this Stalin was opposed. Lashevitch's connection with the Red Army and his impeccable Bolshevik past made his act a matter of state importance. The meeting in the woods was of course attended by under-cover men of the G. P. U., and Stalin was informed of it at once. How dare a member of the Central Committee hold a meeting without the foreknowledge of the secretary-general?

But the new opposition did not sleep. Underground groups were organized, and party documents suppressed by Stalin were circulated surreptitiously. The various factions and currents that had still retained a measure of independent thought were lined up and brought under the Zinoviev-Kamenev flag. The recent recruits to the ranks of the party, mostly ignorant workingmen, were assiduously propagandized, and the responsibility for their hard economic lot and the low wages was rightly or wrongly placed at Stalin's door.

And, finally, Trotsky was approached with a view to the formation of a single anti-Stalin alliance. Kamenev acted as the emissary. It was a sordid chapter. Trotsky had up to now managed to keep his record clean. In spite of the torrents of slander and distortion to which he had been subjected, not a scintilla of proof had been produced that he had really tried to split the unity of the party. But Trotsky decided to play politics. When Kamenev came to see him, Trotsky had been warned by some of his best friends to ally himself with his former enemies because of their innate treachery. "But such questions are finally decided not by psychological but by political considerations," Trotsky writes.

"It is enough for you and Zinoviev to appear on the same platform, and the party will find its true Central Committee," said Kamenev to Trotsky. The latter laughed "at such bureaucratic optimism." Nevertheless, the negotiations were started. Kamenev and Zinoviev agreed to incorporate in the proposed program of the new bloc a retraction to the effect that they had been wrong three years before and that Trotsky was right in his attack against the rule of the machine. On the other hand, Trotsky acknowledged his "mistake" when he had attacked Kamenev and Zinoviev as laggards and opportunists during the seizure of power in 1917.

The united opposition to Stalin became a fact in June, 1926, when a common platform prepared by Trotsky was adopted. The foundation of this platform was the denial of the Stalin theory of the possibility of socialism in one country. The lines were now drawn for battle. The first general skirmish occurred in July, at the plenary session of the Central Committee and the Central Control Commission, the "parliament" and the "senate" of the monolithic party.

IV

Once more Stalin and Trotsky faced each other. After seven years of battling, the two men had undergone marked changes. Since those days at the Tsaritsyn front both had learned a lot. Stalin had received a liberal education, having acquired from Trotsky an understanding of some of the fundamentals of the main economic currents. Gradually he was taking over nearly all his foe's views on the subject. Stalin had decidedly grown bigger with his power. Trotsky had learned from Stalin a few of the principles of practical politics, and was less proud, but also less in stature.

The fighting ground now shifted from the internal to the international field. The opposition started out with a succession of quick and painful jabs. Stalin's régime had become anti-proletarian. Stalin's leadership was rapidly degenerating into one of counter-revolution. "The opposition declared," said Stalin, "that our state is 'far from being a proletarian state.' " This was more serious than anything that had been used in the past. "If Comrade Trotsky before regarded that the rock of obstruction toward socialist construction in our country," argued Stalin, "lay in the contradictions between the proletariat and the peasantry, he now changed his front and retreated to a new base for criticism of the party line, asserting that this obstruction is to be found in the contradictions between our economic system and that of the capitalist world."

The general strike in Great Britain, which occurred in May of that year, had been uncannily forecast by Trotsky in his recent book entitled "Whither England?" He now went after Stalin—who for almost a year had been associated with the Communist International — with a series of onslaughts that sharply discredited his course in the direction of the world revolution. Stalin was shouldered with responsibilities on the theory of missed opportunities. "The party considers that the formula of Comrade Trotsky regarding 'direct state aid of the European proletariat' is a formula of complete rupture with Leninism," replied Stalin. Here in a nutshell was the kernel of the first attack. From this position it was logical for Trotsky to announce that "the theory of socialism in one country is a theoretical justification of national exclusiveness," and that "the working class in Russia would not be able to retain its power." Trotsky, indeed, enunciated a a novel plan. "Let the Soviet government directly help the world revolution, for only in that manner can the Soviet government be preserved!"

The struggle, however, was in its essence one for power. Behind all the maneuvers of the opposition, Stalin perceived the main objective: to dislodge him. His return blow was far more easy to understand. The Inquisition—the Central Control Commission—advanced with a sharp saber. It pointed out the efforts to create illegal, conspirative opposition groups against the unity of the party, such as Lashevitch's clandestine conference.

The ax was brought out. Zinoviev was expelled from the Political Bureau. Lashevitch was thrown out from the Central Committee. Instructions were issued "to conduct the most implacable war against all signs of factionalism." Trotsky, not having had anything to do directly with the meeting in the woods—he had spent a couple of months in Germany undergoing an operation—was left unmolested. The warning, however, was sufficiently clear.

The July, 1927, session which authorized these acts proved fatal to Djerjinsky, who, after a feverish address of several hours, collapsed and died suddenly. There followed a shift in high offices, and at the head of the Control Commission now appeared Stalin's intimate associate, Ordjonikidze. This portended rough work and stern measures on the part of the machine and the G. P. U.

The united opposition did not waver. It advanced with a new load of ammunition. All the critical speeches and documents delivered at the July session were, of course, suppressed by Stalin. But the opposition found ways and means of multigraphing them and giving them as much circulation as possible. From this it advanced to a new method of warfare. Its speakers would appear at various party meetings and without authority address the audiences. This was met by furious counter-blows. Reprisals, arrests followed. Bands of whistlers were organized to disrupt such gatherings. Strings of automobiles would suddenly appear and blow their sirens. The G. P. U. would stop at nothing to make it appear that the masses did not want to hear the anti-Stalin leaders. Booing instead of argument was a common form of rebuttal. There was a decision not to permit a discussion in the party, and the machine would not be intimidated by Trotsky, Zinoviev, or Kamenev.

V

Zinoviev's recipe for democracy, invented in 1924 against Trotsky, when two hundred thousand new and backward members were recruited into the party, now promoted his undoing. This was no longer the Bolshevist army of 1917. This was a gray, stupid mass that had stood away from the revolution during its critical years and that welcomed the privilege of a party ticket when the revolution was established as a successful enterprise. Trotsky knew it. Kamenev and Zinoviev learned it. These masses did not understand the alphabet of socialism, could not grasp the elementals of the issues. Blindly but soundly they sensed that the opposition was trying to upset the government. They were in no mood for experiments. These new recruits had not been in that mood even under the tsar.

And so the glorified masses did not respond. The organized hooting and booing were perhaps essential in universities and similar centers where thinking and independence of spirit were not dead. But these were an insignificant minority. In the course of two or three months, the wave of the opposition spent itself against the blind and petrified and terrorized mass of workers. Stalin had decided that the time had come for another offensive.

The opposition beat a retreat. One of its leaders had come out with the heretical plan of forming a second political party. This was the last straw. A second political party, indeed! What was Leninism coming to? The opposition was scared and disowned the proposer. Had they not for years rehearsed the immortal line of party unity, of monolithic Leninism? The quotations to that effect were still fresh, and Stalin's secretariat had them stacked and filed and ready for the proper moment.

The generals without an army resorted to strategy. Here Trotsky's experience stood them well. On October 4, two weeks before the next plenary session of the two supreme bodies controlled by Stalin was convoked, the opposition sent word to the Political Bureau proposing negotiations and a truce. Zinoviev in Leningrad even then tried to muster his following for the coming meeting. But his wings had been clipped. His henchmen had been removed. He now reaped the fruit of his eight-year rule as boss. The national machine had crushed his own. His "popularity"—of which so many observers had written glowingly for years—as president of the Leningrad Soviet, had strangely evaporated. The prize of dictatorship may be front-page headlines in the government-owned press and eulogies by the pens of gullible visitors, but its price in terms of popular support is zero.

On October 16, the Pravda came out with a declaration of six members of the Central Committee, Trotsky, Zinoviev, Kamenev, Sokolnikov, Piatakov, and Yevdokimov. It was the retreat. The leaders of the opposition renounced any thought or plan of factionalism, they unconditionally subscribed to the theory of an undivided party, they disassociated themselves from the Left elements in the Communist International and from the democratic group of Shliapnikov at home. They undertook to submit without equivocation to the decisions of the party congresses and the Central Committee. But they retained the right to defend their principles and views within the framework of the party constitution.

This gave Stalin a new opportunity to drive a wedge into the demoralized ranks of the enemy. At the plenary session he came out with an analysis of the development of the united opposition, which he found was nothing more than the old Trotskyism, camouflaged! This meant, in the existing régime, "Pull out the guillotine!" Out it came.

Trotsky was expelled from the Political Bureau. Kamenev received similar punishment. Zinoviev was removed from the post of director of the Communist International. The session adjourned.

The opposition still had illusions. Zinoviev suffered from the naive theory that the Communist International was a self-sufficient body, that the forty or fifty so-called communist parties all over the world were independent and had affection for, and confidence in him, Zinoviev. Such is the human capacity for self-deception. Zinoviev had forgotten the way he had conducted himself. Above all, he forgot that it was Moscow that had made the Communist International because it was Moscow that had power, finances, the reins of government, and all the privileges and comforts to offer to the foreign comrades.

In December the executive committee of the Communist International held its session. Trotsky, Zinoviev, Kamenev attempted to carry the domestic struggle into the international organization. It was a doomed hope. The Moscow patronage had extended far beyond the borders of the Soviet Union, although Kamenev did accuse the Stalin régime of the hideous crime of "national reformism."

Stalin's reply made a document of 189 printed pages. He analyzed the Menshevist nature of the opposition. He reiterated that the "basic instrument of the dictatorship of the proletariat is the leadership of a single party." He refuted as un-Leninist the theory that socialism cannot be built in one country. He admitted that "dictatorship in the strict sense of the word is a government relying upon violence," but denied that the violence applied to the proletariat. He argued that the opposition stood for dead Marxism, whereas he stood for creative socialism.

"We start from the premises that the party, the Communist Party, is the basic instrument of the dictatorship of the proletariat, that the leadership of *one* party, which does not share and cannot share this leadership with other parties, constitutes that fundamental condition without which a more or less lasting and developed dictatorship of the proletariat is inconceivable.

"In view of this, we consider inadmissible the existence of factions within our party, for it is obvious that the presence of organized factions leads to the splitting of the united party into parallel organizations, to the formation of seeds and cells of a new party or new parties in the country, and therefore to the disintegration of the dictatorship of the proletariat.

"But the opposition, without openly objecting to these premises, in practice proceeds from the necessity of weakening the unity of the party, the necessity of the freedom of factions within the party, and therefore the necessity of forming the elements for a new party.

"Hence, the sectarian politics of the opposition bloc in its practical work. . . . Hence the question of two parties."

But his telling and terrific wound upon the opposition was inflicted in a casual fashion, so characteristic of Stalin.

"I am speaking of one incident," he remarked, "in which Kamenev was involved when he was still in exile in Siberia, after the March revolution, when Comrade Kamenev joined the prominent merchants of Siberia in sending a telegram of congratulations to the constitutional monarch Michael Romanov, that very Michael Romanov to whom the tsar upon his abdication had turned over 'the right to the throne.' "

Digging up this skeleton from Kamenev's revolutionary past and exhibiting it before the international brotherhood was part and parcel of the campaign the Stalin machine waged against Kamenev and Zinoviev. Once more a thousand presses were let loose. All the handsome epithets that Lenin had ever applied to his two lieutenants were assorted and published in editions of hundreds of thousands. All the slander that Kamenev and Zinoviev had formerly showered upon Trotsky was now revived. The fight became one of mud slinging, but largely on one side. The press and the public platforms were controlled by the ruling apparatus. The opposition was unable to disseminate widely Lenin's testament, nor could it bring out Stalin's dubious connection with the famous Tiflis affair. One by one, however, the former demigods of Bolshevism were being lowered into the slimy depths of mutual recrimination and exposure. The masses witnessed the unfrocking of their priests. The remnants of the bourgeois elements chuckled. The world laughed.

VI

Zinoviev wavered. Early in 1927 he was ready to capitulate and pleaded for mercy. Stalin was sitting in the saddle firmer than ever. Thousands of oppositionists were out of jobs. Hundreds were in jail. And then suddenly Stalin was almost knocked out by a staggering blow from an unexpected quarter. His ally in China, Chiang Kai-Shek, betrayed the cause, turned on the communists, and staged a truly Bartholomean blood-bath. But a few nights before the event Stalin had delivered a speech on the Chinese revolution. It was in type, on the way to the pages of the Pravda. The speech was never printed. The Stalin international course struck a rock. His policy was bankrupt. Because of the immensely magnified hopes that the Chinese revolution aroused in Russia, because of the grand vision of a united block of Soviet states comprising six hundred million people, because of the primitive belief that such a union would deliver a death stroke to the British Empire, a damaging blow to world capitalism, the sudden turn in China was a momentous happening in Moscow.

The opposition took on new life. Its former criticism had been justified. Its charge of opportunism against Stalin now gained an intelligible basis—but only among the upper layers of the party. The masses had never cared for the higher issues in the matter; they knew only that Russia was extending its power into new fields. Zinoviev regained his courage. He even committed the unpardonable sin of addressing a non-partizan meeting held in connection with the fifteenth anniversary of the Pravda. Here, where communists and non-communists alike were present, he dared criticize the Central Committee! Trotsky at the next executive session of the Communist International was even bolder. He accused Stalin of treason to the cause of world revolution.

The recrudescence of underground activity against the Stalin régime for a moment assumed wide proportions. A memorandum of eighty-three opposition leaders, comprising the flower of the old guard, and sharply criticizing the administration for its bankrupt policies, was furtively circulated. Another group, led by Sapronov, drew up a document signed by fifteen labor leaders, in which Stalin's reign was declared anti-proletarian and the G. P. U. was characterized as the organ for the crushing of the working class! Needless to say that the two memoranda had first been submitted to the Political Bureau and were secretly disseminated only after their official suppression.

Trotsky was never so good as in a desperate situation. Stalin was never so deadly an enemy as in meeting such a situation. The skirmishes were turning into a free-for-all, a struggle of life and death. The lines were drawing closer, the predetermined outcome nearer.

Trotsky now called for Stalin's head. All the reams of befogging paper arguments were discarded.

Trotsky invited the opposition to follow the example of Clemenceau in the fall of 1914, when the Germans were enveloping Paris. Clemenceau had then demanded the overthrow of the incompetent government. In Moscow, the fiasco in China was taken as a sign of war. The opposition was urged to follow the example of the French "Tiger." The call was grandiloquent, but in the vaulted chamber of the Stalin dictatorship it was hushed and fell flat.

The Central Control Commission warned Trotsky and Zinoviev of the consequences of their tactics. The opposition leaders were playing for time, to allow their ideas to penetrate into the masses. Again they executed a tactical retreat, and signed a paper in which they once more surrendered to the bugaboo of party unity. In a sense, it was a legitimate move. For they now openly aimed not at splitting the party, but at dislocating Stalin and taking over his machine. They retreated in order to consolidate their lines and to resume the offensive in the last assault for the coveted prize of absolutist power.

CHAPTER TWELVE

THE BLOODLESS GUILLOTINE

I

STALIN did not invent it. He perfected it. The guillotine of the Russian Revolution had been in operation for years. Its weapon was not that of the sword but of the garrote. It had none of the majesty of spontaneity, like the terror of the French Revolution, and all of the turpitude of premeditation. It had none of the challenge of the auto-da-fé and all of the cowardliness of enthroned conspiracy. Its virtue was buried in silence, its judgment was without wrath. Instead of the public square, it preferred the sound-proof chamber. Instead of demonstrative cruelty, it resorted to the hidden dungeon. Thomas More, John Huss, Galileo, Savonarola had set dangerous precedents. They went up to their Golgotha to give newer life to their ideas. Bolshevism learned from the past. It executed petty thieves and terrified spies with flaunting publicity. Great minds, great souls, it immured in holes and surrounded them with a deadening vacuum within and with deadly vilification and distortion without. The twentieth century, the century of mass credulity, of no traditions, of no memory, made it possible to strangle the spirit, scientifically to disintegrate it, and for the perpetrators to go about "building socialism" unbranded and unrecognized.

The Bolshevist guillotine was built by Lenin. Trotsky as well as Stalin, Kamenev as well as Zinoviev, helped in its erection. It was flesh of the flesh of Leninism. Under the blanket of the dictatorship of the proletariat, beneath the deception which that connoted, grew that witch-hunting of heresy within the Bolshevist state monopoly of which the Cheka is the glowing achievement. Not the executions of former nobles and police agents, not the shooting of corrupt bureaucrats, not the staging of trials of counter-revolutionaries, are the signs of the guillotine of Bolshevism. The quiet strangling of all creative thought, the blind suffocation of all dissident opinion, the degradation and imprisonment of all free intellect, the falsifications of records, the venal campaign against the intelligentsia as a class, the hypocritical administrative system of justice, the all-pervading master network of espionage—these are some of the marks of the new guillotine of a new form of dictatorship of our "new" age.

From 1919 to 1925, tens of thousands of fearless idealists whose faith in a new social order could not be bought by government office, whose courage could not be wrenched by the engine of terror, who had believed that the dictatorship of the proletariat meant the genuine rule of all the toilers, who had fought for the revolution in the hope that a people enslaved for a thousand dark years would be guided to freedom and light, had been thrown without trial into prison camps, into exile, into solitary cells. These included hundreds who had languished in irons under the tsar for years and had in good faith formed a coalition with Lenin for the establishment of the Soviet government. They included thousands who had defended the revolution as soldiers in the Red Army.

Before the Trotsky drama reached its well-known climax, by 1925, the guillotine had quietly extended its operations into the Bolshevist Party itself, and hundreds of minor figures of those who chose to stay in jail and keep their convictions rather than to hold office and surrender their beliefs, had been summarily put behind bars or distributed in the desolate tsarist exile places, where Lenin and Trotsky, Stalin and Kamenev, had once abided.

Now this bloodless guillotine would make its world debut. A world that had been inured to mistruth but educated in sensation, a world that had lost its sense of indignation but gained a jazz and cinematographic perspective, would watch with thrilling interest Trotsky, Zinoviev, Kamenev, Rakovsky, Radek, Tomsky mount the scaffold; it would turn its lurid front-page projectors upon the triumphant Stalin, and walk on unmindful of the far more onerous and sinister strangulation of the spirit and the mind of a lost people by the gallows of an unexampled dictatorship.

II

Fear, the soul of dictatorship, now strode across the land. Has there ever been a demonstration of physical panic on such a large scale as that which seized all of the Soviet Union in 1927? The opposition worked under handicaps which the old conspirators would have considered insurmountable. The all-embracing G. P. U. penetrated into the heart of every living cell. The ruling machine was dominated by fear of losing out. Above it all, rang the hysteria of a periodic but monstrous war-scare. The Soviet missions in several foreign countries had been raided. Both Bolshevist camps blew the trumpets of imminent danger. The whole nefarious capitalist universe was plotting, was advancing to destroy that nest of freedom and justice—the "proletarian" dictatorship. The Soviet government was on the brink of perdition, echoed the opposition. The governing apparatus reechoed the wail through its official and unofficial mouthpieces in a hundred countries. Looking back upon the nightmarish utterances of Stalin and Trotsky and their followers in those days, it is impossible to escape the vision of a divided band of conspirators petrified at the sight of their own ghost—the ghost of Bolshevism, the ghost of Leninism, the ghost of terror.

Against this dominating background, the final act of a truly great drama, great because of the magnitude of the country and not of the actors, was staged with florid colors, with picturesque sorties, with high phrases destined consciously for posterity. Beneath the showmanship, deep wounds were mutually inflicted. Beneath the long-rehearsed parts from Lenin's voluminous scrapbooks, the daggers drew blood.

Stalin's guillotine was working at an accelerated speed. The G. P. U. began to reach for the leaders. At first, they were treated to honorary exile, *i.e.,* they were assigned to remote and obscure places to do minor government work. One such veteran, one of the makers of the Soviet power in 1917, a pre-revolutionary member of the Central Committee, Smilga, was ordered to Siberia on such a mission. At the railroad station, Trotsky appeared to bid him farewell, and made a demonstrative speech before the assembled crowd. This was a desperate move. Both Trotsky and Zinoviev were still members of Stalin's Central Committee. The Inquisition now raised the question of their expulsion.

"The Stalin group is leading the party blindfold. Concealing the forces of the enemy, creating everywhere and in everything an *official appearance* of success; this group gives the proletariat no perspective—or, what is worse, a wrong perspective. It moves in zigzags, accommodating itself to, and ingratiating itself with, hostile elements. It weakens and confuses the forces of the proletarian army. It promotes the growth of passivity, distrust of leadership, and lack of confidence in the power of the revolution. . . .

"The direct fault of the Stalin group is that instead of telling the party, the working class and the peasants, the whole truth about the situation, it has concealed the facts, minimized the growth of the hostile forces, and shut the mouths of those who demanded the truth. . . .

"The Stalinists are tracing a line consisting of short zigzags to the left and deep ones to the right. . . . The Stalin course leads, in objective reality, to a retardment of the development of productive forces. . . . The Stalin course is the more dangerous and ruinous in that it conceals a real departure from socialism under the mask of familiar socialist words and phrases. . . .

"The mechanics of Stalin are all designed to present the party membership, upon every sharp or important question that arises, with one single choice: either renounce your own opinion or fall under the accusation of desiring a split. . . .

"The obedience cultivated from above under the name of revolutionary discipline has really nothing whatever to do with revolutionary discipline. . . . The real rights of one member of the party at the top are many times greater than the real rights of a hundred members at the bottom. . . . The dying-out of inner party democracy leads to a dying-out of workers' democracy in general—in the trade unions and in all other party mass organization. . . .

"Every word of criticism against the crude Menshevik mistakes of Stalin is described as a struggle against the party. This, although Stalin has never asked the party any preliminary question, either about the policy in China or about any other important problem. . . . It has become entirely customary to expel oppositionists for speaking at the meetings of their locals, for making sharp exclamations, for attempting to read the testament of Lenin. . . .

"In the organizational sphere, the actual subjection of the Political Bureau to the secretariat, and the secretariat to the secretary-general, has long ago become an accomplished fact. The worst fear expressed by Lenin in his testament—the fear that Stalin would not be sufficiently loyal, would not employ the 'immoderate power' which he had 'concentrated in his hands' in a party manner—has been justified."

These excerpts from the last platform of the opposition, submitted to the Political Bureau early in September, 1927, were strong words to put in writing. Stalin declared the memorandum anti-party, and it was consequently outlawed. However, it was then set up in a secret printing press, just as in the old days, and circulated. The G. P. U. had its informers in the inner oppositionist circles. The culprits were seized, and hundreds of Bolsheviks suspected of the crime and of heresy were arrested and exiled.

In spite of the increasing terror, numerous meetings were arranged for the leaders of the anti-Stalin camp. These were illegal gatherings. "In one day I would visit two, three, and sometimes four of such meetings," writes Trotsky. "They were usually held in some worker's apartment. Two small rooms would be packed with people, and the speaker would stand at the door between the two rooms. Sometimes everyone would sit on the floor; more often the discussion had to be carried on standing, for lack of space."

Whenever Stalinists appeared, they would be asked to participate in the debates. The opposition grew bolder, and decided to carry the fight into the streets. They seized for one evening the building of the Technical College and held a huge mass meeting, under the protection of a crowd of two thousand people outside. Kamenev and Trotsky spoke for two hours. At the same time they proceeded to arrange street demonstrations. Moscow and Leningrad once more witnessed scenes reminiscent of 1902, the early period of struggle against the autocracy.

III

In Leningrad, the All-Union Soviet was holding its session. There was a grand official celebration. Tribunes were erected, and a holiday declared. Kalinin and many other high functionaries were to address the multitude. Suddenly Trotsky and Zinoviev appeared. The masses turned away from the official platform and rushed toward the opposition leaders. All the pent-up discontent with the government was expressed in this silent gesture. Zinoviev and Trotsky mistook it for a sign of popularity. Undoubtedly if Stalin had been in their place and they in Stalin's, the same demonstration would have occurred.

In Moscow, Stalin was wakeful. The G. P. U. worked day and night. It was necessary to find some way to discredit the opposition. The G. P. U. would know how to handle that. It resorted to one of its tested devices. It planted one of its secret agents, a former officer in Wrangel's army, in the opposition ranks, for the purpose of framing up a Trotsky-royalist conspiracy! It then came out with the devastating revelation that the Trotsky-Zinoviev faction had made an alliance with the Whites. But the opposition was more fortunate than similar non-Bolshevist victims. It had its followers in the G. P. U. Trotsky exposed the sordid maneuver. Stalin never took up the cudgels for his stool-pigeon.

Instead the guillotine was brought forward on the stage. Trotsky and Zinoviev rose to dramatic heights at the plenary session which was called to consider their expulsion from the Central Committee.

A RARE PHOTOGRAPH OF STALIN, THE FISHERMAN AND HUNTER, IN SIBERIAN EXILE IN 1916.

Below — STALIN THE TRIUMPHANT, ON THE 13TH ANNIVERSARY OF THE SOVIET REVOLUTION. *To his right is Kalinin, President of the Republic.*

Zinoviev flung the gauntlet down with bravado: "Either let us speak to the party and within the party, or arrest us all! There is no other choice."

Trotsky's impassioned and vitriolic speech was like the lashing of a whip. At every phrase the commotion among the elders of Bolshevism grew wilder. They hooted, shouted, banged, and stamped their feet. Their imprecations were unprintable. The brand of Marxism that flourished in Eurasia now blossomed forth in all its authentic colors.

"My motion to consider independently the question of the officer of Wrangel and of the 'military plot' was voted down," thundered Trotsky. "You decreed that my short speech on the imitation-officer of Wrangel should be expunged from the record—that is, hidden from the party. . . . Rudeness and disloyalty have grown to the size of criminal betrayal. . . . The falsification factory is working night and day in two shifts. . . . You want to expel us from the Central Committee. We agree that this step is in full accord with the present policy at the present stage of its development or, rather, its degeneration. This ruling faction, which is expelling from the party hundreds and thousands of its best members, its unwavering worker-Bolsheviks—comrades who alone could create a party secretariat infinitely more authoritative, more able, more Leninist than our present secretariat—this Stalin-Bukharin clique, who have locked up in the inner prison of the G. P. U. devoted and admirable men . . . this group of officials holding its place on top of the party by violence, by strangulation of the party's thought . . . this through-and-through opportunistic faction . . .

cannot endure our presence in the Central Committee even one month before the party congress! We understand this.

"Rudeness and disloyalty go hand in hand with cowardice. You have hidden our platform—rather you have tried to hide it. . . . What does fear of a platform mean? Everybody knows: fear of a platform is fear of the masses. . . .

"It is true that Stalin inspired Lenin with dread from the very day of his election as secretary-general. . . . That is why Lenin, weighing the prospect of his departure, gave the party his last counsel.

"Banishing and arresting and depriving of employment, the ruling faction is employing both knife and bribe against its own party. The worker-member is afraid to say what he thinks in his own local. He is afraid to vote according to his conscience. A dictatorship of officialdom is terrorizing our party, which is supposed to be the highest expression of the proletarian dictatorship. . . .

"Through the Stalin apparatus, through the Stalinist régime, the forces that are pressing down on the proletarian vanguard are the bureaucrat, the labor faker, the administrator, the industrial manager, the new private capitalist, the privileged intelligentsia of the town and country. . . . The régime of party repression flows inevitably from the whole policy of the leadership. . . .

"The immediate task that Stalin has set for himself is to split the party, to cut off the opposition, to accustom the party to the method of physical destruction. Fascist gangs of whistlers, fist work, throwing of books and stones, prison bars—here for a moment the Stalin régime has paused in its course."

The pause was short-lived. The guillotine performed its bloodless decapitation.

IV

But Stalin did not set the devouring machine to work without invoking the sentiments that go with the high office of the archpriest of Bolshevism. With biting irony, with penetrating political acumen, with a blend of frankness and hypocrisy that historians will for generations endeavor to analyze, with poisoned arrows from the armory of dialectical and historical Leninism, and, above all, with the firm consciousness that the last word would be his in all events, Stalin gave battle to the desperate non-conformists. He took up Trotsky's indiscreet note as to the similarity of the crisis to that in which Clemenceau had figured in France during the world war, and Stalin made use of it in an annihilating fashion.

"Our Clemenceau is Comrade Trotsky and his group!" he exclaimed before the inquisitorial joint session, to the accompaniment of general laughter. "If the enemy should be within eighty kilometers of the Kremlin walls, this newly revealed Clemenceau of ours, this vaudeville Clemenceau, will first try, it seems, to overthrow the present majority, because of the enemy's being within eighty kilometers of the Kremlin, and then take up the matter of defense. And should our vaudeville Clemenceau succeed, that, it seems, would constitute the real and unconditional defense of the Soviet Union. And in order to accomplish it, he, Clemenceau, i.e., Comrade Trotsky, will first endeavor to sweep out the 'rubbish' in the interests of the victory of the workers' state!

"And what kind of rubbish is it? It appears that it is the majority of the party, the majority of the Central Committee, the majority of the government. And so you have it that when the enemy will be within eighty kilometers from the Kremlin, this vaudeville Clemenceau will be occupied not with the defense of the Soviet Union, but with the destruction of the present majority of the party. And that is called defense.

"Of course, it is somewhat laughable to think that this small Don Quixotic group . . . is threatening a party of a million: 'I'll sweep you out!' You can imagine how pathetic is the situation of the Trotsky group when, after sweating blood for four months, it was able to collect but one thousand signatures. I think any opposition group could collect several thousand signatures if it knew how to work. I repeat: this coterie, the number of whose leaders is greater than that of its army, makes one laugh. . . ."

Stalin then outlined his terms for the unconditional surrender of the opposition. "They will say that these are repressions. Yes, they are repressions. In the arsenal of our party, repression was never considered exceptional." And he quoted Lenin to support the employment of violence.

"The opposition retreated, but only to gain a truce," Stalin declared at the next meeting. "It has failed to condemn the Trotsky formula on Clemenceau."

TROTSKY: There never was such a formula.

VOICES: Yes, there was, if you please.

TROTSKY: There was a slogan, but somebody else raised it.

STALIN: Comrade Trotsky must have enough manhood to recognize things as they are.

TROTSKY: But not your slander!

STALIN: All right, we shall see soon whose is the slander. . . . I think that the entire body is deeply convinced that you, by raising the slogan and formula of Clemenceau, made a change in the leadership of the party and the Soviet government the condition for the defense of the country. Only the blind could fail to see it. If you, Comrade Trotsky, lack the courage, the elementary courage, to recognize your mistakes, you have only yourself to thank for it!

"Comrade Trotsky does not understand our party," declared Stalin at the executive session of the Communist International of Sept. 27. "He has no correct conception of it. He looks upon it the way a master regards a rabble, or a bureaucrat—his subordinates. Otherwise he would not assert that in a party of a million, individuals could 'seize power,' 'usurp power' . . . Why then did not Trotsky succeed in 'seizing power,' in gaining the party leadership? Does Trotsky lack the will, the desire to be the leader? . . . Trotsky is inclined to explain it by saying that the party is a blind herd following Stalin and Bukharin. But only people who have contempt for our party and consider it a rabble can think so. It is the view of a forsaken party aristocrat . . . Trotsky paints things so that the present party régime is in principle something different from the régime under Lenin . . . I declare that Trotsky tells plain untruths. I declare that the present régime is an exact expression of the régime established under Lenin during the Tenth and Eleventh Congresses. I assert that Trotsky is fighting the Leninist régime established under and by Lenin himself . . ."

TROTSKY: You are inventing! I did not speak of the Tenth Congress.

STALIN: Comrade Trotsky cannot fail to know that I can prove it with documents.

TROTSKY: You did not prove it on the trade-union issue and you cannot prove it now. You are a liar!

STALIN: Strong words I leave to you. Abuse will only discredit you. The documents in the matter are intact. I will distribute them to the comrades. . . .

Stalin took up the challenge of the Lenin testament a month later, at the climax of the series of inquisitorial sessions. "The oppositionists have cried here that the Central Committee is 'concealing' the testament of Lenin. You know that this question has been discussed a number of times at our joint sessions. Again and again it has been proved that no one hides anything, that the testament of Lenin was addressed to the Thirteenth Congress, that it, the testament, was made public there, that the congress unanimously decided not to publish it. One of the reasons for this decision, among others, was that Lenin himself did not wish or demand it. And nevertheless the opposition has the audacity to declare that the Central Committee is 'concealing' the testament. . . . It is said that Lenin proposed the removal of Stalin. Yes, that it is altogether true." And Stalin then proceeded to read the uncomplimentary part of Lenin's last message relating to him!

"Yes, comrades, I am rude towards those who rudely and treacherously wreck and split our party," Stalin continued. "I did not and do not conceal it. I asked the first plenary session of the Central Committee right after the Thirteenth Congress to relieve me of my duties as secretary-general. The congress discussed the question. Each delegation discussed the question. And unanimously they all, including Trotsky, Kamenev, and Zinoviev, made it binding upon Stalin to remain at his post. What could I do? Run away from the post? This is not in my character. I never ran away from any post and I have no right to run away. That would be desertion. I do not regard myself as a free man, and I obey party orders. A year later I again submitted my resignation, but again I was bound to remain. What could I do? . . .

"They speak of the former Wrangel officer in the service of the G.P.U., who disclosed the counter-revolutionary organization. The opposition is ranting and fuming and storming because the former Wrangel officer . . . turned out to be an agent of the G.P.U. But what is so wrong about it if this very officer does help the Soviet government disclose counter-revolutionary plots? Who can deny for the Soviet government the right to employ former officers in order to use them in unearthing counter-revolutionary organizations?

"Zinoviev and Trotsky overflowed with talk here claiming that we are preparing for the next congress by repressive measures. Strange, that they can see nothing but repressions. . . . Zinoviev and Trotsky apparently think that the way to prepare for the congress is to organize illegal anti-party units, illegal anti-party meetings . . . And when the party takes decisive measures, not stopping at expulsion, against disorganizers and splitters, the opposition cries: Repressions!

"Yes, the party applies and will continue to apply repressions against disorganizers and splitters, for the party must under no conditions be split before or during the congress. . . .You know that in 1922 Lenin proposed the expulsion of Shliapnikov from the Central Committee not for organizing anti-party printing presses, not for alliances with bourgeois intellectuals, but only because Shliapnikov dared criticize at the party meeting the decisions of the Supreme Economic Council. . . .

"They speak here of the arrests of the disorganizers conducting anti-Soviet activity after their expulsion from the party. Yes, we are arresting them and will continue to arrest them if they do not cease digging under the party and the Soviet government. They say that the history of our party knows no such examples. This is untrue. What about Miasnikov's group? What about the Workers' Truth group? Who does not know that members of these groups were arrested with the direct support of Zinoviev, Trotsky, and Kamenev? Why was it permissible to arrest disorganizers expelled from the party three or four years ago, and why is it not permissible now?"

V

The Tenth Anniversary of the Bolshevist government was approaching. Stalin displayed extraordinary restraint and prudence. The manifesto for the occasion already embodied many measures which the opposition had advanced. While the guillotine worked, Stalin was stealing the enemy's thunder.

November 7, the red-letter day of the Soviet calendar, arrived. Ten years had passed since Lenin and Trotsky had brought the Soviet government into being. Lenin lay embalmed under red bunting. Trotsky was about to be embalmed in a new fashion. The roof of the mausoleum where Lenin rested with a mocking smile on his face was the speakers' stand. Stalin and his suite were there. Trotsky was absent, as were so many of the leaders who had battled all their lives for the seizure of power. They were celebrating in the prison cells that they had restored from the wreckage of an old structure.

History had played a trick on Lenin and Trotsky while they thought that they were playing with history. The tide that they had harnessed seemed to flow in their direction. But, behold, it was all a mirage. It was going its own way, and had landed its helmsmen on a lost reef.

Instead of holding the bear by the head, Lenin and Trotsky had been holding his tail. The bear marched on. For the moment a new trainer was guiding it. But the grizzly did not mind it. It had always been in a cage, and whenever it broke out, it quickly and invariably returned to its barred lair.

The well-trained mass of a million that had been

marching regularly twice a year—on May 1 and November 7—to such parades, more than half of the multitude consisting of salaried government officials and the rest of regimented workers and soldiers in the service of the state, filed by the Stalin stand. Several hundred enthusiasts of the opposition vainly attempted to join in the official procession with banners which carried such legends as: "Let us carry out Lenin's Testament!" The placards were torn out of their hands. The demonstrators were beaten up. Trotsky appeared at a window in his apartment to address a crowd that gathered in the neighborhood. Hoodlums broke up the audience. He went out for a ride through the street. A policeman fired at his automobile. An intoxicated fireman jumped on the running-board and smashed the glass of the car. The pogrom of the opposition began.

A week later, Joffe, former head of the peace delegation at Brest-Litovsk, former Soviet ambassador to Germany and other countries, a confirmed Trotskyist and a sick man, committed suicide. He left a letter addressed to Trotsky in which he described how Stalin's aides in the Central Committee had refused to allow him one thousand dollars to go abroad for medical treatment which the party physicians had considered indispensable. The letter was seized by an agent of the G. P. U. before Trotsky's arrival on the scene. Although it was a private and sealed communication, it was confiscated. Only because of the threat of a widespread scandal, did Trotsky eventually receive a photostatic copy of it.

The demonstrations of November 7 were the last straw. Stalin lost his composure.

Trotsky and Zinoviev were expelled from the ranks of the Bolshevist Party.

Such an act in Soviet Russia usually means, and in the case of leaders always means, throwing the ex-members to the mercy of the elements. Every job in the Soviet Union is controlled by the state dictatorship, directly or indirectly. Without money, without quarters, without employment, Trotsky and Zinoviev were doomed men.

But Stalin was merciful. He would solve the difficulty for them. Exile was in the offing.

The bloodless guillotine now worked faster. In December, the Fifteenth Congress met. It meted out the same severe penalty to a group of seventy-five leaders, including Kamenev, Radek, Rakovsky—the Soviet ambassador to France—Piatakov, who was mentioned in Lenin's testament as one of the six most capable men in the party, and others of equal achievement and rank. The official Bolshevist historian, Popov, records that fifteen hundred other secondary chieftains suffered a similar fate.

Zinoviev and Kamenev immediately lost their bravado and became terror-stricken. The fatal blow was delivered on December 18. The following day they and a group of associates already submitted a repentant statement to the congress in which they acknowledged "their fundamental mistake as really threatening the creation of a second party" and pleaded for restoration in the party. Stalin refused to reinstate them without a lengthy period of probation in the provinces. This clemency which they had won by betraying their followers, this shameful surrender, more than anything else marked the ultimate and irrevocable political death of the two men.

The following month Trotsky was ordered by the G. P. U. to prepare for a long journey. The date was set. Word spread around Moscow that Trotsky was being exiled. A crowd of ten thousand gathered at a near-by railway station and blocked the rails. The G. P. U. had to work rapidly and think even more rapidly. It informed Trotsky that his departure was postponed for forty-eight hours. The following day he and his family were forcibly taken out of their apartment and placed aboard a train. This maneuver averted a bloody demonstration. It was a long journey, indeed. The destination was Central Asia, the old Vierny, where for eight years scores of splendid men and women belonging to non-Bolshevist groups had been languishing in isolation. After twenty-two years, Trotsky was once more in exile. During these years the world had changed much, but Russia was still Russia.

The expelled ex-commissars and several thousand minor officials and party members found themselves behind bars. Many of these when in office had distinguished themselves by unwarranted cruelty, by arbitrary rule. The old trail to Siberia, the subterranean dungeons built by Ivan the Terrible on the White Sea in the north, the casemates constructed by the Romanovs had been generously replenished with their aid during the preceding years.

Justice laughed with vengeance. The men and women who had once fought side by side, under separate banners, for the common ideals of freedom and socialism were awaiting the newcomers in their hopeless and eternal servitude. Old friends who had shared the privation and pain of tsarist tyranny now met again, in the same prisons. They who had forged the ring of iron called the dictatorship of the proletariat found themselves entrapped, isolated, and maltreated by the officers of the government they had established, and bitterly derided by their cellmates and fellow exiles.

VI

Then came the epilogue. Trotsky from his distant place continued by devious means to keep in contact with the other members of the opposition. A year passed. A minority had surrendered to Stalin and secured rehabilitation in different degrees. But the majority stuck to its colors. Through loyal inside channels correspondence was carried on among the courageous remnants. Trotsky and his cohort continued the fight; documents were sent abroad, suppressed facts were gathered and made public in foreign countries by the associates of the banished and imprisoned revolutionists. Trotsky in exile became a boomerang to Stalin.

He was ejected from the Soviet Union by the application of physical force.

The Inquisition grew more insatiable. It saw danger where there was none. It was haunted by specters. It could not remain idle. It formed the habit of regarding every criticism of policy as lese-majesty. Out of the bowels of the decapitated carcass of the opposition, a fresh imp sprang.

Stalin's complete victory was promoted by the aid of the Right flank. Some day, history will determine whether Stalin could have won without the tacit and sometimes active support of Rykov, Bukharin, and Tomsky. It is a question whether the three combined had the strength of one Zinoviev, or his cunning. During the onslaughts of the united opposition. Stalin shielded this company and followed a course which was to their liking, both toward the peasantry and in the international field.

But as soon as the opposition was crushed, Stalin executed a staggering political maneuver. He took over the entire opposition program. The long struggle for a unified plan of economy conducted by Trotsky became a reality under Stalin. Forgotten was the doctrine of stabilization of capitalism. The industrialization program championed by his former opponents, which Stalin had characterized as madness, was now written large on his flag. The alliance with the middle peasant was discarded. The war on the *kulak* that Trotsky had urged for years was declared by Stalin and initiated with impetuous speed. The denounced opportunist affiliations in China and in the Communist International were broken, and the latter witnessed a thorough "cleansing" and a turning to the Left. In a word, the whole ship of state and party policy was veered about in one vigorous swing.

How did Stalin meet the issue of democracy? He proclaimed the already familiar slogan of self-criticism. A drive was launched of terrific intensity, and the newspapers of the country were flooded with shocking revelations of bureaucratic misrule. The campaign was initiated from the top, but it is undeniable that for a while it developed with spontaneity.

The exposures published were turned over to the Central Control Commission for action. Innumerable sore spots were in this manner probed and local cures effected. Corruption was in many cases extirpated. Efficiency was increased, and arbitrary administration in the provinces measurably decreased.

The new Stalin course was dictated by two practical considerations. Stalin knew that the way to kill the seeds of the opposition and to demoralize its ranks—even though they were scattered in exile and prison—was to carry out its projects. Moreover, Stalin realized he had lost his way. He learned from his enemies. He did not scruple to use these lessons against them on all occasions, but he applied them nevertheless. He now had a policy! He acquired it, it is true, but it was a policy nevertheless. Stalin had always felt that he could never originate one. How long the course charted for him by his enemies will last is another question, just as it is a question where Stalin will get his future maps and diagrams. It is not within him to create them. That he knows.

Above all, the outstanding characteristic of Stalin is "a tendency toward hurry," as Lenin put it. He retreats rapidly and advances even more rapidly. He proceeded to put into effect the new policy with a precipitancy, a violence, a crudeness, and a wholesaleness which was dizzying. He ordered socialism built even as Peter the Great had commanded St. Petersburg to rise from the swamps along the Neva.

The Right recusancy increased in proportion to the tempo of Stalin's general offensive on the political and economic front, the focal point of which was directed against the *kulak*. In the existing terrorist régime, the middle peasants also suffered from the attack. Hundreds of thousands of homesteads were confiscated, and their owners forced either into state or collective farms or into labor battalions. The scenes of military communism were reenacted in the villages with the aid of armed detachments, except that the purpose was distinctly different.

In the course of the campaign for the promotion of the Five-Year Plan, which is treated elsewhere in this volume, the Right opposition went through all the familiar stages of running the gantlet of the Stalin machine. Its leaders were charged with all the sins against Leninism, with opportunism, Menshevism. They were called saboteurs of the socialist construction, friends of the *kulak,* bureaucrats who ignored the needs of the masses, strike-breakers, obstructors of the rocket flight to a new industrial era.

VII

One by one, the chief actors in the play for power were eliminated from the stage by Stalin. That process of lopping-off which he had repudiated earlier in the performance now became an operation that was indelibly identified in the minds of the people of Russia and of the outside world with the strong arm of Stalin, the man of steel.

Only two years had gone since Stalin, at the height of the conflict with the united opposition, exclaimed at the party congress:

"Why, then, all this indignation against Bukharin? What do they really want of Bukharin? They are out for his blood! That is what Comrade Zinoviev demands when he returns to the Bukharin question with so much acrimony. You want Bukharin's blood? Well, you won't get it!"

Now Bukharin, Rykov, and Tomsky were in the way, and Stalin was after their blood. They presented no such peril as the first enemies, but they were a disrupting influence nevertheless. They would have to go to the guillotine. Stalin gave his reasons for the new slaughter at the Sixteenth Congress held in the summer of 1930. He said of the Right heretics:

"They chattered and shouted about the 'fatal' character of the party policy, the 'probable catastrophe' in the Soviet Union, the necessity of 'saving' the country from the party and its leadership, and so forth. . . .

"We had first of all to put an end to the relics of Trotskyism in the party and the survivals of the Trotskyist theory. We had long ago smashed and thrown out the Trotskyist group as an opposition.

"The essence of Trotskyism consists . . . in the denial of the necessity of iron discipline in the party, in recognition of the freedom of factional groupings, in recognition of the necessity of constituting a Trotskyist party. For Trotskyism, the Communist Party of the Soviet Union must be not a united and single militant party, but a collection of groups and factions, each with their own central organizations, press, and so forth. And what does this mean? It means proclaiming the freedom of political factions within the party. It means that, following the freedom of political groupings in the party, must come the freedom of political parties in the country, *i.e.,* bourgeois democracy. . . .

"Matters are somewhat otherwise with the question of Right opportunism, at the head of which there stand or stood Comrades Bukharin, Rykov, and Tomsky. It cannot be said that the Right deviators do not recognize the possibility of building socialism in the Soviet Union. No, they recognize it. . . .

"The Right deviators do not take the standpoint of the need of forming a new party, and this is yet a further distinction between them and the Trotskyists. . . . Precisely because the Right deviation reflects the resistance of the principal elements of the dying classes, the Right deviation is the principal danger of the moment in our party.

"That is why the party thought is necessary to open a resolute and irreconcilable struggle against the Right deviation. . . . Our task is to continue for the future our irreconcilable struggle *on two fronts,* both against the Left, representing *petit-bourgeois radicalism,* and against the Right, representing *petit-bourgeois liberalism."*

Stalin then outlined a series of demands of the Right leaders to repudiate openly and honestly their "former" views, holding that such an act was not degrading to a self-respecting revolutionist. He continued:

"Is it not a fact that these demands were already once put to them in November, 1929, at the plenary session of the Central Committee? Is it not a fact that they, the former leaders of the Right opposition, accepted these demands at that time, repudiated their line, and recognized its mistaken character?"

After blaming the three Right chiefs for failing

to carry out their pledges and for utilizing the intervening months for political maneuvers, Stalin called attention to their changed attitude at the congress:

"Whence comes such a change and how can it be explained? It is to be explained apparently by the menacing circumstances which have been created in the party for the former leaders of the Right opposition. It is not to be surprised at, therefore, that the congress should form the definite opinion that unless you squeeze these people, you will get nothing out of them."

The squeezing was done by the guillotine. Step by step, it did its bloodless grinding. A holy war was declared against the "deviators," and the G. P. U., on the one hand, the Inquisition of the Central Control Commission on the other, performed their functions, decapitating hundreds of official heads.

Bukharin was gagged. He was dismissed from the office of editor-in-chief of the Pravda, lost his party rank, and was expelled from the executive of the Communist International.

Tomsky, the head of the trade-union federation comprising more than ten million members, soon enough learned what the presidency of such a body under a proletarian dictatorship meant. He was "beheaded" without resistance, and exiled.

The fact of Tomsky's removal was not made known for weeks. The trade unions did not learn until afterward that their president had been ousted and banished. A worse fate befell the prime minister of the Russian Soviet Federation, the main unit in the Union, Syrtsov, who together with several high communists organized toward the close of 1930 a new opposition group to Stalin. The leader and his associates were promptly put in jail.

Rykov, who since Lenin's death, had been prime minister, was removed from his exalted seat. His post was handed over to Molotov, who had loyally served as aide-de-camp to Secretary-General Stalin for eight years.

VIII

Thirty-two years had elapsed since the expelled seminarist in Tiflis had surreptitiously read and disseminated the flaming proclamation of the First Congress.

What a canvas and what an epoch!

The cobbler's widow who had dreamed of her boy as a priest in the service of the state church was still praying to her God and ikons—but in the manor of the former imperial viceroy. Her son, wearing the invisible robes of a dictator, was presiding in the plebeianized Kremlin throneroom over the high conclave of a thousand votaries.

Along the road from the Tiflis haunts to the tribune of the Sixteenth Congress lay the ruins of grand dream-castles, rose fantastic visions come true, thrones and crowns littered the tracks; dark catacombs and fragments of bombs marked the fields of desperate combats; prison cells, exile, escapes, freedom, insurrection, terror, fallen idols, and a sainted prophet were monuments to an encrusted idealism.

Three revolutions had come and gone. Three great wars had been fought in the world. Mountains of humanity had risen and fallen. A winding trail in the background showed a long line of marchers from transient glories to oblivion. In the race for the elusive but undying will-o'-the-wisp one man won out: Stalin.

As he stood there, surrounded by two thousand servile eyes, applauded by two thousand strong hands, satisfied that he had at last subdued all dissension, rooted out all schism, he gave utterance to words which summed up his ascent with a sublime naïveté—the sublime irony of which could not but escape him:

"Never has the party been so united around its Central Committee as it is today.

"All are obliged to recognize now that today our party is more united and single-minded than ever before. . . .

"There is no longer an organized and well-defined opposition, capable of putting forward its own particular policy as against the general policy of the party. . . .

"At our congress, there not only proved to be no more organized opposition, but there was not even a small group, there were not even individual comrades who thought fit to come out on the platform and say that the party policy was wrong."

The great congregation was hushed. Bucolic was the idyl of unanimity. As the shepherd surveyed his flock, he observed with pride that no wayward sheep were to be seen on the horizon. The obstreperous lambs had been removed from the fold, and nothing could mar the tranquil, pastoral scene.

And then the high priest had a thought. He remembered *that* testament of Lenin's. . . .

He delivered the valediction:

"Lenin used to say that a policy of principle is the only correct policy.

"We have emerged victorious from the struggle against deviations because we have been honestly and consistently carrying out *this* testament of Lenin's. . . .

"If we want to be victorious, we must continue to bear Lenin's banner on high, guarding its purity and spotlessness. . . ."

(*Loud and prolonged applause, passing into a general ovation. All rise to the strains of the Red Hosanna—the "Internationale."*)

CHAPTER THIRTEEN

DICTATOR OR BOSS?

I

IN the fall of 1930, after Premier Rykov, of the Soviet Union, had been silently ousted from office and Premier Syrtsov, of the Russian Soviet Federation, quietly lodged in jail, Stalin was asked by an interviewer how he regarded the general conception of himself as a dictator. Stalin laughed. Just another bourgeois misrepresentation of the Bolshevist power. The capitalist ignorance of Soviet principles was appalling.

"It is just very funny," he replied with a grin, and dismissed the subject.

The Russian people, too, think that the question is "just very funny." Under the dictatorship of the proletariat, it is rather difficult to interview the people. What they think of their leader is partly divulged by the Stalin lore which has grown up since his rise and around the barrier that separates the Kremlin from the masses.

Under a dictatorial government, this lore is at least as revealing of the chief of state as his own thoughts on the people are of him. When Lenin was alive and active, the popular saying ran:

"Lenin trusts Stalin, but Stalin trusts nobody."

Following the destruction of the Trotsky-Zinoviev opposition, during the prevailing stalemate in the economic policies toward the peasantry and the industrialization plans, a story gained currency in Moscow on the crisis in the government. A national contest was announced for the selection of a new name for the Kremlin. After long deliberations, the prize-winning title was: "Stalin's Blind Alley."

When Stalin became the undisputed leader and the Kremlin was filled with functionaries brought from the Caucasus, for it is undeniable that Stalin's patronage has caused the installation of a multitude of his countrymen in high office, the story was told of a Georgian bootblack sitting at the entrance to the Kremlin. A customer appeared and extended his foot for a shoe-shine. The bootblack refused with the remark:

"I have no time to bother with shoe-shines. I am waiting here for a political appointment."

In Stalin's native land, in Georgia, the folk humor has been expressed in an anecdote in which a teacher asks a pupil in the classroom to name the famous rulers of Georgia.

"Vakhtang the Wolf-Lion, David the Renovator, Queen Tamara, and Soso the Great," comes the answer.

"Why Soso 'the Great'?" demands the teacher.

"Because Soso was the first to annex Russia to Georgia."

During the conflict with Trotsky, it was generally known that Lenin's widow Krupskaya sided with him. She tried to persuade Stalin not to exile Trotsky. A story given wide circulation was a description of an imaginary conversation that Krupskaya had with Stalin in which she denounced his behavior. Stalin replied with his characteristic rudeness:

"Look here, old hag, if you don't shut your mouth and keep your nose out of this, I shall appoint a new widow to Lenin!"

The feeling that the people entertain for Stalin is best illustrated by a tale recently circulated in the Soviet capital. A man was walking across one of the bridges of the Moscow River when he suddenly heard the cries of a drowning person, "Help! Help!" He jumped into the water and rescued the man. Gratefully the latter turned to his rescuer and said:

"Tell me what you want. You can have anything you wish."

"I don't want a thing," replied the savior.

"But you don't know who I am. I am Stalin."

"In that case, I have a favor to ask of you. Please don't tell anyone that I saved your life."

When a delegation of British capitalists visited Russia in 1929 to inquire into commercial opportunities, the popular imagination gave its account of the meeting of the head of the British group with Stalin.

"What security can you offer to concessionaires?" asked the Briton.

"We have a great deal of wealth in the ground," replied Stalin. "We have oil, iron, coal, and gold."

"True, but what have you above ground?"

"Above ground, we have a strong, well-disciplined Communist Party and a splendid Youth organization."

"I am sorry we cannot do any business, Mr. Stalin," said the Englishman after a moment of reflection. "We could, if it were the other way around."

As against these illuminating inventions of the popular mind, there is a story for which some authenticity is claimed.* During the civil war, one winter day Stalin reviewed the troops on the Petrograd front. He noticed that the soldiers did not greet him with any enthusiasm. One soldier was stamping his feet impatiently. His compressed lips indicated silence. Stalin asked the man why he was so sullen.

"I've been standing here for hours," answered the soldier.

"So have I," said Stalin.

"Yes," retorted the Red Army man, "but you have decent boots." And he pointed to his own feet, clad only in straw sandals. According to one version, Stalin removed his boots, gave them to the soldier, and took his sandals, which he wore all winter. Another version has it that the adventure ended in Stalin's having pneumonia.

In this incident, there is an approximation to truth. It was, of course, unnecessary for him to wear sandals all winter, as it was not difficult for him to secure immediately another pair of boots upon reaching the city. But Stalin is quite capable of such an act on the spur of the moment.

In the spring of 1928, a parade of communist athletic organizations was held in the Red Square in Moscow. The exercises had been scheduled for half past eleven, but in accord with army customs everybody was on hand by eleven. "The boys began killing time," writes Paul Scheffer, "with one of

* Three American writers who have visited Soviet Russia report independently this story. Of them, only Jerome Davis, one of the first to interview Stalin and his mother, tells it as an historical fact. I found no authority for it in my research on Stalin.

the sports young people in Russia most enjoy—girl-tossing. (A number of young men throw a girl high in the air and catch her as she comes down.) All over the square one could see bright-colored shirts, skirts, bloomers sailing skyward and falling again. Stalin was to review the parade. As usual he came late. When he appeared, neither fanfares from the bands, nor a verse of the 'International,' nor the warnings of messengers sent hither and thither, could put an end to the girl-tossing. . . . Stalin stood on the balustrade of Lenin's tomb. Nobody noticed. Nobody was interested in him."

The significant feature of it all was that Stalin did not care. If he is a dictator, he is not of the obtrusive conventional variety. He does not believe in hero-worship and does not practice it. The trappings of power do not tempt him.

II

Stalin is a remarkable imitation of Lenin. Consciously he took over Lenin's ideas of leadership. He had studied his master for years. He suppressed himself in order to acquire the Lenin habits.

Stalin does not seek honors. He loathes pomp. He is averse to public displays. He could have all the nominal regalia in the chest of a great state. But he prefers the background. He is in that respect a replica of the type of political boss which the United States has developed since the Civil War. His omnipotence is execised from an inner office and not from a grandstand. He is the perfect inheritor of the individual Lenin paternalism. No other associate of

Lenin was endowed with that characteristic. Stalin is the stern father of a family, the dogmatic pastor of a flock. He is a boss with this difference: his power is not used for personal aggrandizement.

Moreover, Stalin is a boss with an education. Notwithstanding general impressions, Stalin is a widely-informed and well-read person. He lacks culture, but he absorbs knowledge. He is rough toward his enemies, but he learns from them. Yet he is primarily a politician, and not a statesman.

Stalin has on several occasions expressed his ideas of leadership. In 1925, he was asked to contribute a piece to a volume commemorating Sverdlov, who was the first president of the Soviet Republic. Stalin seized the opportunity to write something which was a masked thrust at Trotsky and at the same time is a revelation of Stalin, the leader:

"There are people, leaders of the proletariat, about whom the press makes no noise, perhaps because they do not like to make a noise about themselves, but who are nevertheless the life-blood and the genuine heads of the revolutionary movement. Sverdlov belonged to this category.

"An organizer to the marrow of his bones, an organizer by nature, habit, revolutionary training, instincts, an organizer in all of his seething activities —such was Sverdlov.

"What does it mean to be a leader and organizer when the proletariat is in power? It does not mean merely selecting assistants, recruiting an office force, issuing orders. To be a leader and organizer in our conditions, means first to know your workers, to be able to size up their qualities and defects, to know how to approach them; and, second, to be able to distribute them so that each will feel that he is in his place, able to give his maximum to the revolution.

"The general direction followed should serve as an expression and realization of the idea in the name of which it is pursued."

In his eulogy of Lenin, shortly after the death of the master, Stalin further amplified his conception of leadership and derided the "aristocratic attitude" of certain political chiefs. He declared:

"The leaders of a party cannot fail to hold precious the opinion of the majority of their party. The majority is a force which a leader cannot disregard. Lenin understood that as much as any other party leader. But Lenin never became a prisoner of the majority, especially when that majority lacked a foundation of principles. There were moments in the history of our party when the opinion of the majority or the trenchant interests of the party came into conflict with the basic interests of the proletariat. On such occasions Lenin, without hesitating, would resolutely take the side of principle against the majority of the party. Moreover, he did not fear at such moments to take issue, literally all alone, against everybody. . . .

"Theoreticians and party leaders who know the history of nations, who have studied the history of revolutions from beginning to end, are sometimes seized by an indecent ailment. This disease may be called fear of the masses, lack of faith in the creative abilities of the masses. It is on this foundation that there sometimes arises a certain aristocratic attitude on the part of the leaders toward the masses. . . . The fear that the elements might get beyond control, that the masses might 'break things too much,' the desire to play the rôle of nurse, to teach the masses from books but to learn nothing from the masses—these are the foundations of that aristocratic attitude.

"Lenin was the complete opposite of such leaders. I do not know of another revolutionist who so deeply believed in the creative powers of the proletariat and in the revolutionary aptitude of its class instinct. I do not know of another revolutionist who could flay so mercilessly the smug critics 'of the chaos of revolution' and of the 'bacchanalia of self-constituted actions of the masses.' I remember how in the course of a conversation, replying to the observation of a certain comrade that 'after the revolution there must be established normal order,' Lenin sarcastically remarked: 'It's a pity that people who want to be revolutionists forget that the most normal order in history is the order of revolution.'

"Hence, Lenin's contemptuous attitude toward all those who looked down on the masses and tried to teach them according to the book. Hence, Lenin's attitude, his tireless preaching: learn from the masses, analyze their actions, carefully study the practical experience of the mass struggle."

Another function of leadership was outlined by Stalin in a speech before the Moscow communist organization in 1928. "To sit at the helm," declared Stalin, "and keep watch, seeing nothing until some calamity overtakes us—this is no kind of leadership. Bolshevism does not interpret leadership in this way.

To lead means to foresee; and to foresee, comrades, is not always so simple. It is one thing when a dozen other leading comrades keep watch and notice defects in our work; but the working masses do not want to keep watch, or cannot do so; they therefore do not notice the defects. Then there is every chance that one may miss something, fail to see everything."

The perennial rebel, eternal militancy and vigilance, the avoidance of all deteriorating personal influences—these form another element of Stalin's conception of leadership. "The old Bolsheviks," he observed once, "enjoy respect not because they are veterans, but because they are at the same time people who do not grow old and who stay ever new as revolutionists."

Stalin's principles and prerequisites of leadership are: organizing and executive ability, an unostentatious and plebeian conduct, foresight, unflinching courage of one's convictions, a never-aging spirit of rebellion; faith in the masses, anticipating their moods and wishes, and learning from them as well as their enemies.

III

Like Lenin, Stalin's method of learning is invisible. He does not want the masses to speak. He seeks to learn their mood. Sometimes he succeeds. He will stay up late in the night reading letters of complaint from peasants or workers in the provinces. He will converse with some ordinary comrade, a visitor from a remote section of the country, and interview him. Stalin is, like Lenin, an acute interviewer. Even in the case of foreign correspondents and callers, he gets more information from them than they from him. He endeavors to keep his ear to the ground. His uncanny sense will suggest to him an idea which his interlocutor was never aware of in relating some incident that occurred in Odessa or Irkutsk.

Stalin's notion of and approach toward learning is typically paternal and didactic. "To build," he wrote for a popular weekly magazine in 1928, "one must possess knowledge, one must master science, one must learn. Learn persistently, patiently. Learn from everybody, from your enemies, from your friends, but particularly from your enemies.

"We are facing a fortress—science, with its numerous branches of knowledge. This fortress we must capture at all costs."

This noble sentiment betrays the primitive aspect of Stalin's viewpoint on acquiring knowledge. Science is not a development of free, creative, untrammeled human life. Science is not an offspring of limitless thought. It is a fortress. It is a completed entity. Hence the battle-cry: Find out all the secrets and capture it.

Yet Stalin does not brag of his own learning. He does not pretend to be the originator of doctrines. He denounces any claim on the part of friends or foes of his having a theory of his own. His doctrine is Leninism—of course Stalin's interpretation of Leninism, for to him there is, and can be, no other. When Trotsky campaigned against him with the ammunition of Stalin's theory of socialism in one country, Stalin produced strings of quotations from Lenin's writings since 1915 which destroyed the allegation. Stalin accused Trotsky of setting up the theory as a disguised method of attacking him, and said:

"Stalin has nothing to do with it; there can be no talk of a Stalin 'theory'; Stalin never pretended to something new in the realm of theory; he always tried to facilitate the complete triumph of Leninism in our party in spite of the revisionist puffings of Trotsky. . . . Trotsky's declaration of a Stalin 'theory' is a maneuver, a trick, a cowardly and awkward trick, calculated to disguise his struggle with the Leninist theory of the victory of socialism in individual countries."

But after all it is the practice of Stalin's power that decides whether there are such things as Stalin theories. They may not be momentous philosophic discoveries, but their impact is felt daily by the masses as well as the advanced elements in the country.

The rank and file of the great communist army does not know what Stalin's course will be tomorrow. There was, for instance, the case of "The A B C of Communism," a popular exposition that had for ten years been used in all the schools of the Union and had been sold in millions of copies. Through the Communist International it had been translated into twenty languages and published in as many countries. But then the authors, Bukharin and Preobrajensky, were found guilty of heresy. The first was a Right non-conformist, the second a Left dissenter. The authors had written it long before any schism developed, four years before Lenin died.

Stalin had the book taken out of circulation. A

new textbook was written and published anonymously. The first admittedly contained no heresy. Apparently Stalin's theory was not in conformity with that of "The A B C of Communism."

And then there was the case of the Young Communist paper whose editors violently attacked Rykov and Bukharin during the early stages of the conflict. But just then Stalin was maneuvering for peace with the Right leaders. A telephone message to the bewildered editors dried up their pens. From that moment on they would have to anticipate Stalin's theories.

It is, of course, possible for a dictator to learn, but is it possible for the masses to teach him? He will learn the things he desires to learn. That is imposed by the character of a dictatorship, by the character of a terrorized country, and by the nature of a people such as inhabits Eurasia.

Stalin scans the horizons from the dark. He is surrounded by walls of fear. He can perhaps penetrate them to a certain degree with his line of conduct. But the people never can. Their light can never reach into his inner sanctum. Hence, the lifelessness within the body of the vanguard, the forward-looking party. Its organ, the Pravda, has under Stalin become singularly thin and narrow in scope. Yet to it a million members must look for guidance.

There is a story in vogue in Moscow of a communist being asked for his opinion on a news event. He answers:

"I am sorry. But I haven't yet read today's Pravda."

IV

Is Stalin a dictator?

Stalin holds no conspicuous official post in the Soviet government. He is not president of the republic. He is not the prime minister of the state. His membership in the council of labor and defense, a military-economic organization created by Lenin during the civil war, dates back to 1918 and constitutes his only formal connection with the government. Yet this council, which is in the nature of a coordinating war-preparedness board, is not administratively related to the Soviet system and the president of the republic, Kalinin, is not even a member of it.

Stalin's power admittedly rests in his position as secretary-general of the Communist Party of the Soviet Union. His direction of the Communist International is incidental to that position.

Is the undisputed leader of a monopolistic party built like an army, in which not even the colonels and generals can question the chief command, a party which exercises unlimited power and enforces an avowed dictatorship, a dictator?

Stalin repudiates the charge, as due to ignorance or slander, when speaking for the consumption of the "bourgeois" world. But the record of his career and his writings for the communist following tell another story.

What is the essence of the dictatorship of the proletariat? Stalin answers by quoting Lenin: "The dictatorship of the proletariat must be a state that embodies a new kind of democracy, *for* the proletarians and the dispossessed." It was Stalin who italicized the "for" in this maxim from his master.

The dictatorship is therefore a rule for the proletariat, and not of the proletariat; for the masses, and not of the masses.

"The dictatorship of the proletariat," writes Stalin, "is the rule of the proletariat over the bourgeoisie, a rule unrestricted by law, based upon force, enjoying the sympathy and the support of the laboring and exploited masses."

It is a rule based not upon the expressed will of the masses, but upon their assumed sympathy; founded not upon the articulate beliefs of the toilers, but upon their presumed interests and wishes. Moreover, the contradiction in Stalin's credo is obvious, for if the proletariat rules over the bourgeoisie it does not need "the sympathy and support" of the proletariat—the laboring and exploited masses.

What is the instrument by which this "benevolent" dictatorship is applied? It is the party, the self-constituted vanguard of the proletariat. This chosen race, according to Stalin, "effectively realizes the dictatorship of the proletariat. It does this, however, not directly but with the help of the trade unions, and through the instrumentality of the Soviets and their ramifications. . . .

"In the Soviet Union, in the land where the dictatorship of the proletariat is in force, no important political or organizational problem is ever decided by our Soviets and other mass organizations without directives from the party."

The party, then, is the governing body. The Soviet system, the various labor corporations, all subservient to the party, are merely blind tools in the hands of the supreme authority. What, then, is their purpose? Stalin replies: to test the sympathy of the masses and to serve as "belts" in transmitting the rule of the self-appointed dictatorship. He writes:

"Without these 'belts' a stable dictatorship would be impossible." And again he quotes Lenin: "The dictatorship cannot be effectively realized without 'belts' to transmit power from the vanguard to the mass of the advanced class, and from this to the mass of workers."

But how does the party generator of power function? It is admittedly constructed on a hierarchical plan. The theory is that the hierarchy elevates the hierarch, who is Stalin. But the fact is that the hierarch makes the hierarchy. Why? Because he has the entire state system, with all its lucrative and greed-arousing elements, at his command.

Stalin at the head of the Bolshevist Party struggling for power would not be a dictator. Stalin as the leader of an exclusive corps installed in office could not but be a dictator. The "plums" of authority, the vast patronage his post controls, would be enough to corrupt any civilized country beyond early recovery. In a backward and primitive continent like Eurasia, the system inevitably breeds subserviency, servility, arbitrary rule, and all the other inescapable fungi of dictatorship.

In the West, the power generated at the center is derived from the fuel of more or less popular will, transmitted by somewhat obstructed yet direct and still throbbing conduits. In the Soviet Union, the very opposite is true. The power is not developed outside, but within. It is originated in the dynamo of the party, which, under Stalin, is Stalin.

The Soviet government is but a dead machine hitched to the live engine of the Communist Party. The party machine, in its turn, is nothing but a system of bureaucratic control under the direct and vigilant hand of its sole "boss"—the secretary-general of the Central Committee, Stalin.

V

How does the dictatorship operate?

At the apex of the extraordinary pyramid of power stands the secretary-general, Stalin. He has two young aides, Molotov and Kaganovitch, who respectively run the Political Bureau and the Organizational Bureau of the Central Committee. The three form the omnipotent secretariat. Both assistants are appointees of Stalin. Originally rubber-stamps in the hand of their chief, they have, during the years of office under him, risen to certain eminence derived from their positions and not their past revolutionary achievements. Neither of the two is distinguished by brilliance of thought, originality of mind, or independence of spirit. Both are capable executives.

The Political Bureau decides and passes upon every important and many unimportant questions of national and international policy, political as well as economic. The Organizational Bureau distributes the immense patronage which the ruling party and the huge government machinery possesses. The members of the two bureaus are all political creatures of Stalin. These twenty-five men are in reality the general staff with which Stalin operates, in the diplomatic service, in the G. P. U., in the Communist International, in the press, in finance, in the administration of justice, in the industrialization efforts, in the collectivization campaign, in the inquisitorial hunt for heresy.

By a system of interlocking directorates, each of these men holds half a dozen responsible posts. They are the backbone of the Central Committee, they are the judges of the Central Control Commission, they are the whips of the most supreme of all the august party bodies—the annual congress which elects the secretary-general.

According to the party constitution, this congress should meet every year. From 1917 to 1925 inclusive, nine congresses were held. From 1926 to 1930 inclusive, a period of five years, only two such congresses have been held under Stalin. This is not a tendency. It is a system.

The twenty-five controllers-general make the opinion of the congresses, mold that perfect unanimity of the one million party members who nominally exercise the dictatorship, but who actually hold state office or party rank which in varying degree affords them privileges, priorities, comforts, and protection denied to others.

The general staff derives its opinions as well as its directions from Stalin. Dissidence makes one liable to the bloodless guillotine, to excommunication. Accord makes for favor with the chief, for more power, and for that seeming security and durability of the whole pyramid with which the lives of its members are so organically identified.

This pyramid is admittedly not set upon a broad base, but is balanced on an inverted plan—the delicate and somewhat hazy system of gaging popular sympathy and support. The apex of the Stalin pyramid of power rests upon the ground; its lower layers are vaguely lost in the clouds.

Is Stalin a dictator? Like the mythical Atlas, he carries the world on his shoulders. That Stalin knows. But he does not regard himself as a dictator. It is unquestionable that his attitude defies the conventional idea of an absolutist ruler. He is not and does not want to be a Nero. He is not and does not seek to be a Napoleon. He has no ambitions of gain. Worldly prowess is alien to his nature. He believes that he is helping create a new order from which some day all happiness will automatically flow to mankind. He believes that it is imperative to traverse a road of untold travail to reach that ideal. The vivisection of 160,000,000 people today he justifies as a sacrifice necessary to bring bliss to double that number tomorrow. To Stalin, only Lenin has charted the right course through the darkness to light. And Stalin is adamant in his belief that he alone understands Lenin's cosmography correctly.

VI

With a pen dipped in his own blood, a young Russian who was raised since the revolution and served as a Bolshevik in the Soviet diplomatic field, S. Dmitrievsky, recently wrote a book which is a cry of agony. The author belongs to the group of "apostates" who under the Stalin régime gave up their affiliation with Bolshevism. His estimate of Stalin is in many ways remarkable.

"I do not know Stalin sufficiently well to have a strong personal opinion of him," he writes. "But I do know that all those who have come in contact with him intimately hold that he is a very decent man. He lives like an ascetic. He works like a giant. To govern Russia sitting on bayonets, and on the shoulders of an unreliable bureaucracy, is not easy. Iron will is needed to bear the ceaseless inner struggle with those near him, as well as with the population of a vast country, and to mark that course which extends a new lease of life to Stalin and his order, and which bars the way to the next pretender. There are many hands reaching for the scepter of Russian autocrat—for Stalin, if not literally, nevertheless holds this scepter. And these hands are all sinuous, their muscles are strong, there is ample blood on them, and it is not a light affair to keep them off. . . .

"Enormous will-power, great experience, clear thinking are needed for the job—regardless of the historical correctness or incorrectness of the course taken. Unquestionably Stalin is greater than all his competitors in the struggle for power.

"That he has remained so long in the shadows made a deep impression in the country with eastern conceptions, where despots have always kept themselves behind thick walls. This created for him a mysteriousness. It gave rise to a belief among sincere people that Stalin seeks nothing for himself. But he has nothing to seek, for he has everything. He has the real power. He understood the secret of power: not the eulogies of admirers, not the enthusiasm of the mob. He knows that tomorrow that mob may cry: 'Crucify him!' that tomorrow his friends may desert him.

"Power rests on bayonets, in an obedient machine, in managing people, in playing on their desires, in a political police, in a system of country-wide espionage and strangulation. That it is possible to govern by moral and intellectual persuasion Stalin does not believe.

"Stalin knows that the majority of his collaborators hate him. But he suffers them, works with them, relies on them, for he holds them in his grip, and he knows that in spite of their hatred they will bend before him and carry out his will. That they will denounce him behind his back is of no account to him.

"In every public address, Stalin shows clearly what he wants. He does not like to make people think, and he saves them the trouble. I believe that in time it will be recognized that Stalin as a writer and thinker was an uncommon man.

"It is said that Stalin has no original thoughts, that he steals others' ideas. Even if it were so, it takes ability to sift all kinds of opinions and organize the selections in the course of a great political game—all the time hanging over an abyss, maneuvering between shoals and reefs. Stalin is not a theoretician. He is a promoter endowed with great intuition.

"He is an oriental statesman of the type of government where one or a few primitive minds think for the even more primitive mass. Without nerves, without sweep, he is a terrible and dominating force, appearing often not as a human being but as a machine.

"Stalin is a great nationalist, not of the future Russia, but of communist Eurasia, the Russia of today. If you were present at a session of the Central Committee during the reading of some editorial from an English paper telling of the danger of the Soviet Union to Europe, you could hear Stalin exclaim triumphantly: 'Aha, at last they understand us!'

"Does Stalin believe in world revolution? He measures everything with money and bayonets. Once there is enough money, a sufficiency of strong bayonets, there will be a world revolution as a result of the victories of our armies and our gold. The little skirmishes which the Communist International now stages are but insignificant rehearsals for the impending tragedy. The great tragedy will come when our troops, the hordes of Eurasia, enter Berlin and Paris. Then Europe will cease being Europe and become part of Eurasia. Such is Stalin's faith in world revolution. He will present it to Europe on the tip of a Russian-Asiatic bayonet. And he will surrender to no western proletariat the hegemony of the revolution, for in the depths of his soul he hates and despises the proletariat of the West as much as he does its bourgeoisie.

"Is Stalin honest? Does he think of the needs and welfare of the people? I am deeply convinced that he aims at the happiness of the people, and sincerely regards himself as the incarnation of the toilers of the country. But what of it? Did not the duke of Alba think that he labored for the people of the Netherlands and was he not surprised when they rose in rebellion? And Nicholas I, the Iron Tsar, did he not regard himself as the people's ruler and was he not bewildered when the peasants revolted?

"Nicholas I, too, attempted to build a state isolated from the rest of the world. It was, in a sense, an attempt to build 'socialism in one country,' in any event, a paternalistic system of state capitalism. How did it all end? With military defeat, the collapse of the whole structure.

"Did Nicholas I think of the people? Of course. He regarded himself as their first servant. He worked from morning until night. In the evening he would literally have to be taken out of his stiff uniform. In his own way, he loved the country and the people. But he brought the people to destitution, the country to ruin. And he fell victim to his own policies. On the day when the news arrived of the collapse of his armies in the Crimean War, he took poison. And with him crashed his entire messianic system of the promised land, of the chosen people, of the supreme state.

"Is it not, after all, an academic question, whether Stalin is honest or not? Of what avail is it that he does not steal, has no mistresses, indulges in no orgies, works hard? It does not make the people's burden lighter. In the end, it is how the people live, and not how Stalin does that counts.

"Stalin is a victim of the strangling centralized bureaucracy which he himself has created. One recalls the horror with which Nicholas I exclaimed: 'Who said that I was the ruler of the country? The country is governed by my bureaucrats!' So far Stalin is the ruler; he sets the general course. But the basic force surrounding him consists of piratical adventurers, careerists who are waiting for Stalin to go, so that they may become the undivided masters of the land. Stalin restrains them. . . .

"Stalin is a blind power, with convictions. There is much in him that resembles Robespierre, with the difference that the latter was a European, Stalin is an Asiatic. He has tightened the reins of the dictatorship to the extreme, and is entangled in them.

"If Stalin's régime of economic and political terror is for the happiness of humanity, I do not want that happiness. I am suffocating in the atmosphere he has created. I cannot and will not live and think while my head rests on the block of the guillotine."

VII

Stalin laughs at being called a dictator. He has fashioned history. How history will ultimately fashion his handiwork it is too early to determine. But already one can say that Stalin is not an accident, one can perceive that he is a link in the chain of the life of Eurasia, that he has summed up a deep past. Stalin has created the post of dictator which the development of Russia has impelled him to create. In his seat of might, Stalin may sincerely laugh at the cry of his being a dictator. But when he vacates that seat, it will be ready for the man who will not laugh.

CHAPTER FOURTEEN

THE HUMAN STALIN

I

THE erect figure of a man of more than medium height, with iridescent, yellowish dark eyes, thick black hair, a furrowed low forehead, a curling mustache half concealing an ironic smile, a heavy and slightly curved long nose, a stubborn squarish chin, an olive skin—this is Stalin at the age of fifty-one.

A metallic, colorless voice, a speech that betrays a non-Russian accent, an absence of flourish, a restrained laugh, a tendency to remain inconspicuous—such are the features of Stalin on the public platform. As an orator, he has none of the conventional attributes. He is not florid; he does not sweep the audience with enthusiasm. Like Lenin, he conveys a sense of compressed energy, of reserved will-power. He is not magnetic, but he impresses one immediately.

Like his great predecessor, Stalin relies upon repetition. He drives his points home with the force of a hammer. His method is that of persuasion by reiteration, which makes resistance on the part of simple minds impossible. He uses elementary words and rehearses them so frequently that they remain pegged in the heads of his listeners.

When sitting on a public stage and watching the multitude, Stalin will as often as not look bored and sometimes embarrassed. Lacking the prestige that Lenin enjoyed, and knowing it, he does not strive for theatrical popularity.

Stalin differs from all the other outstanding leaders of the Russian Revolution in his sense of humor. Lenin possessed it, but he expressed it only occasionally in a phrase or a metaphor. Stalin alone can tell a story. He breaks up the serious dissertations on economics, his keynote speeches at political conferences, with an anecdotal illustration that establishes intimacy with the audience and relaxes the frequently high tension.

Stalin the story-teller is not so well-known to the outside world. On the Russian political scene it is a new phenomenon to have a revolutionary leader talk anything but the gravest kind of high politics. In this respect, Stalin is related to the familiar type of American politician.

The mystery of Stalin is one of the fictions of our day. When Lenin and Trotsky were at their height, they, too, true to Bolshevist traditions, never flaunted their domestic life. For years the names of Trotsky's, Zinoviev's, Kalinin's, Rykov's wives, and their domestic lives, remained unknown to the wide world. In the case of Lenin's wife, the exception was due to the fact that Krupskaya was a prominent revolutionist in her own right. No Bolshevist biographies ever dealt with the non-political pursuits of the leaders' careers.

Stalin has merely lived up to this tradition. The ethics of the party in this regard are applicable to all the prominent figures in the Soviet Union.

Wearing high boots and dressed in a greenish

raincoat, worn over the universal khaki jacket in vogue in Russia, his head covered with a cap set low over his face, Stalin in the spring and summer cannot be distinguished in appearance from thousands of other Soviet officials. In the winter a fur cap and a heavy army coat replace the customary outfit. Stalin's wardrobe does not include any neckties.

Stalin works hard, but he also knows how to relax. The general impression notwithstanding, Stalin is fond of sports and recreation. He hunts, fishes, and reads a great deal.

Stalin's education is broad and continuous. When he was in prison in Baku, he studied Esperanto. A couple of years ago, he took up the study of English, which he pursued for about a year. He reads fiction, both Russian and foreign. He has read Sinclair Lewis's "Babbitt" and applied the term Babbitt in his speeches. He is fond of Chekhov, Gogol, and Heine. The modern Soviet satirists, like Pilnyak and Ehrenburg, he follows, and has on various occasions employed their tales as illustrations for his points.

In the theater, Stalin is not a modernist. He likes, perhaps because of his southern origin, sentimental operas. He has been seen at performances of Verdi's "Aida." He has been reported shedding tears over a revolutionary melodrama.

Stalin is in no sense a "misfit." He won a scholarship as a boy. That feature of his ability is still evident in him. He has an unusual memory. He has an instinct for finding facts and culling from most unexpected sources information which he can use in a practical manner.

Like Lenin he has no personal friends outside of

politics. He lives in his idea and all his associates are those that share this idea. But, unlike Lenin, Stalin is naturally endowed with a great reserve. He can be alone. He needs no confidants. His innate self-sufficiency, more than anything else, is responsible for the Stalin "mystery."

II

In his domestic life, Stalin is exceptionally modest and virtuous. He is fifty-one, his wife is twenty-eight. He loves her deeply. Stalin has a son of twenty-two by his first wife. He has two children, a boy of ten and a girl of five, by his present one, Nadya Alliluieva. His children go to the Kremlin school where most of the commissars' boys and girls get their education. The oldest son, Yasha, was sent by his father to an institute of technology to study railroading.

Stalin has no vices. He smokes a pipe. Like all Georgians, he drinks wine with his dinner. But he is not addicted to alcohol. Women, gambling, and similar pleasures do not exist for him.

Stalin and his family occupy a small two-room apartment within the Kremlin, formerly tenanted by the attachés of the palace. One passes through a dark corridor and climbs up a stairway to reach the Stalin abode. You enter an antechamber. An army coat is on the rack. Stalin is home.

The dining-room, which is also the living-room, is rather small and elongated. The Stalins are at the table. All their meals are brought from the Kremlin restaurant, which supplies all the other high officials.

The dinner is perhaps superior to that of the ordinary Russian restaurant, but it is the kind of food that an American railway conductor would disdain. No luxuries, no delicacies, with the exception of the fine wine.

The furniture in the apartment is of the simplest character. White canvas curtains are hanging over the windows. On the couch in the dining-room the oldest son will go to sleep after dinner. That is his bedroom.

During the meal, there is little conversation. Stalin is not loquacious. He eats heartily. After dinner, he will sit down in an armchair near the window and puff away at his pipe.

The younger child will suddenly begin to cry in the adjoining room. Stalin will not be disturbed. His wife goes into the bedroom to calm the baby. In a few minutes she emerges, only to be disturbed again by the ringing of the telephone, which is included in the limited and strictly private circuit comprising but a few hundred subscribers. Nadya answers the call.

"Hello. This is Stalin's apartment. Who is speaking? Comrade Molotov? Just a minute." She comes out and turns to her husband:

"Koba, Molotov is on the phone."

"I am asleep," says Stalin.

"Comrade Molotov, he cannot be disturbed. He is asleep."

Stalin is put out. Why can't they leave him alone during his few off hours? He had left his near-by office but a short time before, after spending many weary hours at work.

In the summer, Stalin and his family move to the suburban villa at Gorky occupied by Lenin until his death. Here life is different. Living in seclusion in the country, the family can avail itself of the servants on the estate, which is guarded by a special detachment. Every morning at nine o'clock a Rolls-Royce brings Stalin to his quarters at the huge building of the Central Committee. The car is well-protected. It is followed by an open automobile with armed agents of the G. P. U. Stalin remains at work for sixteen to eighteen hours, and returns home late at night.

Once in a long while a few callers drive out to Gorky to spend an evening with the chief. The conversation even then turns to politics. Stalin has no stomach for gossip. Every now and then he invites out the leaders of the Communist Youth League and engages them in long talks, trying to learn the moods and trends of the younger generation.

Stalin is a stern father. His son Yasha has been giving him considerable trouble. When he was twenty, after a poor record in the technological institute, he announced that he did not want an education. Stalin engaged a tutor for the youth, but the teacher was compelled to give up Yasha as a hopeless case. He was then placed in a manual training school to learn a trade.

At the age of twenty-one, Yasha fell in love and eloped. The marriage remained a secret for a while. When Stalin learned of the escapade, he had his son shipped to the Caucasus, where he is reported to be apprenticed to an electrician.

Stalin has a decided puritan bend, and prefers

"clean" plays and stories. On one occasion, after reading a story by a well-known young writer in a leading monthly magazine, Stalin was shocked by the author's "obscenity." The following morning he telephoned the editor and severely reprimanded him for printing pornographic matter. The editor tried to argue in vain that it was literature of a high order. To Stalin, it was a "smutty" story.

Stalin's crudeness crops out even in his kindness. When he learns that one of the inner circle of party leaders has fallen sick, he orders a bucket of cream butter or a keg of honey sent to the patient with a note from him:

"Eat and get well. We need you."

This crudeness of Stalin has on several occasions cost him dearly in reputation. His best intentions were interpreted as diabolical. When Frunze, the successor to Trotsky in the war office, fell ill, Stalin, who valued him highly, displayed unusual care and anxiety for his health. It appeared that Frunze was suffering from severe abdominal pains. Stalin became alarmed and insisted:

"I am telling you that you have an ulcer of the stomach. You must be operated upon. We need you."

Frunze demurred and argued against it. Finally, when his suffering became acute, he yielded to Stalin's urgings. He died under the surgeon's knife.

This episode gave rise to rumors that presented Stalin as a treacherous friend. It formed the subject of a thinly disguised short story by Boris Pilnyak, which was read upon its publication with unconcealed glee. Stalin naturally resented the piece, but the author went unpunished. The false rumor, however, is still making the rounds of the world press.

III

Stalin has a sense of humor. His cynicism is deep, his irony open. He has a genuine appreciation of satire.

Stalin gave his first interview to the foreign press about a year after Lenin's death. The journalist was a Japanese correspondent. When he entered, Stalin rose to greet him with the words:

"Welcome. I, too, am an Asiatic."

Soon after the suppression of the widespread rebellions in Turkestan by the Red Army, a deputation of humbled native notables from that province came to the Kremlin. A group of Soviet functionaries, seated around a table, received the delegates, who were standing. Stalin came in, surveyed the scene, and began to pull up chairs for the visitors. When asked why he was doing it, he replied, looking at his comrades:

"What else, except our courtesy, have we Asiatics to meet you Europeans with?"

When Trotsky was exiled to Turkey and wrote a series of articles for the capitalist press in which he described Stalin as a mediocrity, an American newspaper syndicate asked Stalin for a reply, promising to print it in full. Word was sent by Stalin's secretary that "Stalin was too busy to bother about such trifles."

Stalin's secretary, Ivan Tovstukha, a tall and lanky person, is also his official biographer. One day Stalin suddenly discovered what his secretary looked like. With a solemn expression, he came up and remarked:

"Tovstukha, my mother had a goat. Well, that goat looked exactly like you. Only it did not wear spectacles."

Tovstukha laughed subserviently while Stalin returned to his study.

During his conflict with Tomsky, who was sent to a minor post in remote Mongolia, Stalin received reports of Tomsky's complaints of being exiled in the wilderness. To the merriment of the party congress, Stalin observed:

"I think that Comrade Tomsky's remarks about his being sent into the Gobi Desert to eat wild honey and herbs are the empty jokes of a provincial variety theater, without anything in common with the question of a revolutionist's self-respect."

In the course of a speech, seeking to illustrate the impractical nature of certain leaders looking for easy remedies, Stalin told of an incident during the civil war when the Entente expedition occupied Odessa. The Red soldiers were under the impression that all that was necessary was to capture the "Entente." To the men at the front, the "Antanta," as they called it, was a living being.

"I cannot help recalling an episode in 1919 or 1920, when we drove Denikin out of the Ukraine," said Stalin. "One of our army detachments conducted a furious search in Odessa all over the town for the 'Antanta,' convinced that once they caught her, the war would come to an end."

Stalin's level-headedness makes him turn to satirical sources in his talks. "Who does not know of cases where narrow-minded and unprincipled commercialism has led a so-called Bolshevik into devious ways inimical to the revolutionary cause? Pilnyak describes such types in his story 'The Naked Year.' Here we make acquaintance with Bolsheviks who are full of good will and practical endeavor, who 'function energetically,' but who have no vision, who have no notion of what is seemly to the occasion, who cannot foresee whither their actions will lead, and who, consequently, stray from the revolutionary path . . .

"Who has not had experience of the fatal disease of 'revolutionary' planning, of 'revolutionary' projects which are concocted in the blind belief that a decree can change everything, can bring order out of chaos? Ehrenburg, in his tale 'The Full-Fledged Communist,' gives us an admirable portrait of a Bolshevik overtaken by this kind of sickness. The hero has set himself to produce the ideal man. He is absorbed in his work. Unfortunately the creature is a complete failure. The story is, of course, an extravaganza; nevertheless it is a very shrewd take-off."

When the Japanese mikado Yoshihito died toward the end of 1926, the Soviet embassy in Tokio was in a quandary as to its conduct and participation in the religious and other ceremonies that accompany the death of an emperor in Japan. Stalin cabled instructions to Bessedovsky, the Soviet chargé d'affaires, "to participate in all the ceremonies of the burial, but to conduct oneself so as not to arouse in the Japanese masses an idea of our seeking to curry favor with imperial Japan." Stalin suggested that the customary wreath be placed on the mikado's grave, but that the legend "Proletarians of the World, Unite!" be eliminated for that occasion from the Soviet official coat of arms.

"There was nothing left for me to do," writes Bessedovsky, "but to submit to the virtuous modesty of Stalin." The wreath with the Soviet crest, but without the legend "Proletarians of the World, Unite!" remained on the tomb of the Japanese emperor as a monument to Stalin's Red diplomacy.

IV

Stalin, the raconteur, is not for the fastidious. If his stories lack the esthetic quality required in best society, they at least have a freshness that cannot be misconstrued, and a roughness that in high politics seems novel but serves its purpose admirably.

Speaking at the last party congress on the Right opposition and its leaders, who continued their concealed activities and waited for an opportune moment to strike, Stalin delivered an obituary on the political graves of Rykov, Tomsky, and Bukharin to the roars of his stalwarts' laughter.

"When meeting at their factional assemblies and discussing party questions," related Stalin, "they usually looked ahead in this way: Let's wait till the autumn; maybe the party will come a cropper with the corn supply; then we will strike at the Central Committee. However, the autumn also let them down, and left them 'in the soup.' And, as spring and autumn come round every year, the former leaders of the Right opposition continue to sit quiet, again and again pinning their hopes first to the spring and then to the autumn [*general laughter*].

"They are suffering from the same disease as afflicted that well-known hero of Chekhov, Belikov, the teacher of Greek, the man in the leather case. Do you remember Chekhov's story: 'The Man in the Leather Case'? That hero, you may remember, always went about in galoshes and a wadded coat, with an umbrella, both in hot and cold weather. 'Why do you need galoshes and a wadded coat in July, in such hot weather?' Belikov used to be asked. 'You never know,' Belikov replied. 'Something might happen. There might be a sudden frost; what should I do then?' [*General laughter and applause.*]

"He feared everything new, everything that went beyond the bounds of the daily rut of humdrum life, as he would the plague. A new restaurant was opened, and Belikov was already in alarm: 'It might, of course be a good thing to have a restaurant, but look out that nothing happens.' A dramatic circle was organized and a reading room opened, and Belikov was again in panic: 'A dramatic circle, a new reading-room—what for? Look out, something may happen.' [*General laughter.*]

"We have to say the same about the former leaders of the Right opposition.

"Do you remember the affair of handing over the technical colleges to the economic commissariats? We wanted to hand over only two technical colleges to the Supreme Economic Council. A small matter, it might seem. Yet we met with the most desperate resistance on the part of the Right deviators. 'Hand over two technical colleges to the Supreme Economic Council? Why? Hadn't we better wait? Look out, something may happen as a result of this scheme.' And today all our technical colleges have been handed over to the economic commissariats. And we are getting on pretty well, nevertheless.

"Or, for example, the question of the extraordinary measures against the kulaks. Do you remember what hysterics the leaders of the Right opposition fell into on this occasion? 'Extraordinary measures against the kulaks? Why? Hadn't we better apply a liberal policy toward the kulaks? Look out, something may happen as a result of this scheme.' Yet today we are applying the policy of liquidating the kulaks as a class, a policy in comparison with which the extraordinary measures against the kulaks are a mere fleabite. And we are getting along pretty well, all the same.

"Or, for example, the question of the collective and Soviet farms. 'Soviet and collective farms? What do we want them for? Why should we hurry? Look out, something may happen as a result of all these Soviet and collective farms.' And so on, and so forth.

"And it is this fear of something new, this incapacity to approach new questions in a new way, this alarm that 'something may happen,' these features of the man in the leather case, that prevent the former leaders of the Right opposition from amalgamating properly with the party.

"These features take on particularly ridiculous forms when difficulties appear, when the slightest cloud makes its appearance on the horizon. If any difficulty or hitch has appeared anywhere, they already fall into panic, lest something may happen. A cockroach somewhere stirs, without having time even to crawl out of its hole, and they are already starting back in terror, and beginning to shout about a catastrophe, about the ruin of the Soviet government [*general laughter*].

"We try to calm them down, we try to convince them that nothing dangerous has happened as yet, that it is only a cockroach, and there is no need to be afraid. But all in vain. They continue to shout as before: 'What cockroach? That's no cockroach, it's a thousand wild beasts! It's not a cockroach, but the abyss, the ruin of the Soviet government.' And volumes of paper begin to pour in. Bukharin writes theses on the subject and sends them to the Central Committee, asserting that the policy of the Central Committee has brought the country to a state of ruin, and that the Soviet government will certainly perish, if not at once, then at least in a month's time. Rykov supports Bukharin's theses, with the reservation, however, that he has a very serious difference with Bukharin, namely, that the Soviet government will perish, in his opinion, not in a month, but in a month and two days [*general laughter*].

"Tomsky supports Bukharin and Rykov, but protests against the fact they have not been able to do without theses, have not been able to do without a document that they will have to answer for later on: 'How many times have I told you—do what you like, but don't leave a document behind; don't leave any traces.' [*Roars of laughter of the whole congress, and prolonged applause.*]

"True, later on, in a year's time, when every fool begins to see that the cockroach danger didn't amount to an empty eggshell, the Right deviators begin to recover and, growing bolder, don't mind even boasting a little, declaring that they are not afraid of any cockroaches, and, moreover, that the cockroach was such a cowardly and feeble specimen [*laughter and applause*]."

It remains to be added that this story, told for the edification of a thousand chieftains from all over the country, was delivered and made public by the disdainful political boss at a time when Rykov was still "legally" and nominally the prime minister of the Soviet government. On another occasion, at a gathering of the Communist International, Stalin regaled his listeners with a fable that shows him from a different angle and to better advantage.

"I recall an amusing tale," he began, "which a Swedish comrade related in Stockholm. It occurred in 1906, during our party congress there. This comrade drew a funny picture of the socialist habit of citing Marx and Engels. We, the delegates who heard the story, split our sides laughing.

"It all happened in the Crimea, during the rising of the navy and the army. The delegates of the marines and infantry came to the socialists and said:

" 'You have called upon us for years to rise against tsarism. We are convinced that you are right. We conspired to revolt and now we have come to you for counsel.'

"The socialists became excited, and replied that they could not decide the question without a special conference. The marines made it clear that there was no time to lose, that everything was ready, that if they could not get clear instructions and if the socialists would not undertake the direction of the revolt, the whole thing would collapse. The marines and soldiers left to await the decision.

"The socialists called a special conference. They pulled out the first volume of Karl Marx's 'Capital.' Then they took the second one out. Finally, they turned to the third volume. They searched for directions regarding the Crimea, regarding Sebastopol, regarding a rising in the Crimea. But they literally could not find a single reference in the three volumes of 'Capital,' neither to Sebastopol nor to a revolt of sailors and soldiers. They then began to turn the leaves of the other works of Marx and Engels. But it was all in vain—not a word on the subject! They were at a loss what to do.

"The rebels came back for an answer. But what answer could one give them? The socialists had to acknowledge that in the existing circumstances they could give no directions to the sailors and soldiers how to conduct an uprising.

"And so, finished the Swedish comrade, the revolt of the army and navy ended in a fiasco."

The moral is: We have studied enough. We have had enough scholastic hair-splitting. Let us be practical. Let us attend to business.

V

The business center of the dictatorship is the Central Committee, housed in an enormous new structure on the New Square in Moscow. In this well-guarded edifice, which few non-communists ever penetrate, and which contains secret departments accessible to but a few men, are concentrated the threads of the amazing web which is the Stalin machine. Here there is an atmosphere of intense activity among the thousands of employees that suggests pressure, pressure, and more pressure. Careers are made and unmade by the stroke of a pen, lives are condemned in advance, or saved, before even the judges are picked, assignments are handed out to every part of the world. A direct private wire leads to the G. P. U. on the Lubianka Square. Another such wire runs to the Central Control Commission on the Varvarka. A third goes to the Kremlin. All the orders that require formal passage are transmitted to the proper commissariats, such as that of foreign affairs, finance, the war office, the Communist International, and are issued under their seals and official signatures.

On the third floor is Stalin's office. He rarely works here. Near by is the secretariat presided over by Molotov. Here even important party members enter by special permit and maintain a respectful attitude. In the secret section are the files. Here there is a card system that catalogues all the tens of thousands of the leading communists in the entire Soviet Union. Every card has a corresponding biographical record.

Stalin has a special dossier. He makes his headquarters at the office of the Political Bureau in the Kremlin. Here the chief executive is in daily conference with his associates. In a safe in the same room are the accurately filed records of the several hundred key leaders. These record information on the pasts of the men, on their sins, errors, and blots collected by the vigilant secret service of the G. P. U. The order and completeness of the file is sufficient to arouse the envy of the director of Scotland Yard. When the president of the Ukrainian Soviet Republic, Petrovsky, a veteran Bolshevik, began, for example, to display disobedience, Stalin pulled out his dossier and read from it:

"We know everything. In 1905, you caroused with the police chief in Pavlograd. . . . Look out, it might prove unpleasant."

It was from this archive that Stalin secured the telegram of congratulations which Kamenev sent to Michael Romanov, the short-lived tsar.

According to Bajanov, who served for several years as a junior secretary in the Political Bureau, Stalin at the meetings of this high tribunal maintains his usual reserve. He seldom generalizes. He sees only concrete problems and seeks practical solutions. He attacks few questions and rarely makes mistakes.

"At the meetings of the Political Bureau," he writes in his revelations, "I always had the impression that Stalin was much more inclined to follow events than to direct them. During discussions he would keep silent and listen attentively. He never would give his opinion until the debate was over and then would propose in a few words, as if it were his own idea, the solution on which the majority of his assistants had already agreed. For that reason his opinion was ordinarily adopted.

"When I was present for the first time at a meeting of the Political Bureau, the struggle between the triumvirate—Stalin, Kamenev, and Zinoviev—and Trotsky was already unleashed. Trotsky arrived first. The others were late, conspiring. . . . Then Zinoviev entered. He passed in front of Trotsky. Each pretended not to see the other. Kamenev upon entering the room exchanged a slight bow with Trotsky. Finally Stalin came in. He approached the table where Trotsky was sitting, addressed him with a very friendly gesture, and shook hands across the table."

Trotsky's relations with Stalin were never personal. His estimate of the figure that had so ingloriously defeated him is nevertheless illuminating of Stalin the man of affairs. "He is gifted," writes Trotsky, "with practicality, a strong will, and persistence in carrying out his aims. His political horizon is restricted, his theoretical equipment primitive. . . . His mind is stubbornly empirical, and devoid of creative imagination. . . . Because of his enormous envy and ambition, Stalin could not help feeling at every step his intellectual and moral inferiority." Trotsky then observes that he was repelled by Stalin's "narrowness of interests, coarseness of psychological make-up, his peculiar cynicism, that of a provincial whom Marxism has freed from many prejudices without, however, replacing them with a philosophical outlook thoroughly thought out and mentally assimilated."

Stalin is not imaginative, but he is stedfast. He is not brilliant, but he knows his limitations. He is not universal; he is single-tracked. These properties may be defects, but in Stalin's position they are sources of strength. He is a "big business man," a type new in Russian political life. He is the carrier of that modern "ism" which has invaded the Old World—Americanism.

Chapter Fifteen

STALIN'S AMERICANISM

I

STALIN'S breadth and limitations, his searching mind and his fixed horizon, his Leninist duplicity in dealing with the non-Bolshevist world, his evangelism, are revealed in his relations with the United States and in his—Americanism.

Stalin knows three living aspects of contemporary America. He knows the American intelligentsia, the "petit bourgeois liberals and radicals," whose brethren in Soviet Russia he had pulverized as a class—professors, trade-union leaders, and economists who have been making pilgrimages to the Red Mecca.

Stalin knows the American communists whom America does not know. He takes seriously the American Communist Party! The staged and wire-pulled demonstrations of communists which make the front pages of the American newspapers, even as a sensational murder or "Al" Capone does—but which in American life have the same significance—when cabled back to Moscow assume there the proportions of a great social upheaval, and make impressive reading.

Finally, Stalin knows the American engineers, the efficiency experts, the energetic if somewhat adventurous specialists in industry, who are mostly first cousins to our Alaska pioneers, California gold-rush prospectors, the "Burning Daylights" of Jack London. This is the American "bourgeoisie," the enemy from whom, according to Lenin, one must learn.

In the fall of 1927, an American trade-union delegation, consisting of half a dozen liberal labor leaders, a dozen advisors holding various Ph.D. degrees, and a secretarial staff of college graduates, altogether about twenty-five men and women, went to the Soviet Union to conduct an inquiry into the entire system of government there. An unusual interview was arranged with Stalin. It lasted about five hours.

"I have never seen a politician so anxious to be explicit, so little inclined to be cryptic or laconic, as the proverbially taciturn head of the most powerful party in the world," writes Anne O'Hare McCormick, who was in Moscow at the time and who was present at the session.

"When we arrived at the party headquarters, we were all carefully scrutinized and shot up in detachments to the top floor. A Red soldier waited at the landing, and, after the whole party had assembled, the door was opened from within and we were guided through several antechambers into a large light room like a directors' room in a bank. Stalin entered at once and took his place at the head of a long mahogany table. The rudeness Lenin complained of is probably the roughness of his steamroller methods. His manner as he greeted us was affable and self-possessed, almost gentle; and in contrast to the carelessness affected by many Bolsheviks, he was trim and well-groomed in his neat khaki uniform. He does not look Russian at all, but Turkish; he reminded me of no one so much as Mustapha Kemal or Ahmed Zogu, the young mountain chief who is president of Albania. Stalin, too, as he took out his black pipe and ordered rounds of tea and plates of thick caviar sandwiches, was like an Oriental tribal chief dispensing hospitality. The Caucasus is in him, and the mountains—in his easy vigor, the glance of his quick eyes, in some core of calmness which he shares with Lenin. He was the steadiest and most assured of all the Soviet leaders I saw. In the thick of the last bitter battle with the opposition he was unworried, under the tedious ordeal of the long pauses in a translated interview he was not fidgety. His low brow was clear under a squarish brush of black hair that made his head oddly cubist. His smile was frequent and genuine, but it was the reserved smile of the East rather than the open smile of the West. The Slavs in the communist councils are dominated by something much more immovable than themselves. Lacking brilliance, Stalin gives an impression of craft and suppleness. He is the shrewd manipulator, quite obstinate, ruthless without passion. Trotsky is the agitator, bold and vivid, and Stalin is the organizer, composed and wary. . . . The Bolshevik chief answered questions like a teacher. He was bland and patient."

Stalin in the course of the lengthy interview showed, as far as the published minutes are concerned, his unmistakable superiority to the entire American delegation. His answers to the questions propounded to him make a fine web of truths, half-truths, and evasions, which the American examiners hardly attempted to resist by cross-interrogation.

Perhaps the only unequivocal statement made by Stalin was: "The revolution needs the G. P. U., and the G. P. U. will live with us to the terror of the enemies of the proletariat."

But when Stalin turned the tables and interviewed his guests, the conference assumed an illuminating aspect. It was not only that the replies he received were a pathetic commentary upon the intellectual paucity of the Americans who endeavored to enlighten him. Stalin's probing questions, which follow, show a stubborn and honest desire to penetrate and understand the American scene. He asked:

"How do you account for the small percentage of American workers organized in trade unions? I think there are about seventeen million industrial workers in America. I think that about three million are organized. Personally I think that the proportion of American workers organized in trade unions is very small. In the U. S. S. R. ninety per cent of all the proletarians in the country are organized in trade unions.

"I should like to ask the delegation whether it regards this small percentage of organized workers as a good thing. Does not the delegation think that this small percentage is an indication of the weakness of the American proletariat and of the weakness of its weapon in the struggle against the capitalists in the economic field?

"How do you explain the absence of a special mass workers' party in the United States? The bourgeoisie in America have two parties, the Republican Party and the Democratic Party. But the American workers have no mass party of their own. Do not the comrades think that the absence of such a mass workers' party, even if it were like the British Labor Party, weakens the working class in its political fight against the capitalists? Then, again, why do the leaders of the Labor movement in America, Green and the others, so strongly oppose the establishment of a Labor Party in America?

"How do you explain that on the question of recognizing the U. S. S. R. the leaders of the American Federation of Labor are more reactionary than many bourgeois? How do you explain that bourgeois like Mr. Borah and others are in favor of recognizing the U. S. S. R., while American labor leaders like Gompers and Green have conducted and still conduct reactionary propaganda against the recognition of the first workers' republic, against the recognition of the U. S. S. R.? How do you explain that even a reactionary like the late President of the United States, Woodrow Wilson, was able to 'greet' Soviet Russia, while Green and other leaders of the American Federation of Labor wish to be more reactionary than the capitalists?

"Can we regard it as normal when the leaders of the American Federation of Labor desire to be more reactionary than reactionary Wilson?"

The record does not show whether any of the Americans pointed out to Stalin that the "reactionary" President Wilson extended de facto recognition, in March, 1918, to the then living and representative Soviets of the Russian people in their struggle for "freedom" and not for a Stalin dictatorship. But it does show that none of the American labor leaders was able to suggest to Stalin that the heretical development of American capitalism might conceivably indicate the bankruptcy of Marxian politics and the Leninist theory of power.

"But it is the skilled workers mainly whose material conditions are guaranteed," said Stalin, in a sincere attempt to analyze the American social scene as presented to him by his visitors. "There is a contradiction here. On the one hand, it would appear that there is no necessity for organization because the workers are provided for. On the other hand, it is said that the more secure, the skilled workers, are organized in the trade unions. Thirdly, it would appear that the unorganized workers are those least provided for, namely, the unskilled workers who most of all stand in need of organization.

"I cannot understand this at all," confessed Stalin with resignation.

II

In the comic opera of "American" communism, the rôle of Stalin is one of sublime burlesque. The big boss of Bolshevism has actually perpetrated two revolutions in America—in Union Square. The first took place in 1925, when a cablegram from Moscow swept aside "the desires and votes of two-thirds of the American Communist Party . . . and appointed the group representing the remaining third of the party to lead it." It all happened during the Trotsky-Zinoviev-Stalin struggle.

The second Stalin revolution occurred as recently as 1929. Again a cablegram from the Communist International "wiped out the desires and votes of nine-tenths of the party membership." The group appointed "to direct the party's destinies" represented the remaining tenth. Incidentally, the membership of this grand army of the world revolution is about five thousand, of whom eighty per cent are not naturalized citizens.

In his interview with the American delegation of labor leaders and intellectuals, Stalin said in answer to a question: "The assertion that the American communists work under 'orders from Moscow' is absolutely untrue. Some people believe that the members of the Communist International in Moscow do nothing but sit and write instructions to all countries. . . . And the American labor leaders believe that with this ridiculous legend they can cover up their fear of the communists and conceal the fact that communists are the bravest and most loyal workers in the labor movement in America."

Thus spoke Stalin, with a serious mien, to a representative group of the American "petit-bourgeois" intelligentsia, in September, 1927. More than a year later, on the occasion of the national celebration of his fiftieth birthday, his right-hand man in the Communist International, Manuilsky, paid Stalin the following official tribute: "The time has not yet come to tell in detail how the leadership of Stalin has saved a number of communist parties from political errors. The entire history of Stalin's work in this field lies hidden in the archives of the Communist International. Not a document of importance, possessing big international significance, was issued from the Communist International without the most active participation of Stalin in its formulation. His marginal notes on these documents show how quickly and sharply he seizes the weak sides of a premise in a document, how he is able to center attention upon the fundamental, the decisive, in each question, how he has taught each of us the art of 'not running all over the place,' and of formulating tersely and accurately our proposals. All this applies to the realm of routine work."

Well, these "hidden archives" have partly been opened. The "big international significance" of the Stalin coup d'état in America can now be revealed. That "ridiculous legend" of the Moscow dictators who "do nothing else but sit and write instructions" can now be verified in the opera bouffe of the "bravest and most loyal workers in the labor movement in America"—the "American" communists.

It all happened at the Sixth Congress of the Communist International in 1928. Trotsky in his place of exile prepared a lengthy document on "the strategy of the world revolution." It was a criticism of Stalin's guidance, of course. It was sent on to the congress. Finding it impossible to suppress the document, Stalin had one section from it eliminated and turned over the balance to a limited number of foreign delegates. Now it further happened that the "American" representatives were divided at the assembly. Two recalcitrant comrades managed to smuggle out a copy, in a manner "the description of which would read like a romance."

But it was the "American" question that formed the stage for the farce. Moscow never gave orders to the foreign communist parties, Stalin assured the American liberals. But in the special commission of the Communist International which was set up to deal with the "crisis" in the American Communist Party, Stalin said:

"A month has already passed since the American delegation arrived in Moscow. For almost a whole month we are occupied with it." Stalin took the two wrangling factions to task, and virtually spanked both of them. He accused one group of "hair-raising feats" in outdoing the other in loyalty to Moscow. He exclaimed:

"Another game of rivalry—who can spit farthest . . . Let them know over there in Moscow how to play the stock market . . . But, comrades, the Communist International is not a stock market. The Communist International is the holy of holies of the working class." (*No laughter.*)

Stalin revealed what went on behind the scenes when the contesting "leaders" from Union Square had private interviews with him, and later used these conferences to create a mysterious atmosphere of each side having won over Stalin. It appeared that one of these stalwarts, an American "brave" whom Stalin had characterized as "a sly attorney, a pettifogging lawyer," was to be detained in Moscow with the aid of the G. P. U. This "loyal" revolutionary chief came to Stalin to plead that "the decision to withdraw him from America be rescinded . . . He promised to be a loyal soldier of the Communist International."

"But, my dear comrades," implored Stalin, "that is disgraceful. Do you know that there are no 'Stalinites,' that there must be no 'Stalinites'?" Well, these Americans were practical and would not be persuaded. Had not the G. P. U. already detained several non-Stalinites in the holy of holies? Stalin came down with an ultimatum:

"In order to put an end to these foul methods and place the American Communist Party on the lines of Leninist policy, it is necessary first of all to put an end to factionalism." The end was effectively put. The majority was thrown out. And then came the moment for the solemn benediction—a revelation of Stalin's profound understanding of American conditions:

"The American Communist Party is one of those few in the world upon which history has laid tasks of a decisive character from the viewpoint of the world revolutionary movement . . . I think that the moment is not far off when a revolutionary crisis will develop in America. And when a revolutionary crisis develops in America, that will be the beginning of the end of world capitalism as a whole. It is essential that the American Communist Party should be capable of meeting that historical moment fully prepared and of assuming the leadership of the impending class struggle in America. Every effort and every means must be employed in preparing for that, comrades. For that end the American Communist Party must be improved and Bolshevized.

"The fact of the matter is that we have an accentuation of the class struggle in all capitalist countries, a growing revolutionary crisis in Europe . . . Yesterday this was signalized by a general strike in Lodz. Not so long ago we had a signal from Berlin. Tomorrow we shall get signals from France, England, Czecho-Slovakia, America, India, China. Soon the ground will be too hot for world capitalism."

Stalin is a true Leninist. In this farce of "American" communism he walks in the narrow, incurable path of Lenin the nationalist, the Eurasian. Lenin had spent fifteen years in the West and had all his time there been identified intimately with the German socialist leaders and politics. Yet when the World War broke out he made a bet with Zinoviev in their residence in Austria. Zinoviev bet that the German socialists would not dare vote against the kaiser's government and would therefore abstain from balloting in parliament when the question of war credits came up. Lenin declared that the German socialists could not be such rascals and bet that they would vote against the kaiser if only to save their standing with the masses. Both Lenin and Zinoviev lost their bet. The German socialists voted in favor of war and war credits.

Lenin retained to the end of his days a provincial, an exclusive Russian mentality. That was his strength and his weakness. Stalin is a wax image from the Lenin panopticon. His circumscribed vision is his greatest natural asset and source of power in a primitive land.

In a cosmic world that does not conform to a single formula, Stalin is lost. He cannot find his bearings in a world developed beyond the perceptions of elementary Eurasia, a world bewildering in the variety of its living colors, a world in which the warm, deep currents of a flowering individualist culture are intertwined with the civilization of a machine age in a manner that defies rudimentary generalization.

III

If Stalin, despite his efforts, could learn nothing of the character of American civilization from the products of American universities and trade-union reformers; if Stalin has not been able to extract from the "braves" of the American Communist Party any light on the confounding indifference to Bolshevism of the American proletariat; he was at least able, in his pragmatical mind, to seize upon, from his contacts with the dynamic American builders of electrical and metallurgical plants in Russia, an expression of Americanism that he instantly elevated into the "American spirit." This Stalin found applicable to his realm.

The spirit of the cowboy turned oil magnate, the spirit of the American foreman driving the slaves in the rubber plantations in Liberia and the coolies in the concessions in China, the spirit of Billy Sunday, of the braggadocio that makes some town in the Middle West boast of the largest garage in the world, and of a "patriotism" that makes two New York corporations race for the highest tower in the world —this American spirit Stalin understood quickly, embraced without hesitation, and wrote it large upon the banner of . . . Leninism.

In his lectures on Leninism at the Sverdlov University, in Moscow, which were later incorporated by him in his major work under that title, Stalin elaborated upon Leninism as a school where the study of theory and practice is characterized by two peculiarities, namely:

"(a) Revolutionary zeal, inspired by the Russian

spirit. (b) Businesslike practicality, inspired by the American spirit. . . .

"Revolutionary zeal is the antidote to laziness, routinism, conservatism, apathy of thought, slavish adherence to tradition and to the belief of our forefathers. Revolutionary zeal is a life-giving force that stimulates thought, spurs on to action, throws the outworn into the limbo of forgotten things, and opens the portals of the future. Without such zeal there can be no advance. But it has a drawback, seeing that in practice it tends to vent itself in revolutionary talk, unless it is intimately combined with level-headedness and businesslike action imbued with the American spirit. . . .

"The best antidote to revolutionary fantasy is practical work imbued with the American spirit. Such businesslike, practical endeavor is an unquenchable force, one that recognizes no obstacles, one that, by sheer common sense, thrusts aside everything which might impede progress, one that invariably carries a thing once embarked upon to completion (even though the affair may seem a puny one), one without which any genuine work of construction is impossible.

"But the practical, businesslike American spirit is liable to degenerate into narrow-minded, unprincipled commercialism, if it be not allied with revolutionary zeal. . . .

"In party and government work, a combination of the Russian revolutionary zeal with the practical American spirit is the essence of Leninism."

A political boss, a rigorous master, a paternalistic hierarch, Stalin at the head of the Bolshevist oligarchy is a new type of dictator in a primordial, preadamite world. Like King Solomon, who sent his trading vessels to the fabulous land of Ophir in quest of ivory and gold, so Stalin sends his envoys to the legendary Ford in America in search of magical tractors and the alchemical formula of transmuting an archaic order into the millennium.

CHAPTER SIXTEEN

STALIN AND THE FIVE-YEAR PLAN

I

LIKE a shooting star, the Five-Year Plan has risen on the horizon of the world. It has been hailed as a challenge because of the provocative force of the idea of planned and coordinated national economy. It has been advertised as a menace because of the powerful entity which the Soviet Union will represent upon the completion of the five-year course. It has elevated Stalin to the status of a world figure.

Where did the Five-Year Plan come from? Is it a discovery or a development? What are the forces that drive it—human will-power or the deeper and unbridled dynamics of the revolution itself? How and where is Stalin guiding it? Finally, since we are not concerned here with the challenge of the idea of national planning itself, is it making Russia a mighty menace to the capitalist civilization?

The origin of the Five-Year Plan in the Russian Revolution, like the origin of political Bolshevism, is to be found in the history of modern western civilization. The planning idea is an outgrowth of western capitalist progress.

In the United States, the land of violent economic individualism, the idea of rational economics was first given bone and flesh by President Wilson when he introduced the Federal Reserve System. During the World War, it was further expressed by the creation of the War Industries Board and the Food Administration. In America, however, the experiment in government control and operation lacked the basis of government ownership.

In Germany, the land of advanced industrialism, efficiency, state centralization, state paternalism, and classical socialism, the planning idea was first given a scientific interpretation.

In 1898, a young professor of economy in the Berlin University, Karl Ballod, published a book entitled "The State of the Future." Although this work had an introduction by Kautsky, it was far from communist in character. The learned author attempted to prove the possibility of a socialized and coordinated economic system on the basis of the human advance in applied sciences.

Ballod in many ways anticipated the tendencies now observable in America, such as standardization and a shortened work day. He advocated the regulation of production by the state in conformity with the needs of the population, the purchase of all industries by the government, the regulation of labor, universal labor discipline, but he also proposed the retention of the Prussian military system which existed at the time.

The technical plan of Professor Ballod did not envisage revolution, but an agreement between the state and the private interests. Lenin studied the scheme in the original German soon after its appearance. The book was first published in Russia in 1906. It was republished, at Lenin's instance, in 1919, at the beginning of the era of military communism. It is the direct progenitor of Lenin's famous Electrification Plan, which in turn is the parent of Stalin's present Five-Year Plan.

"In order to appreciate the full magnitude and the full value of the work accomplished by the state commission for the electrification of Russia, let us look at Germany," wrote Lenin in February, 1921, in his essay on "The Unified Economic Plan." He continued: "There an analogous work was performed by a certain scientific authority, Ballod. He prepared a scientific plan of the socialist reconstruction of the entire national economy of Germany. In capitalist Germany, the plan was suspended in mid-air, and remained literature, the achievement of one individual. We gave it a state character, we mobilized hundreds of specialists, and in ten months—of course not in two as proposed originally—we were presented with a single economic plan on scientific lines."

Lenin then outlined the history of the various planning schemes initiated during the period of civil war. In March, 1919, the new program of the Russian Communist Party provided for the planned development of national economy, the maximum exploitation of all the labor power in the country, the universal mobilization of all able-bodied workers, and the coordinated distribution of the various activities.

In February, 1920, the Soviet Executive Committee passed a resolution authorizing the preparation of an Electrification Plan. "We have so many planning commissions that it is impossible to wade through them," declared Lenin. He insisted that the Electrification Plan should become the paramount effort, serving as a bridge from the primitive economy of the country to advanced socialism. That plan outlined a ten-year program for the transformation of the peasant land into a modern industrial empire.

Thus was a western theory transplanted and cultivated on the steppes of the Russian revolutionary dictatorship. It was taken over in a moment of distress, in a day of blockade, war, famine. It was given its start by a bureaucracy which Lenin viciously derided as imbued with "conceited stupidity," which he fought without realizing that it was of the substance of the power that he had established. The Electrification Plan became known as the Electrifiction. Professor Ballod, incidentally, continued to write books in Germany and to expand his original thesis without, however, admitting its applicability to Soviet Russia.

II

During the critical period of military communism, from the middle of 1918 to the spring of 1921, all the aspects of the present Five-Year Plan were developed in Russia. According to Popov, the official historian of the Bolshevist Party, the years of the civil war were essentially an era of nothing more nor less than a system of planned economy in a land of impoverished resources, in a state of isolation from the rest of the world externally and from the producing elements internally.

The crying need for bread was the first dictator of planning, compelling the creation of a network of state-controlled agriculture. A relentless drive was instituted to organize large government farms, which socialism always regarded as superior economically.

A campaign against the kulaks * was conducted without mercy. By the end of 1921, there were 4,316 Soviet farms (*sovkhozi*) and 15,121 collective farms (*kolkhozi*) in existence, covering a total area of over 10,000,000 acres, and employing 1.5 per cent of the rural population of the country. In the conditions of civil war, lacking capital and technical personnel, this was no mean political achievement on the part of the dictatorship.

"During the first complete year of our rule, from August 1, 1918, to August 1, 1919," declared Lenin in 1921, "the state collected about 2,000,000 tons of grain; during the second, about 4,000,000; during the third, more than 5,130,000.

"Now, already possessing practical experience, we made it our objective and plan to collect 7,200,000 tons. Only by becoming the actual owner of a sufficient food reserve can the workers' government stand firmly on its own feet in the economic sphere, and to safeguard the persistent although slow restoration of 'heavy' industry and to create a correct financial system."

These figures are of transcendental value in gaining an historical perspective of the agricultural foundation of the Five-Year Plan in 1930. One should remember that due to the Kolchak, Denikin, and other vast occupational advances by hostile armies into the Soviet realm, the cultivated area was reduced by at least one-half. One should further bear in mind that the population of the Soviet Republic during the civil war, while fluctuating with the fortunes of the front, was by a considerable percentage lower than that of our own time.

* Prosperous peasants.

In the direction of industry, the era of military communism gave birth to numerous planning bodies, of which the Gosplan, the state planning commission, developed into one of widest scope. The needs of the army for munitions and other equipment, the disastrous decline in the production of the nationalized industries dictated drastic measures and chimerical plans. In 1920, although Russian industry employed 43 per cent of its prewar force, its production amounted to but 18 per cent of the prewar output. "Especially catastrophic," adds Popov, "was the condition of the 'heavy' industries. In 1920, the pig-iron production amounted to 2.8 per cent of the prewar total. The terrific crisis of the beginning of 1921 paralyzed even the pitiful remnants of industry preserved during 1920."

Lastly, military communism witnessed the blasting of the hopes entertained by Lenin in 1917-18 for immediate world revolution. Bolshevism was ushered in by Lenin in the sincere belief that the West, especially Germany, was ripe for social revolt. This was proclaimed again and again. Now it was a matter of weeks, as Trotsky recalls. Now it was a matter of months, as Stalin corrects him. Lenin knew better than any other Soviet leader what it meant to build socialism in a backward peasant land. It was his firm conviction that it could be accomplished by hitching the primitive Russian wagon to the modern German dynamo. But the dynamo would not turn East. The crisis compelled Lenin to try to make the Eurasian horse outstrip the European engine by means of . . . electrification.

In the meantime, the plight of the country was worse than ever. Immediate and not visionary schemes were needed to save the situation. It was in connection with this pressing crisis that the governing party witnessed its first violent conflict since the Brest-Litovsk peace issue. During 1920 and the early part of 1921, Lenin and Trotsky fought their battle over the latter's proposition of the "militarization" or "state-ization" of union labor in the restoration of the ruined economy of the country. Stalin supported Lenin. Stalin brought his rancor against Trotsky from the front to the new contest, and opposed the Trotsky program because of its violence and bold sweep! Trotsky had the support of Bukharin, Djerjinsky, and a whole array of Bolshevist stars.

Lenin won. The victory was not due to planning, but quite the contrary, to inchoate forces. "The danger consisted," writes Popov of the Trotsky plan, "in the extreme tightening of the compulsory machine of the state, in too much pressure and too much of a stranglehold. The Soviet power would have exploded if it had followed that road. . . . There was only one road left open: to surrender the system of military communism, *i.e.,* to renounce the policy of immediate realization of socialism. . . . It was necessary at all costs to meet the peasantry halfway. . . .

"The insufficiency of bread became more acute. The village was starving and gave almost no grain to the city. It became more and more difficult to extort from it every slice of bread. Risings were spreading. The workers in the cities, getting almost nothing from the state, demanded freedom of trade."

Such was the situation which compelled Lenin

not only to fight Trotsky's plan, but to beat a retreat. Socialism or no socialism, the Soviet government had to be saved. At this very moment, Stalin addressed a letter to Lenin that throws a flood of light upon the man and the Five-Year Plan that he was to sponsor eight years later.

"During the last three days I had an opportunity to read the volume 'The Plan for the Electrification of Russia,'" wrote Stalin. "My illness has been a help. (There is no evil without good!) It is an excellent, well-composed book. A masterful sketch of a really *unified* and really *statesmanlike* economic plan *without reservations*. It is the only Marxist attempt in our times to put under the Soviet superstructure of an economically backward Russia an actually realistic and only possible industrial technical basis in the existing conditions. You remember last year's 'plan' of Trotsky (his theses) of 'the economic regeneration' of Russia on the basis of applying en masse to the wreckage of prewar industry the labor of unskilled masses of workers and peasants (the labor armies). What wretchedness, what backwardness as compared with the Electrification Plan! An artizan of the Middle Ages, imagining himself an Ibsen hero, called upon to 'save' Russia by an ancient saga. . . . And of what value are the scores of 'unified plans' which now and then, to our shame, appear in our press—mere babbling of elementary school children? . . . Or for instance, the middle-class 'realism' (really fantastic dreaming) of Rykov, who is still 'criticizing' the Electrification Plan, sunk as he is in the mud of routine. . . .

"My opinion:

"1. Not to waste another minute on jabbering about the plan;

"2. To *begin* the immediate *practical attack* on the business;

"3. To subordinate to the interests of this attack at least one-third of our work (two-thirds will be consumed by current affairs) in the direction of importing material and men, restoring enterprises, distributing labor power, securing supplies, the organization of equipment and bases for equipment, etc.;

"4. Since the members of the electrification commission, with all their good qualities, lack healthy practical spirit (one feels professorial impotence in their articles) it is indispensable to introduce into the planning commission men of live practical experience who can act on the principle of 'reporting performance,' 'executing on the date fixed,' etc.

"5. To bind the Pravda, Izvestia, and especially the Economic Life to popularize the Electrification Plan, both as to its premises and concrete aspects, bearing in mind that there is *only one* 'unified economic plan,' which is the Electrification Plan, and that all the other 'plans' are but empty and injurious jabber."

In this letter, Stalin the man and the leader are revealed in striking outline: his tendency to act precipitately, as remarked by Lenin; his personal rudeness on a question of policy toward Trotsky and Rykov, who at the time were far more important than he; his elementary interpretation of a complex problem, such as his insistence on but one plan at a time when the matter required further study; his enthusiasm for bald and concrete targets without bothering about calculating the distance; his anxiety to attack practical tasks; his didactic description of the plan as the only Marxist scheme; and finally his complete, incredible insensitiveness to what was going on in the country at that very moment.

The letter was dated March, 1921. Several days later the roars of the Kronstadt cannon, fired by Bolsheviks and other Soviet adherents, sounded what seemed the funeral salvo of the dictatorship and the Lenin régime, and knocked out all the visionary, long-range plans. Lenin announced the New Economic Policy. The Stalin message was buried and forgotten until seven years after the death of the man to whom it was addressed and who had consigned it to the archives.

III

The New Economic Policy was a complete reversal of the course of the dictatorship. Economically, it was a retreat from a wide front to commanding heights—not a planned retreat, but a precipitous flight executed by a master strategist. It opened the floodgates of private initiative in the village and to a considerable degree in the commerce of the country. The government retained its hold upon the basic resources and industries, the transport system, and the monopoly of foreign trade. The socialist agricultural sector was restricted to the cooperative system and the moribund state and collective farms.

The new era, which lasted about six years, witnessed a boisterous renascence of elementary national economy, despite the heavy hand of the political dictatorship. This spontaneous renewal of prostrated cells in the body of the nation was reflected in the process of disintegration within the body of the dictatorship. Perhaps the greatest planned achievement of the period was the establishment of a new and stable currency.

The population of the Soviet Union, reduced by war, famine, and pestilence, began to increase rapidly. The birth-rate not only made up for all the losses of a decade of havoc, but continued to rise without interruption.

The devastated agriculture witnessed a similar rebirth. In 1917, there were in Russia 15,000,000 individual peasant holdings, In 1927, there were 25,000,000 such homesteads. The untrammeled peasant economy was making giant strides toward capitalism.

But what was happening to socialism? The nationalized industries, controlled by the state, with the exception of coal and oil, which are obtained by primitive power, suffered from lack of capital and even greater lack of technical efficiency and guidance, and lagged behind the rural advance at an increasing pace. Yet Marxism teaches that socialism can be built on industry only.

The growing petty capitalism in the village was overtaking the slow-moving state industries. The latter were unable to supply the needs of the vast peasant market. The gap between the produce of the country and the products of the city grew wider. Trotsky gave this price disparity the winged name of "scissors." The dictatorship was being threatened by an accumulation of capital in the village. The old peasant problem was a bone in the throat of Bolshevist theory. The Soviet Union would be drifting back to capitalism. Its artificial socialist structure, imposed from above by political pressure, would be strangled by the moujik.

Stalin during the "NEP" forgot all about the Electrification Plan. He was too preoccupied by the struggle for power to think of planning in the economic field. He displayed the same mental attitude as during the months following the overthrow of the tsar. In the first half of 1917, he was swayed by the surrounding popular environment and stood for an understanding with the Kerensky régime. During the spontaneous expansion of the "NEP" he was equally swayed by the drift toward an understanding with the private capitalist in the village. From the viewpoint of consistent Marxism, this was opportunism, heresy, weakness. From the viewpoint of creative, unplanned life, this was a tribute to Stalin's adaptability, to his strong instinct of self-preservation and the preservation of the dictatorship.

Trotsky struggled with Lenin for two years prior to his death, urging the adoption of the principle of endowing the Gosplan with executive powers. Lenin was almost converted to this view when he was stricken the last time. Stalin fought that. In 1923, Trotsky sounded the call to industrialization, and made a national issue of it. That year a partial five-year plan was introduced in the metallurgical industry. In 1925, Trotsky outlined a five-year plan on a national scale. It was a moderate but comprehensive scheme. For political reasons, Stalin kept Trotsky away from the coveted post of economic dictator. When Trotsky was crushed, Stalin began to take over most of his enemy's ammunition. The Gosplan was instructed to prepare a new five-year plan, which would cover the span from October, 1926, to October, 1931. A revised version of this plan was approved without ballyhoo by the following congress of the Communist Party. But it is not *the* Five-Year Plan.

Events, unforeseen by Stalin, unplanned by the Gosplan, derived from the uncontrolled depths of the Russian village and the equally uncontrolled fears of the Bolshevist dictatorship, came thick and fast, and forced the Stalin hand to write the newest and yet unfinished chapter in history.

IV

The cry for bread, the emergency of war, and the economic isolation were the three sources from which the planned efforts of the period of military communism sprang.

The year of 1927 saw the recrudescence of these three elemental powers. The cry for bread went up once more. The abundance of grain in the village and the famine of goods in the city led the peasant to retain his reserves. The "scissors," the disparity in prices of manufactured articles and rural produce, grew wider than ever. The state was deprived of its greatest medium of exchange abroad—the export of grain. The city workers suffered intensely. The peasants had no incentive to surrender their bread. The grain collection program of the government showed an enormous deficit. The winter of 1927–8 was ushered in with all the appearances of an internal catastrophe.

"We had but two or three months left before the spring thaw," declared Stalin several months later in an address delivered at Leningrad. "We therefore faced this alternative: either to make up the losses and reestablish the normal rate of grain collections for the future, or be confronted by the inevitability of a serious crisis in our entire national economy."

So serious was the crisis, according to Stalin, that even the favored Red Army was not getting its food supplies regularly. The cities and factories were in a worse condition. The Political Bureau and the Central Committee held frequent sessions. The grain question, the specter of starvation, was defying all peaceful theories.

At the same time a series of episodes that partly grew out of the activities of the Communist International in China and elsewhere created a "war cloud" on the Soviet horizon. In the year 1927 were recorded the raid on the Soviet embassy in China, on the Soviet trade mission in London, the assassination by a "White" Russian of the Soviet ambassador in Warsaw, and the rupture of diplomatic relations between Great Britain and the Soviet Union. This gave rise to a war hysteria in Russia that was as blind as it was deep. All the groups in Moscow vied with each other, for internal political reasons, in magnifying the scare. A dictatorship ruling by terror is the first to yield to panic. Stalin's proclamations of the period illumine the man and the system he heads.

"Another imperialist war is unquestionably impending," wrote Stalin in July, 1927. "We refer not to some indefinite, vague 'danger' of a new war, but to the real and imminent threat of a new war in general, and of a war against the Soviet Union in particular. . . . England prefers wars fought with the hands of others. . . . Now and then she has actually found fools to pick her chestnuts from the fire."

The Soviet theory of the sinister plot against it was simple. His Majesty's government had Marshal Pilsudski and Marshal Chang all set to attack in concert. The shot of a Russian refugee in Warsaw, according to Stalin, "was intended by its authors to play the rôle of Serajevo and draw the Soviet Union into a war with Poland."

Stalin had no difficulty in assorting a string of genuine and assumed incidents to buttress his simple theory. "The entire international situation," he wrote, "all the facts in the field of the British government's 'operations' against the Soviet Union, the fact that it organizes a financial blockade of the Soviet Union, that it conducts secret conferences with the Powers on a policy against the Soviet Union, that it subsidizes the *emigrés'* 'governments' of the Ukraine, Georgia, Azerbaijan, Armenia, etc., for the purpose of raising revolts in those states of the Soviet Union, that it finances groups of spies and terrorists to blow up bridges, set fire to factories, and terrorize Soviet legations abroad—all this undoubtedly proves that the British Tory government has definitely and concertedly undertaken to organize a war against the Soviet Union."

Stalin did not deem it prudent to mention in his article the political activities in China of Borodin, the Chicago adventurer who represented the Communist International and the Political Bureau. Stalin made no reference to General Bliukher of the Red Army, who was training and equipping Chinese communist brigades. Nevertheless, Stalin's sincere fear of war was undeniably equaled by a deep desire for peace. Stalin's internationalism would never take him to war for the sake of world revolution. His policy of peace at any price is imbedded in the love of power, in the anxiety to retain that power in any event—of course, all for the ultimate benefit of world socialism.

"Your task is to prevent at all costs the united Anglo-Japanese intervention in China, in the event of the further development of the Chinese revolution," declared Stalin to Bessedovsky, when the latter was appointed counselor to the Soviet legation in Tokio. Stalin was even ready, in case of need, to surrender Northern Saghalien and Vladivostok to Japan for its neutrality, holding that England would not go to war without Japan. "I am not a diplomat and I do not pretend to give you practical suggestions," he said. "If there should be a Soviet government in Peking, then, to save it from intervention, we might be ready to surrender to the Japanese not only Vladivostok but Irkutsk as well. It would all depend on the balance of power at any particular moment of the revolution. Brest-Litovsk will yet be repeated in various combinations. It may become necessary in the Chinese revolution as much as it was in the Russian. I want to give you one piece of advice: talk with the Japanese as little as possible and telegraph us as often as possible. And don't think you are more clever than anybody else."

Later, when China turned against Bolshevism, Stalin sent one frantic cablegram after another to Bessedovsky, urging him to secure a mutual non-aggression pact with Japan. The fear of war in Moscow was actual. The Japanese government gave the Soviet representative a formal verbal assurance that it had no intention of attacking Soviet Russia. This commonplace statement, which only confirmed what the whole world knew, that Japan and Great Britain were not preparing to launch a war against Russia, was hailed in Moscow as a tremendous diplomatic achievement. Stalin, in the name of the Political Bureau, congratulated Bessedovsky upon his success, and had him promoted and transferred to Paris.

The war scare did not subside in the Kremlin. Stalin, who gradually became the sole guide and guardian of Soviet foreign policy, thought of one plan after another to avert the "impending war." He proposed the sale of that famous bone of contention, the Chinese Eastern Railway, to Japan—in order to augment the antagonism between Japan and the United States. He suggested and caused the initiation of negotiations for the legal cession of Bessarabia to Roumania, the annexation of which the Soviet government had never recognized, in order to win the friendship of Roumania's ally France, and to disrupt the "planned attack" against Russia.

In addition to the fear of starvation in the cities, the fear of war in the Kremlin, there was a third fear which motivated Stalin and the dictatorship, and which led to the economic isolation of the Soviet Union.

Despite Stalin's earlier cry that Great Britain

was organizing "a financial blockade of the Soviet Union," the negotiations for the settlement of the debt question between Russia and France were moving to a successful end. The Soviet ambassador in Paris, Rakovsky, a firm adherent of Trotsky, and the French industrialist, Senator de Monzie, virtually agreed on a plan that had the support of the government of France. In exchange for recognizing the old debts on a highly reduced basis of valuation, the Soviet government was to receive new credits immediately amounting to $120,000,000. Rakovsky returned to Russia to participate in the political fight, and landed in prison and exile, where he has been ever since. His mission was carried on by Bessedovsky, who favored the agreement. He pointed out to Stalin that the short-term credits secured by the Soviet government abroad were in themselves a worse penalty than paying the debts, because of the excessive rates of interest and discount which European and American capital charge for Soviet transactions.

It is axiomatic that the first requisite for the successful industrialization of Russia is capital. The opportunity which presented itself in France to open up the money market of the profit-seeking capitalist world for the insatiable state industries of Russia was turned down by Stalin.

Stalin insisted that one must be naive to think it is possible for the Soviet Union to secure long-term loans without political strings. "They will put up conditions such as will make it impossible for us to conduct our economy as we desire it," he declared. "Not we would be the leaders, but they would lead us. You must understand that short-term credits, as expensive as they are, free us from political vassalage. We do not need large foreign loans. . . . A Bolshevik, a real Bolshevik, cannot think otherwise."

This quality of naïveté in the arch-Bolshevik, as far as international affairs are concerned, is not new. It has been strikingly illustrated in his "Americanism." Stalin's policy won in the Political Bureau. The self-imposed economic isolation from the financial resources of the West stands as a monument to the Leninist bugaboo of the capitalist dragon.

At the same time, the growing isolation of the Soviet Union from the revolutionary workers of the world was moving to a climax. Stalin's policy in this direction suffered one defeat after another. The Chinese hope turned into a debacle. The opportunity of fanning a revolution in Germany, which had existed after the French occupation of the Ruhr, was missed. Several minor sorties of this nature in the international field ended in disaster. The whole Communist International was on the decline. Its member parties were splitting and losing their followings. In Germany, the masses flocked to Hitler's Fascist banner. In that fortress of world imperialism, Great Britain, the vanguard of the proletariat, the British Communist Party, which attained during the General Strike a membership of 10,000, was melting away. At this writing, it has dwindled to less than 1,000. Something was evidently wrong with the world revolution. Attention had to be centered upon the national revolution. The "building of socialism in one country" had to be stressed more than ever, to inspire the young generation, to hold out the vista of a promised land to a weary and restless multitude, to strangle the opposition, to maintain power, and, above all, to justify the original Leninist purpose of the revolution. The dictatorship had grown into a habit, and it was humanly impossible to relinquish it.

The grain and goods famine in the cities, the panicky rush to war preparedness, and the blasted hopes of world revolution were the three organic premises, all springing from the heart of the dictatorship, which brought about the emergence of the phenomenon that was to become known as the Five-Year Plan.

V

How did Stalin answer the peasant boycott of the city and the threatening famine in the urban stronghold of Bolshevism?

The general policy proclaimed had as its immediate aim the transformation of the petty, individualized, subdivided, private holdings into united, combined, collective or state-owned large farms, with modern mechanical equipment capable of intensified agriculture.

This note Stalin struck again and again in numerous speeches and articles. He described it as "the only way out of the situation." He characterized it as the road "to overcome the capitalist elements in the village." Tractorization became a pillar of light. The theory of Stalin merely disguised the need for bread in the city, and the equally sharp need for grain to export in order to secure purchasing power for the development of the lingering industries.

"We must not for too long a period of time base the Soviet power and the socialist structure on two different foundations, on the foundation of the largest and most unified socialist industry and on the foundation of the most divided and backward petty peasant farming. It is necessary gradually but systematically and stubbornly," declared Stalin in November, 1928, "to remake agriculture on a new technical basis, on the basis of big production, pulling it up to the socialist industry. Either we solve this problem, and then final victory is guaranteed, or we retreat from it without solving it, and then the return to capitalism may become an unavoidable development."

How did Stalin meet the fear of war? The country was suffering from a shortage of goods. This dictated concentration upon the restoration of light industry. But the panic in the Kremlin switched the center of gravity to the heavy industry. "The center of industrialization, the cornerstone," declared Stalin, "lies in the development of the fuel resources, metallurgical production, finally in the development of machinery and tools for production." Instead of satisfying the famine for manufactured articles, the Five-Year Plan was directed toward rebuilding the heavy metal and chemical industries.

"Either we will achieve this," announced Stalin, "or we will be wiped out. This is true not only from the standpoint of building socialism. It is true also from the standpoint of preserving the independence of our country encircled as it is by capitalism. It is impossible to preserve this independence without possessing a sufficiently industrialized base for defense. It is impossible to create such an industrial base without commanding higher technique. That is why we need and that is what dictates to us the rapid tempo of industrialization."

And, finally, how did Stalin face the debated issue of building socialism in one country?

"To overthrow the power of the bourgeoisie and to establish the power of the proletariat in one country does not yet mean to safeguard the full victory of socialism. After consolidating its power and leading the peasantry, the proletariat of a victorious country can and must build a socialist society. But does that mean that it can achieve the complete, final victory of socialism? Does it mean that it is able by its own powers to consolidate the final socialism and guarantee the country against intervention, and therefore against Restoration? No, it does not mean that. To insure that, it is necessary that the revolution be victorious in several other countries. Therefore, it is an essential task of our victorious revolution to develop and aid revolution in other countries. Therefore, a victorious revolution in one country must be regarded not as a self-sufficient force, but as a prop, a medium for the hastening of the victory of the proletariat in other lands."

The Soviet government will perish if the individual farms are not socialized and controlled by the state. The Soviet government will perish if the "heavy" industry is not restored to provide a base of national defense. The Soviet government will perish, even if it builds socialism in one country, so long as there is no revolution in the advanced industrial nations. Such are the three remarkable theories with which Stalin met the three-winged crisis confronting the dictatorship in 1928.

That year Russia imported grain from the Argentine.

The Stalin offensive on the internal front was not a planned move, but a counter-attack against the kulak. The frenzied pace with which the world identifies the Five-Year Plan was not artificial in origin, but compulsory. Artificial stimuli were resorted to later to keep the pace up. But the original start was made because of the necessity to secure bread at all costs and under the threat of war.

Fifteen months before the Five-Year Plan was set up as a goal in a race, stern warfare was declared by the Bolshevist power against the kulaks. A state of military communism was introduced at the commencement of 1928. The grain-collection methods employed were those of confiscation and requisitioning by force. These extraordinary measures, carried out as they were by a blind bureaucracy, involved the customary cruelty, arbitrary misapplication of instructions from Moscow, imprisonment and exile of hundreds of thousands of peasants. Although the official theory was that only 3 per cent of the rural population were kulaks, 12 per cent were treated as enemies. This Stalin acknowledged later as a mistake. The line of demarcation between a kulak and a middle peasant is more theoretical than real. How could one expect the armed proletarians to distinguish between a peasant that had two horses, two cows and an old cabin, and one that had only one horse, one cow, and a new cabin?

Nearly three million peasant homesteads suffered

in varying degrees from the campaign. The Stalin policy created a serious crisis in the fall of 1928. There were insistent demands in the Political Bureau for his resignation. Indeed, there were reports that he was ready to retire, that he was seeking an understanding with Bukharin, that the Right group would take over the reins.

Stalin shifted his course. The middle and poor peasants were organized and united against the kulaks. The need for bread in the cities was as acute as ever. New measures of violence were applied. "These measures," writes Popov, "were considerably different from the extraordinary measures practiced in 1928, such as the mass raids upon homesteads, the closing of markets, etc. First of all, the measures of the year before had been applied by government organs from above. Second, they had been applied not only toward the kulak, but toward the middle peasant as well."

At the same time, Stalin returned to the war chest of the old military communism to look for remedies. Once more the state farms, the *sovkhozi,* were taken up, but on a larger scale, modeled after the great American farms, with proper technical equipment and expert personnel. "Yet, ambitious as this scheme was," writes Michael Farbman, one of the most competent observers of the economic trends of the Soviet Union, "it was intended originally merely as a stop gap."

Greater attention was given to the revival of the moribund *kolkhozi,* the collective or cooperative farming societies. These were to be mechanized or tractorized at the expense of the state in return for their yield of grain to the state at a fixed price. Largely by accident, as a result of an experiment conducted on his own initiative by the manager of a modern state farm, it was discovered that the government could supply to the *kolkhozi,* which represented combines of many settlements, tractor energy from central stations. "This simple discovery, and its implications when properly understood," writes Farbman, "were hailed with the greatest enthusiasm by the Bolsheviks, who believed that the high road to socialist agriculture had at last been found."

All the while the Gosplan was struggling with the execution of the minimum five-year plan approved in principle in December, 1927. Its industrialization program was being pushed in vain by its scientific sponsors. The lack of capital was the primary handicap. The inefficiency and lack of technical personnel were other obstacles. The famine of elementary goods in the country was increasing. The scarcity of bread in the cities was growing. The year of 1929 opened with an implacable mass drive against the entire kulak class.

VI

Stalin rose to the occasion. He remembered his Leninist schooling. "Lenin was born for revolution," he declared in 1924. "He was truly the genius of revolutionary explosions and the greatest master of revolutionary leadership. He never felt so free and happy as in a period of revolutionary upheavals. . . . Hence, the 'amazing' lucidity of his tactical slogans and the 'dizzying' boldness of his revolutionary schemes."

Stalin turned the cumulative momentum of the quest for bread from a defensive into an offensive operation, from a counter-attack into an advance. With a driving force of unbridled intensity and sweep, Stalin launched the Five-Year Plan as a law and the supreme effort of the state. He lifted the old plan out of the hands of its commissions, and incorporated in it all the features of the industrialization scheme which Trotsky had fathered. The newly dressed child was entrusted to the iron arms of the political dictatorship. It was sent out into the world under messianic banners that promised the fulfilment of unprecedented objectives.

Stalin became the spokesman of a novel social strategy—the new tempo. It was the rate of the advance, the speed, and not the plan itself, which became paramount. That was inevitable because of the origin of the movement. He was swept along by the velocity he had helped to develop. It was this tempo which caused the cleavage with Bukharin, Rykov and Tomsky. Again it was this tempo which constituted Stalin's constant refrain, echoed from the front pages of thousands of newspapers, during the first two years of the Five-Year-Plan period.

"When, in the summer of 1929, I first came into contact with the new situation," writes Farbman, "I was not quite certain whether I was moving in an atmosphere of revolution or of war. The atmosphere seemed to contain elements of both. The enthusiasm and the vibration of temperament was symptomatic of an upheaval; but the concentration of effort, the intensity of activity, the appeal, and even the imperative demand, for making the supreme effort and sacrifice—all recalled the experiences of the war years.

"My impressions when I revisited Russia in the summer of 1930, were essentially the same, only intensified. The outlook was sterner and grimmer, the privations of people were accentuated, the tasks seemed more formidable and onerous; but while a certain 'war weariness' was unmistakable, the enthusiasm in many quarters appeared unabated. Propaganda, however, had become more intense, more insistent, and the drive more bitter and ruthless. The country still seemed midway between revolutian and war. Yet the whole spirit of the time was different from that of either revolution or war. The significant feature of the situation was that an attempt was being made to play on mass psychology for the accomplishment of a vast economic plan."

The press files of the world record the spectacular bulletins issued from the Kremlin, announcing victories won on the front of the Five-Year Plan. They are reminiscent of General von Kluck's march on Paris in the fall of 1914.

On the agricultural front, the first year was marked by a formal class war against the kulaks. The war-cry was: "Finish the enemy for good!" The resistance of the shrewd farmers was as amazing as their versatility. Those who had escaped confiscation of their property or exile, sought shelter in the *kolkhozi*. In fact, the collectivization drive became an enormous success because of these recruits. The crusaders were instructed to eliminate the kulaks. The country was speeding to socialism under the Stalin whip. The high-water mark was reached when it was announced that 60 per cent of all the peasant holdings had been collectivized.

The spring of 1930 came. The sowing season was approaching. The state farms and the fifteen million collectivized holdings were demanding seeds, tractors, money. The peasants had not joined the "voluntary" cooperatives to become wards of the state in order to sweat for their bread. Moreover, several revolts broke out. Anxiety spread in the Kremlin. It was found that the victory was somewhat exaggerated. The tens of thousands of closed churches that went with the communist drive now offered little comfort to the Stalin power.

Stalin executed an immediate retreat. He came out with his manifesto, "Dizziness from Success." Three months later the number of collectivized farms dropped to 25 per cent of the total. On October 1, 1930, only 21 per cent of all private holdings remained within the collectivized sector.

In 1920, the last year of military communism, the year of the Polish and Wrangel operations in the fertile Ukraine, the Soviet government collected from a war-ravaged and depopulated country 5,130,000 tons of grain. In 1930, after a decade of reconstruction, repopulation, and perfection of the dictatorial machine of state, the Soviet government collected 8,766,000 tons of grain.

On the industrial front, the achievements of the Five-Year Plan are more tangible and the failures more blatant. Scores of electrical, metallurgical, chemical, tractor, tool-making, and similar plants are rising all over the Soviet Union. The coal mines and oil fields are being modernized. Virtually the entire wholesale trade of the country was taken over by the state. The major and overwhelming part of the retail trade was captured either by the state directly or by the government-controlled cooperative system.

During 1929, nearly the entire surplus capital accumulated in the country in the years of the New Economic Policy was squeezed out by the state and invested partly in the mechanization of agriculture and largely in the promotion of the industrialization program. In 1930, the Soviet government was driven in its desperate quest for capital to export commodities badly needed at home and to issue paper currency, according to the official figures, six times the amount provided for in the Five-Year Plan.

The situation in the Soviet Union at the close of 1930 presented a striking similarity to that of the period of military communism of a decade before. There was no unemployment. There was a shortage of bread. The transportation system was breaking down. The rationing system in the cities included all articles of first necessity. In front of the government stores and cooperatives, long queues waited for hours to get food and other vital goods at the official price. In the restricted open market, the prices were twenty to forty times higher. The gold rouble had depreciated so that on the "black bourse" the dollar fetched forty roubles instead of the two paid by the State Bank. Yet even the favored proletariat was forced to buy food from the speculative private traders. "The workers are forced to satisfy about 25 per cent of their requirements of agricultural produce in the private market, paying higher prices," declared

Stalin in the summer of 1930. Even according to this official estimate, the discrepancy was enough to reduce the workers' wages to an insignificant fraction of their real value.

VII

Despite grave internal straits, the Soviet Union externally is hailed or attacked either as a challenge to capitalism or as a potent menace to civilization. The former is the view of "friends" of the revolution; the latter is the stand of commercial interests directly affected by certain Soviet exports.

All the protestations of Stalin and his spokesmen that the Five-Year Plan aims to mitigate the colossal commodity famine in Russia, that it would take generations of development to supply the home market so as to leave a healthy surplus for export, cannot down the bugaboo of the "Red" menace.

Perhaps Trotsky, from his retreat in Turkey, has best expressed the official mood in Moscow on the subject. "That the world capitalist press has painted the growth of Russian export as a system of dumping for the purpose of overthrowing the foundations of civilization," he writes, "is a matter of routine. . . . Not the villainy of the 'dumping menace' is surprising, but its stupidity which, incidentally, is also nothing to wonder at. . . . The liberals and democrats who represent Soviet 'dumping' as a threat to world economy thereby recognize that Soviet industry has become so potent that it can shake the world markets. Unfortunately, that is not so."

The Soviet "trade menace" happened to fall on fertile soil. The economic crisis in America and certain European countries during 1930 revived the familiar "Red" peril as a convenient scapegoat. The monarchist Russian refugees were once more able to inspire and spread their propaganda. In the West, this propaganda remains nothing more than talk. In the Soviet Union, it becomes a "White" peril.

The tremendous increase of Soviet foreign trade was dictated by the new Stalin tempo of industrializing the country, on the one hand, and by the acute lack of capital, on the other. The isolation of Russia from the financial markets of the world is a Stalin policy. It was sound Leninism in the days of military communism, because of the conditions then prevailing in the world, but Stalin has retained it out of fear for the safety of the dictatorship. He has vetoed the projected favorable settlements of the old Russian debts, barring the Soviet Union from the international money market. Yet the penalty he makes the country pay amounts to a sum almost sufficient to defray the interest on all of Russia's pre-Bolshevist debts. It is conservatively estimated that the Soviet commercial credits secured abroad during 1929 and 1930 totaled $1,000,000,000, all in short-term notes averaging about twelve months. These are discounted by the holders for cash at rates ranging from 25 to 30 per cent. Such is the bonus which the Stalin régime is paying for the failure to recognize the former Russian debts in principle and to negotiate terms of settlement with the conflicting individual countries.

But the Stalin policy of "importing" capital at

excessive cost is paralleled by his policy of exporting goods below cost of production. The stripping of the country of its barest necessities, the marketing of these articles abroad, are desperate measures dictated by the urgency of meeting foreign bills. And this frenzied "dumping" is represented as a sign of progress, a challenge to capitalism!

The violent expansion of Soviet foreign trade not only denuded the population of vital commodities, but intensified the vortex in which Bolshevist economy finds itself. Selling below cost, the Soviet government was compelled to make good the deficit by issuing more paper currency at home. This depreciated money was in turn passed on to the producers whose purchasing power diminished in proportion to the increasing scarcity of goods.

VIII

The Stalin Five-Year Plan already has developed its own law. Its velocity is in direct proportion to the existing economic distress. Yet Stalin claims to have already piloted the Soviet ship into the harbor of socialism. To be sure, the vessel is not yet moored.

"Have we, in fact, entered the period of socialism?" asked Stalin at the Sixteenth Congress of the Communist Party in the middle of 1930. He proceeded to answer:

"Our period is usually called the period of transition from capitalism to socialism. It was called the transition period in 1918. . . . It is called the transition period today in 1930, when . . . the new order in the sphere of industry and agriculture is growing and developing with unprecedented speed. Can it be said that these two transitional periods are identical, and are not radically different from each other? Clearly it cannot. What did we have in 1918, in the economic sphere? Ruined industry and mechanical cigarette-lighters, no collective or Soviet farms as a mass movement, the growth of the 'new' bourgeoisie in the towns and the kulaks in the country.

"What have we got today? Socialist industry, which has been restored and is being reconstructed, a widespread system of Soviet and collective farms, embracing over 40 per cent of the total sown area in the Soviet Union in the spring-sowing alone, a dying 'new' bourgeoisie in the town, a dying kulak class in the villages. The first was a transitional period, the second is a transitional period. And yet they are as far apart from each other as heaven and earth. And no one can deny that we are on the eve of liquidating the last serious capitalist class, the kulak class.

"It is clear that we have already passed out of the transitional period in the old sense, and have entered the period of direct and full-fledged building of socialism all along the front.

"It is clear that we have already entered the period of socialism. . . ."

From his place of exile in Turkey, Trotsky challenges his mortal enemy. He writes:

"The second year of the Five-Year Plan is being described in speeches and articles as one in which 'the national economy of the country has entered the period of socialism.' It is declared that 'fundamentally' socialism has already been achieved.

"It would seem that 'fundamentally' a socialist

order of production is one which is conducted to serve the immediate needs of humankind. Yet, in spite of the frightful famine of goods in the country, our 'heavy' industry has shown an increase during the last year of 28.1 per cent and our 'light' industry of only 13.1 per cent, not even attaining the basic program. Even if these proportions should be regarded as ideally correct—perish the thought!—it would still remain a fact that in the interests of the peculiar 'primary socialist accumulation' the population of the Soviet Union is compelled to tighten its belt to an ever-increasing degree. . . .

"Is it not monstrous? The country cannot emerge from the famine of goods, the supply system breaks down at every step, there is not enough milk for the children, and nevertheless the official philistines proclaim: 'The country has entered the period of socialism.' Is there a more vicious way of compromising socialism? . . .

"The reports of the grain collection campaign are printed in the Pravda day after day under the Leninist epigraph: 'The struggle for bread—is the struggle for socialism.' But when Lenin uttered this phrase he was far from the thought that the country 'has entered' the period of socialism. The very fact that it is necessary to struggle for bread, for bare bread, indeed to fight for it, means that the country is still very, very far from a socialist régime.

"For the first time it has been officially acknowledged that the financial system is shaken as a result of the empirical and planless leadership during the first two years of the Five-Year Plan. The currency inflation means nothing but that the first two years obtained without security a loan from the future, and that the ensuing years will compel payment on account of that loan."

From their place of exile in Siberia, Rakovsky and a group of other oppositionists addressed a daring memorandum to the Central Committee in which they characterized Stalin's collectivization campaign as agrarian capitalism and his industrialization efforts as state servitude for the workers. "The situation has not been so serious since the period of civil war," declared the authors of the provocative document.

Is it possible that Stalin has placed the cart of national economy before the iron horse of the dictatorship? Only the future can tell. But one thing is certain: the development of the "heavy" industry first is not an accident, but springs from the nature of the dictatorship, and dooms the country to an ever-growing famine of articles of elementary necessity. A new kind of socialism!

Or is Stalin building state capitalism? If so, where will the required capital come from? The taxable elements in the village have been annihilated. The taxable commercial class in the cities has been wiped out. Even if the festering sore of cost of production and operation of the state-controlled agriculture and industries be left out of reckoning, the rate of advance dictates huge capital investments for the mechanization of the rural economy and even vaster outlays for the completion and maintenance of the insatiable state industries and the restoration of the disorganized transportation system. The future will determine who will pay for Stalin's Five-Year Plan.

Stalin himself characterizes the difficulties as due to growth, to progress. "Our difficulties," he declares with emphasis, "are of such a kind that *they contain within themselves the possibilities of overcoming them.*" How? "Organize the *offensive* against the capitalist elements *along the whole front!*" In other words, the velocity carries its own objective; the remedy for speed is more speed, a social theory of perpetual motion.

"Some comrades think that the main thing in the socialist offensive is repressions," observed Stalin at the last congress, "and if repressions do not increase there is no offensive. Is this true? Of course, it is untrue.

"Repressions are a necessary element in the offensive, but an auxiliary, not a principal, element. The principal element in the offensive of socialism, in our present-day conditions, consists in increasing the rate of development of our industry, increasing the rate of development of the Soviet and collective farms, increasing the rate of the economic squeezing out of the capitalist elements in town and country, mobilizing the masses around the cause of socialist construction, mobilizing the masses against capitalism.

"You may arrest and exile tens and hundreds of thousands of kulaks, but if at the same time you do not do everything necessary to hasten the building of new forms of economy, replace the old capitalist forms of economy by new forms, blow up and liquidate the productive origins of the economic existence and development of the capitalist elements in the villages—the kulaks will be reborn and grow just the same."

IX

The latest sky-rocketing pace set by Stalin, for the third year of the Five-Year Plan, is hailed by his followers as a miraculous performance and denounced by his critics as stark madness. Only time can decide what will happen to the different variants of the plan, whether the objectives of the original moderate draft or the newest Stalin goals of realizing the Five-Year Plan in three years will be achieved, and only time can pass judgment upon the dazzling array of statistical tables issuing forth from Moscow.

It is the historical forces which dictate an ever-accelerated pace that concern us. If the velocity carries within it the seed of its own triumph, is it not possible that it also bears the makings of its own destruction? Is Stalin driving history, or is history driving Stalin?

The newest rate is a development, first of all, of the rising economic distress. During 1930, the country was stripped of its elementary food reserves, which were dumped abroad in the frenzied search for capital. At the end of the year, the meager gold reserves of the state were being exported. This process must continue, so long as the rate of the Stalin offensive continues. Since the socialized industries and agriculture are at best non-profit-paying, since the immense expansion program calls for corresponding capital investments, and since the "heavy" industry even when put in operation will not supply the vital needs of the people, the Five-Year Plan must in the main draw upon the printing presses for currency within the country and for exportable food taken from the mouths of the population to secure dollars and pounds. The cry for bread and the famine of elementary goods dictated, in the beginning, the Stalin drive in the form of the Five-Year Plan. In turn, this offensive creates an ever-growing goods famine and an increasingly distressing cry for bread.

The second factor in stimulating the new tempo is the fear of war, the constant harping on the menace of a capitalist attack, and the consequent war preparedness and the tense atmosphere that goes with it.

"We must remember that the danger of intervention continues to remain quite real," declared Kaganovitch, secretary of the Central Committee, mouthpiece of Stalin, on December 24, 1930, in the preamble of his report on the program of the Five-Year Plan for the following year. "Recent facts, such as the visits of French generals in Poland and Roumania, the campaign against our 'dumping,' the increase in armaments on the part of Poland and Roumania—all these facts show that we are dealing with sufficiently stubborn attempts of the imperialists to organize intervention against us.

"That is why, while pursuing our firm policy of peace, we must draw all the necessary conclusions regarding the strengthening of the defensive ability of our country. We are conducting and will continue to do so a policy of peace. But the more plants and the more factories we build, the more will we fortify our inner power, the greater will be our confidence that we shall not be caught by surprise, that we shall be ready at any moment to strike back at the imperialist robbers.

"In our general scheme of work for the raising

of the socialist economy, we are devoting the maximum of attention to the task of the all-sided strengthening of the Red Army and the fortification of the country's defense."

It would appear that the concentration upon the "heavy" industry is dictated not by economic but political considerations, and is carried on not in the interests of socialism but in the interests of the safety of the state. Instead of furnishing the population shoes and clothing, hardware, glassware, soap, furniture, and all other vital necessities, the Soviet government is building chemical and metallurgical plants—for defense.

The third force making for the new Stalin rate of advance is derived from . . . the economic crisis in America. The Bolshevik God, as Bukharin remarked in 1919, is magnanimous and wakeful. There was no world revolution, so he presented Stalin and the Five-Year Plan with a gift from across the Atlantic.

In the beginning, it was the failure of the proletarian revolution in the world that turned Stalin to the building of socialism in one country. But gone is the "stabilization period" of capitalism. The latest Stalin theory, consequent upon the economic crisis in the United States, is the decline of world capitalism, the rise of Soviet socialism, the need that the latter outstrip the former without delay. For the world revolution, after all, is lurking around the corner, and the mighty communist Soviet Union must lead it to victory.

It seems that the world is witnessing the *turn of the tide.* The emphasis in all cases is Stalin's own.

"We in the Soviet Union have a *growing advance* in socialist construction, both in industry and agriculture," declares Stalin. "They—the capitalists—have a *growing crisis* in their economic life, both in industry and in agriculture. . . . The most varied 'theories' of the crisis are being thought out . . . The bourgeois oppositions point to the bourgeois governments, which, it appears, 'did not take all possible steps' to prevent the crisis. Democrats accuse Republicans, Republicans accuse Democrats, and both together accuse the Hoover group with its Federal Reserve System, which failed to keep the crisis 'in check.' There are even wise men who see the cause of the world economic crisis in 'Bolshevik plots.' . . .

"The crisis has struck deepest of all at the *principal country* of capitalism, its citadel, the U. S. A., which concentrates in its hands not less than half of the whole production and consumption of the world. Obviously this circumstance cannot but lead to a colossal extension of the sphere of influence of the crisis, to the sharpening of the crisis, and the accumulation of 'unbudgeted' difficulties for world capitalism. . . .

"The present economic crisis is developing on the basis of the *general crisis* of capitalism, which began during the period of the imperialist war, undermining the foundations of capitalism and facilitating the oncoming of the economic crisis."

Stalin, supported by Kaganovitch and many minor figures, then produces evidence in the form of selected statistics to show the people of Russia that capitalism is dying in America while socialism is flourishing in the Soviet Union.

"It has been observed long ago," wrote Lenin in his "Unified Economic Plan" in February, 1921, referring to the "conceited stupidity" of many of his aides, "that the defects of people are mostly bound up with their qualities. Such are the defects of many leading communists. We have been doing for decades a great work, preaching the overthrow of the bourgeoisie . . . a work of great universal, historic character. But it is enough to exaggerate a little bit, and the result is the confirmation of the truth that there is but one step from the sublime to the ridiculous."

The citadel of capitalism, the United States, is crumbling. Therefore: "Catch up with and surpass in the briefest possible time the most advanced capitalist countries!" This is the slogan of the newest Stalin offensive.

"We shall yet see which countries are to be ranged among the most backward and which among the most advanced!" challenged Stalin with undisguised braggadocio.

"It is only the acceleration of the rate of development of our industries that will permit us to catch up with and surpass technically and economically the advanced capitalist countries," he declared at the last party congress. The cry has been echoed, in all seriousness, by a thousand adventurous economists in the Soviet Union.

"The great task set by the Five-Year Plan," proclaims Grinko, of the state planning commission, in his book, "is that of attaining and surpassing the technical and economic level of the advanced capitalist countries, thus assuring the triumph of the socialist system in its historic contest with capitalism."

In Russia, the propaganda race between the Soviet Union and the United States became a bureaucratic stampede. It fitted in well with the general precipitancy of the Stalin pace. "In reality," writes Trotsky, "the economic turn toward industrialization and collectivization took place under the lash of administration panic. This panic still rages. It is enough to see the front pages of all the Soviet papers today; there is a complete adaptation to the slogans, formulas and battle-cries of the civil war: front, mobilization, breaches, cavalry, etc. Now and then this is seasoned with sporting snobbishness, such as start, finish, etc. . . . The mass propaganda continues in the spirit of bluff and deception."

Trotsky cites some well-known figures to illustrate the contest between the Soviet Union and the United States. In the former, four-fifths of the population are engaged in agriculture; in the latter, for every farming person there are 2.7 engaged in industry. The net production per person in the United States is nearly ten times that of Russia. In the latter country, the power of primary mechanical installation is 4,600,000 as against 35,800,000 in America.

The metal output per person in the Soviet Union in 1929 was close to a third of what it was half a century ago in the United States. The metallurgical production in the Soviet Union is one-eighteenth of the agriculture production. In the United States, metallurgy exceeds agriculture by 28 per cent.

The coal output in the Soviet Union is 7 per cent, in the United States 68 per cent of the world total.

The foreign commerce of the Soviet Union is 2 per cent of the international trade. The merchant marine of the Soviet Union constitutes one-half of 1 per cent of the world tonnage; that of the United States, 22.5 per cent. In the railroad network the discrepancy is almost as great. The gold reserve of the Soviet Union is now insignificant, not more than 2 per cent of the world supply. The per capita wealth of Russia is about 1 per cent of that of the United States.

What a race! Upon the full consummation of the Five-Year Plan, the Soviet Union will have 158,000 automobiles!

But the Stalin general staff is undaunted. At the ninth national congress of the Young Communist League of the Soviet Union, an organization with a million members, the pride and hope of Bolshevism, Stalin's spokesman, Kaganovitch, unfolded in the presence of his chief the following reel of the historic contest:

"We in Soviet Russia are buying new machines; we are building works and factories in order to set going new and more rapidly working machines. In America things have come to such a pass that they are prepared to place people at slower-working machines, to lay idle hoisting cranes and other machines, in order to employ as great a number of people as possible. We, on the other hand, want to erect new works for the construction of cranes and other means of transport.

"In America, they no longer wish to have shorthand typists, but to have everything written by hand. We, however, are building typewriter factories and propose also to manufacture typesetting machines. We are going forward to a new technique. In America, however, they are seeking to find a way out by means of technical retrogression!"

Some day an H. G. Wells will write a novel on the gulf that separates socialism and socialists. Some day a G. B. Shaw will pen a comedy on the abyss that lies between communism and communists. In the meantime, the world is treated to the grand spectacle of a race between the Soviet Union and the United States.

In Moscow, there is current a story of a man, all out of breath, running headlong in the street. He bumped into a friend.

"Where are you running?" he was asked.

"I am carrying out Stalin's orders. I am running to overtake the United States."

X

The seeds of political Bolshevism, carried from a century of western revolutionary movements into the soil of Russia, developed there into a grotesque and misshapen plant. The tissue of economic Bolshevism, borrowed from a century of western capitalistic growth, blossomed out on the eastern plains into a fantastic, preposterous body kept in perpetual motion. Both are deeply rooted in the fear that is the essence of the dictatorship, which in turn is even more deeply imbedded in the despair that has for a thousand years fertilized the land of Eurasia.

Conceived in distress, propelled by panic, fed on false promises, driven by emotional and not rational means, the Five-Year Plan in the hands of the Stalin dictatorship is like a rocket proceeding to the moon, with the aid of charts prepared by a group of astronomers.

The military communism of the period of the civil war ended in the Kronstadt rebellion and the New Economic Policy.

How will Stalin's adventure end?

Whither Stalin?

Chapter Seventeen

STALIN HAS A VISION

THAT night Stalin could not sleep. His health had been waning perceptibly. The physician had suavely warned him what the dizzy spells and the numbness in his fingers portended. He would have to give up his work or be prepared for the inevitable.

It was quiet in the Kremlin. The stillness irritated Stalin. Was it a surface calm? Night had descended upon an inchoate continent which had for fifteen years twitched in the throes of revolution. Was it the calm of night? Or what? Do great revolutions go to sleep? Do they wake up? What of tomorrow? But will there be a tomorrow? He did not trust those physicians. They were bourgeois courtiers. For a long time they had assured him that he was all right when he knew he was not. And now they gently warned him to be careful. Did it mean that a stroke was near? Will there be a tomorrow?

Stalin sat up in bed, but fell back upon his pillow. Those pestiferous memories! He could subdue a volcano, but he could not banish memories. His supreme power could not stop their ravaging work. Oh, let them come, let the film unroll. . . .

There was once a youth in the Caucasus who climbed no glittering snow-capped peaks, but tunneled subterranean passages. . . . There was the thrill of the first missive from the mountain eagle

Lenin in 1903. . . . Yes, this is 1931. . . . He had then found a faith, he had been loyal to the same faith all these years. Yet . . . yet, it wasn't the same. It then had a different color. What was it? . . .

Lenin. . . . He was but a short distance away, outside the high wall, lying lifelike but dead. Dead! . . . There was Trotsky, a proud but worthy enemy, languishing on an isle in Turkey with ulcers in his stomach and spasms in his heart. There was Kavtaradze, a boyhood friend, who courageously risked his life in the Tiflis bombing, now turned oppositionist and isolated in a cell as a counter-revolutionist. There were Kamenev and Zinoviev, impaled on their own treacherous lances, politically putrid, but names that belong to history nevertheless. And Rykov and Tomsky, and Bukharin, their heads bowed low over the grave of a great dream. Rakovsky, Muralov, Beloborodov, and a host of others scattered in exile and prisons from Turkestan to the Polar Circle, all old grenadiers of an heroic past. . . .

The night drew closer around Stalin, and its still minutes grew longer. His forehead was moist with warm beads. He could not stand it any more. He turned on the light, took up a book, opened it, and read:

"We have captured the dictatorship of the proletariat and by doing so we have created the political base for the advance to socialism. Can we, with our own powers, create the economic base, the new economic foundation, indispensable to the erection of socialism?"

THE RED SQUARE IN MOSCOW NOW DOMINATED BY LENIN'S MAUSOLEUM. *The Red Army and Workers Celebrating the Anniversary of the Soviet Revolution.*

Stalin was startled. "Can we?" Who said that? Why, these were his own words. He was reading his address at the Executive Committee of the Communist International in December, 1926. "Can we?" Will the pyramid of the dictatorship prove a durable base . . . without Stalin? Perhaps the physicians were wrong, after all. Indeed, what could happen? In what direction will the wind carry the vessel he had riveted? Stalin pondered and dozed off.

He was at a crossroads. What had happened to his Revolution? Which of the four directions had it taken? He must find out. He turned east. Out of the darkness an arresting figure of a man rose before him, with eyes that scraped one to the bone, a diabolical, haughty figure. Yet the stranger greeted him benignly.

"Have you seen my Revolution?" asked Stalin.

"It is safe and sound, and marching on to success. You have built on a solid base by building socialism in one country. Your reward is already here. The Revolution has swept as far as Arabia, Korea, Ceylon, and China is now part of the Soviet Union. You have created the state supreme where justice is ministered by the rod and equality by pressing machine. Private greed has been rooted out, private initiative subordinated to the sublime ideal. You have created a society of perfect order. Its power is the envy and alarm of the despicable merchants of the world. You have continued my labors and advanced them nobly. I, too, slept on a bed of boards and worked day and night for my ideal. I was a little ahead of my time. I brought from Byzantium the Alexandrian Library, the greatest storehouse of human knowledge ever assembled, and I studied Plato and Aristotle, the Mosaic law and the Roman Republic, Josephus and Herodotus, and concluded that the only wise rule is the rule for the people and not by them. I leveled the boyars. I laid out a school system. I unified taxation and extirpated all independent sects and separatist government. I introduced the first printing press, I set up one militant political party endowed with the authority of the state. When I entertained the English shopkeepers, the Fletchers and Jenkinsons, and courted Queen Elizabeth, they thought I was a barbarian, those petty traders! But I subdued the Tatar kingdoms in Kazan and the Crimea, and conquered Siberia, so that Muscovy became an empire that reached to the Black Sea and the borders of Mongolia, an empire that is now gathering the dominions cultivated for us by the British lion. You have carried on my mission to the terror of the anointed money-grabbers.

"Your dictatorship is a success! The flag of the Soviet Union is waving over the cradle of humanity—Asia. As to the West, it has no soul, and will never understand us."

Stalin staggered. Who was that Mephistophelian speaker? He looked familiar. Had he not seen his portrait on the walls of the great hall in the Kremlin? . . . Why, he looked like— Yes, of course . . . Ivan the Terrible!

Stalin shuddered. "Success!" It could not be!

He fled, and was back at the crossroads. He faced the west.

A gigantic, muscular figure, with a cherubic face,

stood there. . . . Danton! He knew those features well. Danton! Stalin shrank.

"You would know what has happened to your Revolution? Recall my last talk with Robespierre when he asked me whether we could not come to an understanding.

" 'Is not power forced to become cruel in extreme danger?' asked Robespierre.

" 'Yes, but it should never become pitiless,' I replied. 'The wrath of the people is an explosion. Your guillotine is a system. . . . The Committee of Safety is shedding blood drop by drop, as if to sustain the terror and the habit of execution. You are executing the innocent as well as the guilty.'

" 'Has there been one man executed without trial? Has one head been severed without condemnation by law?' challenged Robespierre."

Danton laughed bitterly.

" 'Innocents! Innocents! You regard mere hatred of you as a crime! All your enemies you have declared guilty!'

" 'No,' said Robespierre, 'and the proof of it is that *you* are still alive!'

"We parted. My friends urged me to open war against Robespierre. And you remember what I said:

" 'It will mean more bloodshed. Enough of it! I shed blood when I thought it useful. I would rather be guillotined than be the executioner. . . . In revolutions power falls into the hands of great bandits. I would rather be a simple fisherman than govern people.'

"Robespierre executed the French Revolution.

He paid for it with his head first, but it was a small price. Then came the Thermidor, Napoleon, and . . .

"You have learned nothing. You blind son of Asia who would out-Robespierre the original Robespierre! You condemn to death without trial, and your executioners do not behead in public but shoot their victims from behind in the backs of their heads. But conspiracy will not avail you!

"Your Revolution has been captured by the man on the white horse!"

Stalin slunk away. He faced the south. A pair of cold eyes, looking out from beneath the massive dome of the head of Karl Marx, greeted him.

"Master," spoke Stalin, "I have lived up to your precepts. Where is my Revolution? Where is it going? Where has it gone? Show me the way."

"You know every word of my writings by heart," sneered Marx, "but you understand none of them. I sought a dictatorship of the proletariat, and not for the proletariat. I wanted all the toilers to rule, and not a rule for them by professional politicians. I sought the destruction of private property so as to make all people happy, for when all begin to work freely for their own commonwealth they will be happy. You have commanded them to be happy! You have destroyed private capital, but you have concentrated it in the hands of a terrorist state. Your workers are your slaves. You are not building socialism, but some Asiatic monstrosity.

"You recall my correspondence with Engels? A government of terror is the rule of people who are imbued with fear. Terror is largely a series of futile cruelties perpetrated by men for their own peace.

You can open the road to socialism by force, by a dictatorship, but you cannot build socialism by compulsion. Once all capital resources are nationalized and the bourgeoisie deprived of its property, the ex-capitalist, the workingman, the peasant become equal, and their equality, their common humanity, should be ennobled and not trampled under by the state.

"Instead of giving every worker, every non-propertied man and woman a voice in the government, you have filled your prisons and exile camps with scores of thousands of honest socialists who have not the slightest interest in reestablishing private property—capitalism. Ninety per cent of your population are proletarians who should have secret suffrage, a free press, as many political parties as possible, so long as their platforms do not call for the state to surrender to private capital its land, industries, resources, and foreign commerce.

"A true proletarian revolution must be a revolution of and by humanity. And you have created a new privileged class, a bureaucracy of backward workers armed with official powers. You call it the dictatorship of the proletariat! But you cannot create by violence the conditions, cultural and economic, you cannot leap across the historical stages, which make for socialism.

"I never did think that Russia was headed for socialism, and said so, but you misinterpreted my words. My theory of social revolution referred to industrial countries, and not peasant countries. However you may try to solve the peasant problem by political means, there is only one solution in the end: the village must follow the city, agriculture must follow industry, and you have the process reversed. You are being pulled by an ox-cart. And you imagine that you can make a stream flow uphill with the power of your political dictatorship!

"You conspired to seize power under false pretenses, under the Soviet banner, and then you gradually substituted the Bolshevist banner and deprived the masses of their rights.

"I see a new revolution, a true uprising of the toilers, not an insurrection, but a revolution, as spontaneous as that which overthrew in March, 1917, the tsarist autocracy. I see the masses in vast revolt, sweeping away the chains of your dictatorship, but keeping off the vultures of imperialism and capitalism, and marching to genuine social democracy. . . ."

"You are a renegade. You are a traitor to socialism. You talk like Kautsky in his dotage," interrupted Stalin, and turned north. The familiar face of Lenin, with that ironical glint in his eyes, was staring at him.

"Comrade Lenin," said Stalin, "where is your Revolution bound for?"

"It is mine no longer. It is yours now. You remember what I said during the civil war? On page 374, volume 4, of the Journal of the Lenin Institute, you will read:

" 'Ten to twenty years of correct relations with the peasantry, and victory will be guaranteed on a world scale (even if the growing proletarian revolutions are delayed)—otherwise, twenty to forty years of the torments of White Guard terror.' "

"Yes, I remember it very well," replied Stalin.

"Did I interpret it accurately in my defense of Leninism against Trotsky in 1926?"

"What did you say then? I wasn't there," said Lenin.

"I explained your meaning," replied Stalin, "in the following words:

" 'A. If we establish correct relations with the peasantry, our victory—the victory of socialism—is assured within ten to twenty years.

" 'B. This victory will be a victory not only in the Soviet Union, but a victory on a world scale.

" 'C. In the event we do not achieve such victory within that period, it will be a sign that we have been smashed, and the régime of the dictatorship of the proletariat will be replaced by a régime of White Guard terror which will last from twenty to forty years.' "

"That is correct," observed Lenin.

"Would that mean the restoration of the monarchy?" asked Stalin.

"Yes, with a vengeance."

"How soon?"

"Figure it out for yourself."

"We have been in existence over thirteen years. You said from ten to twenty. But has my policy toward the peasantry been right?" inquired Stalin.

"Well," chuckled Lenin, "the peasant has not answered yet."

. . . .

The telephone rang sharply. Stalin woke up. It was morning. Nadya was on the phone. She seemed quite agitated.

"Koba," she turned to her husband, "it is Molotov. They've discovered an underground press of Trotskyists in the Sverdlov University, and stacks of incendiary leaflets and reprints of Lenin's Testament."

Stalin leaped out of bed.

"Tell him I'll be over right away."

THE END

STALINIANA

(The sources listed below are limited to such biographical items only as contain some vital or first-hand facts on Stalin's life and work. Scores of additional writings on Stalin were perused. Of the numerous general works on the Russian Revolution consulted in the preparation of this volume, two deserve special acknowledgment: "An Outline of the History of the Revolutionary Movement in Russia," by Prof. M. N. Pokrovsky, Associate Commissar of Education; and "The Ethical Face of the Revolution," by I. Z. Steinberg, Commissar of Justice of the Soviet Republic in 1917–18.)

* *All items marked by an asterisk are in Russian.*

ADORATSKY, V. *Stalin as the Theoretician of Leninism. *Proletarskaya Revolutzia,* December, 1929.

ALDANOV, M. A. Stalin. *Contemporary Review,* May, 1928.

ALLILUIEV, S. I. *Reminiscences. (The author is Stalin's father-in-law.) *Krasnaya Lietopis,* Nos. 5, 8, and 9. Leningrad, 1923.

ARSENIDZE, P. *Political Parties in Georgia. *Volia Rossii,* Prague, No. 2, 1927.

BADAYEV, A. E. *The Bolsheviks in the Duma. Moscow, 1929.

BAJANOV, B. With Stalin in the Kremlin. *La Revue de France,* Paris, Sept.-Nov., 1930.

BESSEDOVSKY, G. *On the Road to the Thermidor. Vol, 2, Paris, 1931.

BIEDNY, DEMYAN. *On Stalin. *Pravda,* Feb. 7, 1928.

BIEDNY, DEMYAN. *Fragments. *Pravda,* Dec. 21, 1929.

BUBNOV, A. *The Leninist, the Organizer, and the Leader. *Pravda,* Dec. 21, 1929.

CHAMBERLIN, W. H. Soviet Russia. Boston, 1930.

CHASE, DUNN AND TUGWELL, Editors. Soviet Russia in the Second Decade. New York, 1928.

DAVIS, JEROME. Ten Years. *The Survey,* February 1, 1927.

DAVIS, JEROME. Stalin, Russia's Ruler. *Current History,* March, 1929.

DAVIS, JEROME. Interview with Stalin. *N. Y. American,* Oct. 3, 1926.

DMITRIEVSKY, S. *The Fate of Russia. Stockholm, 1930.

DOBB, M. Russian Economic Development since the Revolution. New York, 1928.

DURANTY, W. Interview with Stalin. *N. Y. Times,* Dec. 1, 1930.

EASTMAN, MAX. Since Lenin Died. London, 1925.

EFFENDIEV. *Reminiscences. From the Past of the Baku Organization. Baku, 1923.

FARBMAN, M. Piatiletka. Russia's Five-Year Plan. New York, 1931.

FISCHER, L. The Soviets in World Affairs. New York, 1930.

GAISINSKI, M. G. *Sverdlov, Y. M. Moscow, 1929.

GERMANOV, L. *Reminiscences. *Proletarskaya Revolutzia,* No. 5, 1922.

GERTIK, D. *Reminiscences. *Pravda,* May 6, 1927.

GLASSMAN, L. M. The Bolsheviki as Humorists. *Current History,* 1930.

GOLUBEV, N. *Reminiscences. *Proletarskaya Revolutzia,* No. 6, 1922.

HOOVER, CALVIN B. The Economic Life of Soviet Russia. New York, 1931.

JAKOV, M. *Reminiscences. *Proletarskaya Revolutzia,* No. 6, 1922.

KAGANOVITCH, L. *Stalin and the Party. *Pravda,* Dec. 21, 1929.

KAGANOVITCH, L. *The December Joint Plenary Session of the Central Committee and the Central Control Commission. Moscow, 1930.

KALININ, M. *The Helmsman of Bolshevism. *Izvestia,* Dec. 21, 1929.

KNICKERBOCKER, H. R. The Red Trade Menace. New York, 1931.

KRASINA, LUBOV. Leonid Krassin. London, 1928.

KRUMIN, G. *The Theoretician and Man of Affairs. *Pravda,* Dec. 21, 1929.

Kuibishev, V. *Stalin and the Industrialization of the Country. *Pravda,* Dec. 21, 1929.

Kuusinen, O. *Stalin and the Bolshevization of the Communist International. *Pravda,* Dec. 21, 1929.

Lenin, V. I. *Complete Works. Moscow, 1923-25.

Lenin, V. I. *Letter to Karpinsky. *Leninski Sbornik,* Vol. 8. Moscow.

Lenin, V. I. *Correspondence with Maxim Gorki. *Leninski Sbornik,* Vol. 1. Moscow.

Lyons, E. Interview with Stalin. *N. Y. Telegram,* Nov. 24, 1930.

Manuilsky, D. *Stalin. *Pravda,* Dec. 21, 1929.

McCormick, Anne O'Hare. The Hammer and the Scythe. New York, 1928.

Medvedeva-Ter-Petrosian, S. F. *A Hero of the Revolution. Published by the Historical Commission of the Communist Party. Moscow, 1925.

Mikoyan, A. *The Steel Soldier of the Bolshevist Guard. *Pravda,* Dec. 21, 1929.

Mitrevitch, A. * Reminiscences. *Proletarskaya Revolutzia.* No. 4, 1922.

Nelidov, N. *Reminiscences. *Proletarskaya Revolutzia,* No. 3 and No. 7, 1924.

Nelidov, N. *On Sverdlov and Stalin in Siberia. In collection entitled Sverdlov, Y. M. Moscow, 1926.

Nevsky, V. I., Editor. Biographical Dictionary. Leningrad, 1923.

Ordjonikidze, S. *The Rockribbed Bolshevik. *Pravda,* Dec. 21, 1929.

Pestkovsky, S. *Reminiscences. *Proletarskaya Revolutzia.* No. 6, 1930.

Pestkovsky, S. *Reminiscences. *Proletarskaya Revolutzia.* No. 10, 1922.

Podvoisky, N. *Reminiscences. *Krasnaya Lietopsis,* No. 6, 1923.

Poletayev, N. *Reminiscences. *Pravda,* May 6, 1927.

Popov, N. *Stalin and the National Question. *Pravda,* Dec. 21, 1929.

Popov, N. *An Outline of the History of the All-Russian Communist Party. Moscow, 1930.

Proletarskaya Revolutzia. Stalin Miscellany. No. 7, 1922, Page 239; No. 4, 1923, Davtian Reminiscences; No. 4, 1925, Page 204; No. 6, 1925, Page 148; No. 11, 1926, Miliutin Reminiscences.

RAKHIA, E. Reminiscences. *Pravda,* Nov. 7, 1927.
SAMOILOV, F. *Reminiscences of a Bolshevik Duma Deputy. *Proletarskaya Revolutzia,* No. 3, 1924.
SAVELIEV, M. *Stalin—the Continuator of Lenin's Work. *Pravda,* Dec. 21, 1929.
SCHEFFER, PAUL. Stalin's Power. *Foreign Affairs,* July, 1930.
SEMASHKO, N. *Reminiscences. *Proletarskaya Revolutzia.* No. 1, 1924.
SHLIAPNIKOV, A. *Nineteen Seventeen. Vol. 2. Moscow, 1925.
SHUMYATSKY, Y. *Turukhanka. Sketches from the Life of Exiles. Moscow, 1926.
SPIRIDOVITCH, A. I. History of Bolshevism in Russia. Paris, 1922.
STALIN, J. *About Lenin and Leninism. Moscow, 1924.
STALIN, J. *Address at Sixth Congress. In article entitled "July Days of 1917." *Proletarskaya Revolutzia,* No. 5, 1923; *Krasnaya Lietopis,* No. 7, 1923.
STALIN, J. *Address of October 19, 1928. *Pravda,* 1928.
STALIN, J. *Address on Tenth Anniversary of Soviet Government. Moscow, 1927.
STALIN, J. *Article on Sverdlov. In collection entitled Sverdlov, Y. M. Moscow, 1926.
STALIN, J. *Collection of Articles. Tula, 1920.
STALIN, J. *Correspondence with Lenin and Krupskaya. Included in The Dawn of the Zvezda and Pravda, Vol. 3. Moscow, 1923.
STALIN, J. Interview with the First American Trade Union Delegation in Soviet Russia. New York, 1927.
STALIN, J. *Lenin, the Organizer and Leader. *Pravda,* No. 86, 1920.
STALIN, J. Leninism. Translated by Eden and Cedar Paul. New York, 1928.
STALIN, J. *Letter to Lenin. *Zarya Vostoka,* Tiflis, Dec. 23, 1925.
STALIN, J. *Memorandum on Brest-Litovsk Peace. *Leninski Sbornik,* Vol. 11. Moscow.
STALIN, J. *Numerous articles in *The Life of the Nationalities,* the Journal of the Commissariat for Nationality Affairs. Moscow, 1918-1923.
STALIN, J. *On the Komsomol—the Young Communist League. Moscow, 1929.
STALIN, J. *On the Opposition. A Collection of Articles and Addresses for 1921-1927. Moscow, 1928.

STALIN, J. *On the Problems of the Agrarian Policy. Moscow, 1930.

STALIN, J. *On the Road to October. Leningrad, 1925.

STALIN, J. *On Science. *The Journal for Everybody,* Moscow, September, 1928.

STALIN, J. Reminiscences. *Pravda,* May 5, 1922.

STALIN, J. Report on Fourteenth Conference. Moscow, 1925.

STALIN, J. Speeches on the American Communist Party. New York, 1930.

STALIN, J. *The National Question. Article included in volume entitled The October Revolution and the Dictatorship of the Proletariat. Moscow, 1919.

STALIN, J. The Sixteenth Party Congress. London, 1930.

STOPANI, A. *Reminiscences. From the Past of the Baku Organization. Baku, 1923.

SUKHANOV, N. *Notes on the Revolution. Vol. 2. Berlin-Moscow, 1922.

SVERDLOV, Y. M. *Letters from Siberia. *Pechat i Revolutzia,* Vol. 2, Moscow, 1924.

SVERDLOV, Y. M. *Three Letters from Siberia. *Proletarskaya Revolutzia,* No. 4, 1922.

SYROMOLOTOV, F. *Reminiscences. *Pravda,* May 5, 1922.

TOVSTUKHA, IVAN. *Biographical Sketch of Stalin. (Official.) Moscow, 1927.

TROTSKY, L. The Real Situation in Russia. Translated by Max Eastman. New York, 1928.

TROTSKY, L. *The Bulletin of the Opposition. Paris, 1929-30, Nos. 1-18. Contains numerous articles by Trotsky.

TROTSKY, L. My Life. New York, 1930.

TROTSKY, L. The Strategy of the World Revolution. New York, 1930.

TROTSKY, L. The Draft Program of the Communist International. New York, 1929.

TSYAVLOVSKY AND MELGUNOV. *Bolsheviki. Collection of Okhrana Documents. Moscow, 1918.

ULIANOV, I. I. *The Cossacks and the Soviet Republic. Moscow.

VERESTCHAK, S. *Reminiscences of Stalin. *Dni,* Paris, Jan. 22-24, 1928; *Pravda,* Moscow, Feb. 7, 1928.

VOROSHILOV, K. *Stalin and the Red Army. *Pravda,* Dec. 21, 1929.

YAROSLAVSKY, E. *History of the Communist Party of the Soviet Union. Moscow, 1927-1930.

YAROSLAVSKY, E. *A Revolutionary Bolshevik. *Pravda,* Dec. 21, 1929.
YELOV, B. *Reminiscences. *Krasnaya Lietopis.* No. 7, 1923.
YENUKIDZE, A. *Underground Printing Presses in the Caucasus. Moscow, 1925.
YENUKIDZE, A. *Fragments of Reminiscences. *Izvestia,* Dec. 21, 1929.
YERMANSKY, O. A. *From the Past. Moscow, 1927.

INDEX